T0247819

CELEBRATING

50 YEARS

Texas A&M University Press
publishing since 1974

UVALDE'S DARKEST HOUR

UVALDE'S DARKEST HOUR

Craig Garnett

Texas A&M University Press
College Station

First edition

♾ This paper meets the requirements of ANSI/NISO Z39.48-1992 (Permanence of Paper).
Binding materials have been chosen for durability.

Library of Congress Cataloging-in-Publication Data

Names: Garnett, Craig, author.
Title: Uvalde's darkest hour / Craig Garnett.
Description: First edition. | College Station: Texas A&M University Press,
     [2024] | Includes index.
Identifiers: LCCN 2024030624 (print) | LCCN 2024030625 (ebook) |
     ISBN 9781648432996 (cloth) | ISBN 9781648433009 (ebook)
Subjects: LCSH: Uvalde School Shooting, Uvalde, Tex., 2022. | School
     Shootings—Texas—Uvalde. | School police—Texas—Uvalde. | School
     crisis management—Texas—Uvalde. | Police-community
     relations—Texas—Uvalde. | Gun control—Political aspects—United
     States. | BISAC: SOCIAL SCIENCE / Violence in Society | HISTORY / United
     States / State & Local / Southwest (AZ, NM, OK, TX)
Classification: LCC LB3013.33.T4 G37 2024 (print) | LCC LB3013.33.T4
     (ebook) | DDC 364.152/3409764432—dc23/eng/20240718
LC record available at https://lccn.loc.gov/2024030624
LC ebook record available at https://lccn.loc.gov/2024030625

Cover design by Noah Van Soest

This book is dedicated to Alexandria "Lexi" Aniyah Rubio,
daughter of Leader-News reporter Kimberly Mata-Rubio,
and her eighteen classmates and two teachers who were killed
on May 24, 2022: Nevaeh Bravo, Jackie Cazares,
Makenna Elrod, Jose Flores, Ellie Garcia, Uziyah Garcia,
Amerie Jo Garza, Xavier Lopez, Jayce Luevanos,
Tess Mata, Maranda Mathis, Alithia Ramirez,
Annabell Rodriguez, Maite Rodriguez, Layla Salazar,
Jailah Silguero, Eliahna Torres, Rojelio F. Torres,
Irma Garcia, and Eva Mireles.

Contents

Author's Note

The rampage killing at Robb Elementary School on May 24, 2022, shattered our small town. In the space of four minutes, nineteen fourth graders and two of their teachers were mortally wounded in a fusillade of high-velocity bullets that ripped apart flesh and pulverized bone. Nine children survived but at great physical and mental cost.

As chaotic reports of an active shooter flooded social media, parents swarmed to the modest neighborhood school. A phalanx of officers pushed back as relatives begged them to "go in the building or let us go in to rescue our children." That did not happen for 73 minutes, and the sense of betrayal added immeasurably to the subsequent grief and anger.

The law enforcement debacle spilled over into the city's other institutions, especially the Uvalde Consolidated Independent School District. School police chief Pete Arredondo, in an active shooter plan he coauthored, named the acting school district police chief as the incident commander in the event of an attack. Nevertheless, on May 24 and afterward, Arredondo denied that he had been in charge or that he knew who commanded the 376 law enforcement officers who flew to intervene that day.

A seventy-seven-page Texas House Investigative Committee report released two months later identified the failure of law enforcement, including local police and Texas Department of Public Safety, to force an end to the worst school shooting in Texas history. The Uvalde school district was singled out for a culture of complacency in terms of security and administrative preparedness. "Robb Elementary was unprepared for an armed intruder on the campus," the report read. The committee pointed to the school's five-foot perimeter fencing as inadequate and doors that either malfunctioned or were routinely left unlocked for convenience—which was against school policy but appeared to be tacitly condoned by school police and administrators.

For families of victims, the report validated what they had seen in person that day. Hundreds of police surrounding the school and positioned in the hallway outside the besieged classrooms for more than an hour without acting to end the carnage. A school administration that had failed not only to protect its students with adequate security but in the aftermath refused to provide victims' families with basic answers or to even console all of the wounded children and teachers.

This book is the story of May 24 and subsequent events as families fought to learn what had happened in Classrooms 111 and 112. At what moment had their children been wounded and died? How might they have been saved if police had responded with leadership and determination? And especially, why law officers would allow more than an hour to crawl by as children called 911, pleading for help to save their wounded and terrorized classmates and a dying teacher.

The loss of staff reporter Kimberly Mata-Rubio's ten-year-old daughter Lexi crushed our tight-knit staff, and in the opening hours and days we struggled for direction. Afterward we were determined to find answers for families that had been misled and relegated to the dark by local and state institutions. We fought for information of the most fundamental nature—the names of students enrolled in each classroom and the school records of the eighteen-year-old responsible for the horror.

Others will have a different view of events. But this is how our journalists and I reported a tragedy that has become far too familiar across America. A troubled teen with a weapon of war, purchased legally along with almost 2,000 rounds of ammunition, went largely unnoticed until it was too late.

I am indebted to our staff for their courageous reporting and assistance with information and fact checking. And to the many families of victims, surviving students and teachers, and officials who shared their incredibly painful stories. Without them there would be no accounting of Uvalde's darkest hour.

UVALDE'S DARKEST HOUR

CHAPTER 1

Sounds of Emergency

The police scanner is the exposed nerve of a small-town newspaper. When the dispatcher keys the mic, all ears bend to the receiver, especially if the radio voice rises an octave or quavers in the least. On May 24, 2022, at 11:28 a.m., a dispatcher in Uvalde, Texas, relayed a 911 call that a pickup had crashed into a drainage ditch behind Robb Elementary School and that the driver had fired on the two men who approached to render aid. Minutes later, the dispatcher heard a second, more ominous message from the same caller: "He's walking to the school. Oh my God! Please hurry!"

Kimberly Mata-Rubio was sitting in front of her computer working on a story for the *Leader-News* when the first radio transmission sounded in the newsroom. The words "gun" and "Robb" in the same sentence galvanized the thirty-three-year-old mother of five. Two of her youngest children were at the school following the end-of-year awards ceremonies that morning. Still, the veteran police reporter listened with practiced calm, telling herself it was probably another incident where a vehicle transporting suspected illegal immigrants had crashed during a police pursuit, and the driver and passengers fled on foot. These "bailouts" had become so frequent that campus lockdowns were almost routine.

Earlier that morning, I had joked with Kimberly about her desk still being a perfect fit. In 2010, at age twenty-one, the Uvalde High School graduate had accepted a job as our receptionist. She had been so eager to begin work that she had skipped an appointment the same day to renew her birth control. The result would be the birth ten months later of Alexandria "Lexi" Rubio.

Our new receptionist dispatched her routine duties with ease and devoured books during slow times. And even though her only writing experience had been penning stories to herself as a child, we soon offered her a position on our crime desk. "Rubio," as most of us called the striking, petite woman (it was less confusing after we hired another reporter named Kimberly), dove into the work with an eagerness that would mark all of her undertakings. In Kimberly's words, she came to us as a "clean slate," and managing editor Meghann Garcia, who had earned a bachelor's degree in political science from the University of Texas at Austin in 2008, assumed the role of writing coach. Kimberly proved a quick study, cranking out accurate and informative copy well before deadline.

The new reporter and Meghann would grow ever closer, not only because Kimberly was a managing editor's dream but also because the young women shared a common culture (Kimberly's parents were Hispanic and Meghann was born of an Anglo mother and Hispanic father) and because they shared a passion for gossip, food, and local journalism, in no particular order.

Our circulation manager, Pete Luna, and Kimberly engaged in a daily game of intellectual "I got you." The playful Luna's disarming wit confused some people but Kimberly relished the sparring. Months after the tragedy, when most were trying to tiptoe across a minefield of grief, Luna made a point of treating "Rubio" with the same wry humor. She responded by laughing again—if just a little.

In 2019, Kimberly had shocked us with plans to resign to complete an associate of arts degree at Southwest Texas College, followed by a bachelor's in public history at St. Mary's University in San Antonio. During her college course work, Kimberly joined us on holidays and summer break. Each time she left, we resisted the urge to search for a replacement. We simply were not ready to give up on Rubio as part of our family.

By late morning on May 24, the newsroom—normally pulsing with friendly banter about stories under way or the next lunch menu—had grown silent. Melissa Federspill, who covered education and sat close to the scanner, moved even nearer, hoping to decipher the emergency. Sadly, one did not need a police scanner to know something extraordinary was happening. Sirens screamed from every quadrant of the city and overhead, the whomp-whomp-whomp of helicopters added confirmation.

Luna, who was also a prize-winning photojournalist, was running errands during his lunch break when he received the first of two messages. A friend who was hardwired into Uvalde's first-responder scene texted "Are you listening?," referring to police scanner chatter about a shooting on Diaz Street three blocks from Rob

The second message came from the *Leader-News's* graphic designer, Neil Sturdevant, who had just departed for lunch and was waiting behind a car at a stoplight at North Camp and Main Street. When the light turned green, the car in front of him turned left onto the highway and smashed head on into a vehicle stopped in the oncoming lane. A police officer in a cruiser directly behind Sturdevant jumped the curb to pass on the right and raced through the intersection, ignoring the wreck. A former professional MMA fighter, Sturdevant did not spook easily, but the cop's maneuver stunned him. As the newspaper staffer continued south in the path of the police car, the unfolding chaos became more profound. Sturdevant texted Luna at 11:42 a.m.: "cops and border patrol no joke doing 100 mph on south getty."

Pete Luna and our managing editor are a couple, and Pete dropped Meghann off at the home they had long shared on the city's main north-south thoroughfare—North Getty Street—and hurried to the office to collect more gear. As he pulled into the parking spaces in back of the newspaper's offices, Pete noticed Kimberly outside talking on her cell phone.

The drive from the *Leader-News*'s downtown office to Robb Elementary took a matter of minutes. Enough time for Pete to theorize that a suspect had fled from a domestic disturbance, crashed his vehicle, and run toward the school for cover. With long practice in approaching crime scenes, Pete parked on the street a block north of Hillcrest Memorial Funeral Home and carried his Canon camera with a 300 mm telephoto lens and a separate video camera as close to the scene as possible. At six feet three inches and 250 pounds, Pete stood out in a crowd, but he worked hard to blend in and do his job efficiently without disrupting those who were trying to do theirs.

Police had cordoned off the school campus on the north perimeter along Geraldine Street to hold back the swelling crowd of terrified parents and members of the media, of which Pete was the sole representative. He had a clear view of the fourth grade wing about seventy-five yards away and set up for what he thought would be the perfect angle to catch the suspect being led from the campus in handcuffs.

The school district posted on its Facebook page that Robb students were being evacuated to the high school auditorium. Kimberly, who was without a car, grabbed a ride with her younger sister, only to learn that the information had been changed. When school officials became fearful of a follow-up attack, they shifted the site to the city-owned Ssgt. Willie de Leon Civic Center two blocks from the newspaper.

Meanwhile, Kimberly's maternal instincts had shifted into overdrive. Mothering is what had driven her since the day when as a fifteen-year-old she held her firstborn, Kalisa. When Kimberly had learned she was pregnant at age fourteen, she was terrified of what her parents and others would think, but she had never wavered in her determination to keep the baby.

"The real fear came when they placed her in my arms," Kimberly said. "I just felt so much love and needing to protect her . . . to provide for her and how do you do that as a fifteen-year-old? What if I can never give her anything? What if I can't get a job? What if I can't feed us or buy a house for us? How do I make sure that you have a better life than I did?"

Kimberly remembered her parents being supportive, especially her mother, Cindy, as her father was often away as a truck driver. Cindy's main concern was that Kimberly not get married. She also wanted her daughter to attend Excel Academy, an alternative school for students who were struggling. Kimberly rebelled at both suggestions. She married Kalisa's father (they would remain together for three years) and insisted on attending Uvalde High School "because I needed to prove that I could do it and still graduate."

Her memory of the first day at home with Kalisa was still vivid. It was late in the afternoon and Cindy, who later became a registered nurse, showed Kimberly how to give the baby a sponge bath while being careful of the umbilical cord. The house was laid out in such a way that one part could be closed off from the other, and when night came, Cindy "came in, closed it off and said 'Okay, I'll see you in the morning.'"

"My family was very strict on 'This was your decision. You're mom, you're gonna wake up all night with her and there's nobody gonna come help you.' People would joke and tell me the first baby is the good baby. Not Kalisa. . . . I think I was getting thirty-minute increments of sleep. She had to be on me and when I finally put her down, she would realize and wake up again."

Through those sleepless nights and weary days at school, the fifteen-year-old had discovered her identity. She was a mother determined to succeed for her child.

As she raced to protect her two youngest on May 24, Kimberly received good news about her eight-year-old-son Julian. His teacher texted that the boy was safe with his class at the civic center. That news freed the journalist to summon her sister for yet another ride, this time to her grandmother's house on Geraldine Street, just beyond Robb.

"I was really, really late there," Kimberly said about her arrival at the school. "And then I remember when I think it hit me for the first time how serious it was. I don't know who told him, but Angel Garza just starts crying and running. It's because somebody had just told him that his stepdaughter [Amerie Jo Garza] had been shot."

CHAPTER 2

The "Mexican School"

R obb Elementary was a neighborhood school in every sense of the word. Getting there involved turning away from major roads and into the heart of a quiet, pecan-shaded community of modest homes inhabited almost exclusively by Mexican Americans, many of whom had been there for generations. The campus, with its low-slung brick-and-mortar building, occupied the equivalent of two city blocks in the center of the enclave. Hillcrest Memorial Funeral Home, situated across the street from the playground, was the only commercial structure in the immediate vicinity.

The school was named for popular Anglo teacher and civic leader Annie Robb. She was among the first three Uvalde students in 1891 to graduate high school. When the new elementary school opened in 1956, two years after Robb's death, there were no bilingual teachers at the school, despite the fact that few students spoke English. Furthermore, children who spoke Spanish at school were often subjected to punishment. Olga Charles (or Charlés), who served as the coordinator for our Newspapers in Education program, found an important calling at Robb, often referred to as the "Mexican school." Because her parents were bilingual, Olga, became the de facto translator for her friends and classmates at the age of seven, in 1958.

The Robb community, with its shared culture and neighborhood stores, lived insulated from the rest of the city, even though Uvalde covered only a handful of square miles. Children on bicycles could easily span the city limits in half an hour, but few ventured beyond the security of their neighborhood.

Once Olga departed Robb to attend fifth grade at West Main School, with its iconic vaulted dome, she noted a marked difference. The facilities, including playgrounds, were more modern and better kept, there were more books in the library, and she now had white classmates. In the intervening years, Olga was not aware of discrimination, even though Spanish was still forbidden among students and those who traveled outside of the West Side neighborhood encountered signs excluding "Mexicans" from restaurants and stores.

Rogelio F. Muñoz, an attorney who for many years served as chair of the Uvalde County Democratic Party, remembered a trip in the 1960s to play a varsity football game against the Eagle Pass Eagles. Muñoz and one of his friends, a starting lineman, were caught speaking Spanish during the seventy-mile bus trip. As punishment, the coach sidelined the starter for the entire game.

When the all-Anglo school board refused in April of 1970 to renew the contract of Josué "George" Garza, one of the few Hispanic and bilingual teachers in the district (who later became the city's mayor), the decision triggered a student walkout. Mexican American organizers had warned of the outcome if the board followed the recommendation of the principal at Robb, where Garza taught fifth grade. They also insisted on thirteen other conditions for ending the protest. Those included hiring more Hispanic teachers, requiring teachers to learn how to pronounce the names of Hispanic students, and teaching Mexican American history.

In the beginning, the protest was confined to Uvalde High School, where 200 left their classrooms. That number would soon swell to 650 Mexican American students across all the grades, about 18 percent of the city's student body.

Elvia Perez, one of Olga's former classmates, told me the protest remained peaceful, with two marches staged in front of the high school and one at Robb. Even so, Texas Department of Public Safety troopers, also known as state police, and Texas Rangers were deployed to Uvalde to maintain order. Texas Rangers are an elite branch of the Department of Public Safety with jurisdiction over local and state police.

Perez recalled walking three blocks from her house on Oak Street to attend a school board meeting held in a downtown building at 313 N. Getty. As she crossed the street, she looked up into the barrel of a rifle trained on her by a Texas Ranger positioned on the rooftop. "That was my most vivid memory of the walkout," she told me.

Perez's father had opposed her participation but her mother, "a devout Catholic," believed Elvia, who attended Catholic school until eighth grade, should follow her convictions.

"I was a school girl. I loved school, and I knew that I was going to be a teacher one day." Perez described herself as a "naïve and idealistic" seventeen-year-old who wanted to help effect change for other students even though she, like Olga, had never experienced discrimination. "I had no idea what the consequences would be."

Six weeks after the protest began it ended when the school year ended. High school administrators flunked the seniors who had participated, including Perez, who stood at the top of her class as valedictorian. Students were forced to repeat their final year but many never returned or earned a degree through the GED program.

Perez was fortunate to have won an academic scholarship to Our Lady of the Lake University in San Antonio before the walkout. Despite not having earned a high school degree, she began classes in the fall. Several years later she was required to take the GED as part of the college's requirement for graduation. "I had been a college student for years," Perez laughed at the irony.

That summer, local activist Genoveva Morales filed a class action lawsuit against the Uvalde Consolidated Independent School District, claiming that it discriminated against Hispanic students by not offering them an education that was equal to the education white students received. The suit also alleged that Hispanic students had been segregated from attending two better-funded elementary schools on the east side of town, Dalton and Benson.

Federal district judge John H. Wood Jr. of San Antonio ruled against Morales, writing that he saw "no evidence of discriminatory intent, past or present" on the part of the district. Morales appealed, and the Fifth Circuit Court of Appeals in New Orleans ruled in 1975 that the school district had in fact segregated its schools, violating the civil rights of Hispanic students. That decision threw the case back to Judge Wood, who ordered school officials to devise a plan to desegregate the schools. That plan was followed for forty-two years until July 2017, when the suit was finally settled.

The Uvalde school walkout, one of the longest in US history, clearly brought about long-needed change, but the collateral damage many Hispanic students suffered proved significant. It also resulted in a schism between students who had participated and those like Olga who had remained in school (her father had insisted).

"Many felt that the adults who arranged the walkout got off without getting hurt. It was the kids who suffered the most," Olga said.

By the time our two children attended fourth and fifth grade at Robb in 1990–93, the school district was fully integrated. Hispanics counted for more than 85 percent of the district's enrollment, which meant that Anglos were a minority. Our children told us about sporadic incidents of racial teasing, but most student skirmishes tended to be among friends. In other words, Hispanic students fought largely among themselves, which was the same for Anglos.

Of course, among Hispanic leaders, especially those like George Garza and Gilbert Z. Torres, who had championed the walkout twenty years earlier, the community was far from free of its racist past. Torres, a feisty forty-seven-year-old with close-cropped graying hair, became the first Hispanic Uvalde County Commissioner in 1975. He served in the Precinct 2 post for more than twenty-four years.

When I joined the newspaper in 1982 as general manager, I covered the county and Torres disliked virtually everything that I wrote. He called our newspaper the Mickey Mouse Liar-News and called me a racist. Nothing would change, he told me one day in my office, "until the Leader-News is owned by a Mexican."

Garza, who had earned a master's degree in education, practiced a different kind of advocacy. As the city's mayor from 1996 to 2008 (he was defeated in 1998 and reelected in 2000) he was far more diplomatic in the way he articulated the need for Latino inclusion in the form of better wages and housing. However, when the position of city manager became vacant in 1997, he refused to go along with four council members (three Hispanics and an Anglo) who had determined that one of the three applicants, an Anglo, was the best qualified. Garza insisted that the new city manager must be bilingual and Hispanic, "that an Anglo would not be relevant to Uvalde."

In 2022, more than fifty years after the walkout, the racial divide had been patched over but certainly not erased. It was not unusual to hear snide comments about "Mexicans" from Anglos who clearly had not accepted the fact that the majority Hispanic population was here to stay or to admit that they had actually gotten here first. Nevertheless, most residents had learned to adhere to their practiced roles in the dance between the races.

Besides, a different kind of racial tension had exploded just 65 miles away along the nation's southern border with Mexico. As immigrants fleeing impossible conditions in Central and South America scrambled for asylum in the United States, the influx overwhelmed the US Customs and Border Patrol, the Texas Department of Public Safety, and local law enforcement.

Almost overnight, a new, more lucrative business than drug smuggling presented itself to Mexican cartels. Thousands of undocumented immigrants who daily crossed the Rio Grande needed to distance themselves from "La Migra" (immigration). And while their paltry resources only went so far, many had planned ahead for the steep price of a car ride to freedom.

The impact on Uvalde County was staggering. The city sits at the intersection of two of the longest highways in the United States—US Route 83 and US Route 90—a perfect funnel in the route away from nearby border cities such as Eagle Pass and Del Rio.

Virtually every day, our police scanner erupted with the sounds of a car chase as drivers tore over county roads and even through the heart of the city with as many people as could be squeezed into cars, pickups and sometimes vans. In one notable chase, a driver had packed eight people inside a Mini Cooper that was eventually stopped following a chase on West Main Street.

Far more tragic consequences often ensued. In September 2022, a Toyota Tacoma pickup transporting nine immigrants slammed into an 18-wheeler that was turning at the downtown intersection. The seventeen-year-old female driver and a front-seat passenger died at the scene. Eight passengers in the pickup bed flew across the pavement but somehow survived. Police found a message on the driver's cell phone telling her how to claim her $600 payment. A similar crash the previous April at the same intersection—Main and Getty—had damaged four vehicles and sent several people to the hospital.

In the meantime, area farmers and ranchers recorded millions of dollars in damages as drivers carrying human cargo plowed through gates and fences in an effort to evade capture. Our twenty-two-acre home site at the city limits experienced two such incursions. On several occasions we found discarded cell phones and packs containing food and clothing. One morning, we discovered a nineteen-year-old Honduran huddled in the crook of a fallen mesquite. He wept openly as he described to me how his family was forced to pay a monthly fee to Honduran cartels to avoid death.

The Border Patrol station in Uvalde, which employed 150 Border Patrol officers, was operating at the limits of its capacity, as were stations across the entire border region. There was not a vacant hotel room in the city due to an enormous influx of state police who had been dispatched to interdict immigrants as part of Gov. Greg Abbott's Operation Lone Star. By late 2023, the state of Texas had spent $10 billion in a futile effort to stem the tide.

Fifty percent of the incidents published in our twice-weekly crime report were connected either directly or indirectly to human smuggling. The district judge maintained a backlog of 3,000 cases, most of which were related to human smuggling or the narcotics that the smugglers were transporting and/or consuming.

Collateral damage extended to the school district, where each chase and bailout near a school triggered a new emergency. The district's director of student services reported in the summer of 2022 that schools had been secured or locked down forty-seven times since the previous February, of which 90 percent were attributed to bailouts. The district's Raptor Alert system, which was designed to allow any school employee to report danger over the mobile app, had a distinct flaw. The messaging did not differentiate its signals between bailouts and other kinds of alerts, such as an active shooter.

Since its founding in 1856, Uvalde had served as the commercial and recreational hub for Southwest Texas. It was a veritable oasis of giant oaks and pecans, bountiful wild game, and more miles of crystal-clear running rivers that any county in the state. Those attractions had only grown with time, and now we could claim the dubious distinction as a major staging area for law enforcement in the fight against illegal immigration.

CHAPTER 3

Celebration

The 2022 school year would end in two days, and the prospect of summer spread its intoxicating magic across the Robb campus. Excitement had begun to build the day before on May 23, when almost one hundred graduating seniors from Uvalde High School arrived at Robb Elementary around mid-morning for the annual "victory walk."

Dressed in their snappy maroon caps and gowns with silver sashes, the older students formed a procession that paraded past adoring second, third, and fourth graders. Shouts of encouragement and high fives followed the visitors' spirited jaunt, which began at the west door of the more modern fourth grade wing and continued via covered walkways to the lower grades. The seniors waited briefly for the locked exterior door to be opened. Once inside, they were accosted by more than 500 admiring, giggling children.

"They were so happy to see us. They were so happy to see their siblings and their cousins. And it was just so nice . . . so sweet," senior Ariana Diaz told me in a bittersweet interview. The bubbly teenager had attended Robb in fourth grade and although she did not have popular Room 112, where Irma Garcia and Eva Mireles co-taught, she knew them by reputation as "such good educators" and was friends with Irma's son Jose. "The teachers were so happy—their energy also matched the students."

The fourth graders had created congratulatory signs and banners that festooned the blue-on-green hallway. They insisted that their pictures be taken with their teenage relatives. Kadence Kubish could hear little sister Makenna Elrod calling to her—"Sissy, Sissy, Sissy, Sissy!"—but the seventeen-year-old could not locate her in the crush of elementary students and fellow seniors. Finally, Makenna tugged at Kadence's gown and they embraced and posed for a picture. As the older girl walked away, she heard Makenna telling her Room 112 classmates: "This is my sissy! This is my sister!"

Another friend of Diaz, Briana Mata, stopped for a quick picture with her ten-year-old cousin, Lexi Rubio. And then the swiftly moving procession was gone, striding into the sunlit walkways of the lower grades.

In those fleeting minutes, images of the smiling faces in front of Classrooms 111 and 112 had been etched in Diaz's mind. "If you ask, do you remember somebody from the end of the hall, I literally can't remember. . . . [but] I remember distinctly seeing the people in these classrooms. I don't know the science behind that. But I do know that I remember their faces."

The following day, Robb hummed with even more energy as parents and extended family funneled into the small cafeteria-cum-auditorium to watch their "babies" finish off the year in a shower of honors. Attendance, good citizenship, and of course grades topped the agenda.

Kimberly and husband Felix visited at 8 a.m. for Julian's second grade ceremony and returned at 10:30 a.m. for the fourth grade version with daughter Lexi. The night before, Kimberly had messaged Meghann that she might be a little late due to the Robb festivities. Garcia had replied that it was not a problem.

Lexi was recognized with a good citizenship award and for making the All-A Honor Roll. When the ceremony ended, the proud parents took a picture with their daughter and another at 10:54 a.m. of Lexi with her favorite teacher, Arnulfo Reyes. Kimberly and Felix said goodbye with a kiss and a promise of ice cream when they picked Lexi up at the end of the day.

Gloria and Javier Cazares awoke to drama the morning of May 24. Their nine-year-old daughter, Jackie, in uncharacteristic fashion, wanted to skip school. The couple sought a compromise. If Jackie would attend class and stay through the awards ceremony, she could then go home with them. The girl agreed, but when the ceremony rolled around, no awards came her way. Earlier in the year, she had been moved from Reyes's Room 111 to Garcia and Mireles's class to help her sharpen her math skills. And while she had returned to Mr. Reyes's class months earlier, her awards remained with Room 112.

Jordan Olivarez's mother, Virginia Vela, had the day off as an emergency medical technician with Uvalde EMS. She and her husband, Bobby Olivarez, watched the ceremony for Room 112 as Jordan received a good citizenship award. Jordan's third grade cousin, Aria Guerrero, had joined the family for the occasion, and by the time Vela walked the special needs student back to her classroom and returned to the cafeteria, Jordan had disappeared. "He didn't even ask to go home with us," his mother said.

Khloie Torres was new to Uvalde, having arrived fifty-four days earlier with parents Jamie and Ruben Torres. The dark-blonde ten-year-old was delivered to school by her grandmother and recognized with a good citizenship award. But she had previously secured something even more valuable. An outgoing, always-smiling Girl Scout named Amerie Jo Garza had taken the new student in Room 112 under her wing.

On the morning of May 24, Miah Cerillo missed the ceremony due to a doctor's appointment. She had complained of a cough, so her mother, Abigale Veloz, took the child out of class for an appointment with pediatrician Roy Guerrero. Although the doctor cleared the eleven-year-old to return to Robb, her mother offered home as an option. Miah chose school. She had left her phone and backpack in Classroom 112.

By 11:30 a.m., the awards ceremonies had concluded and the children had downed a quick lunch. Back in their rooms, the eighteen students in Garcia and Mireles's class were watching *Lilo & Stitch*. Inside Room 111, which was connected to Room 112 with an interior door, teacher Arnulfo Reyes stood at his kidney table while his remaining eleven students settled onto the floor to continue where they had left off watching *The Addams Family*.

Over the next 5 minutes, an act of unimaginable violence descended on the modest neighborhood school that left nineteen students and two teachers dead or dying and almost a dozen wounded. Over an hour later, the campus was crawling with hundreds of law enforcement officers and even more parents screaming, fighting, and crying for their children to be rescued.

That would not happen for 77 minutes, a delay that ranks as the most damning police response to a mass school shooting in US history. That second tragedy left the community to grieve twenty-one beautiful souls as well as the failure of the very institutions that helped hold the town together.

CHAPTER 4

Into Darkness

Eight years earlier, a skinny fourth grader with unusually cropped hair who "talked funny" and often wore the same clothes for days at a time had spent the school year in Robb Elementary Classroom 111. Salvador Ramos's mother, Adriana Reyes, had implored his teacher to protect the boy from bullies, who she said had bedeviled him since kindergarten. The educator claimed to have delivered, telling investigators that Ramos had had a good year and that he had made friends there. His cousin, who was in the same classroom, gave different testimony. She said he was made fun of and bullied despite the teacher's purported efforts. At one point, a girl had tied Ramos's shoelaces together so that when he stood up, he fell over. Everyone laughed except the teacher and the cousin.

The boy completed fourth grade (he would tell friends later that he had bad memories from that year) and continued through elementary and middle school. Classmate Ariana Diaz said that they were not friends but that most students knew of him. She acknowledged that he had a distinct speech impediment in the form of a lisp and remained mostly to himself.

Family stability presented an enormous challenge. Adriana Reyes held a variety of jobs as a server in the food service industry, scraping over a rocky bottom that featured inadequate wages, drug abuse, and fraught relationships, not the least of which was with her son. Ramos's father had been largely absent since his son's birth on May 16, 2004, in Fargo, North Dakota. With help from other relatives, especially Reyes's mother, Celia "Sally" Gonzales, the family lived from one day to the next, albeit often shakily.

By the time Ramos entered his sophomore year, his dress resembled that of other students, but that was the extent of his conformity. Ariana Diaz, who shared an elective leadership class with the young man, observed that he sat apart from the others, near the door, and was always on his phone. His clothes consisted of jeans, T-shirts, and Jordans. He was also chronically absent, missing around one hundred days a year beginning in 2018. The leadership class teacher, who was strict about attendance, questioned the teenager's absences but got no answers. Diaz described Ramos as someone you tried to avoid talking with unless you wanted to get your feelings hurt. "He was just so mean," she said.

During what Ariana described as "peak COVID," the summer of 2020, she was scrolling through TikTok and stumbled on a video of Ramos. But the images she encountered were so shocking that it took a few moments to register that it was the same person. He was wearing eyeliner and was dressed in a black muscle shirt, black pants, and combat boots. And he was lifting up his shirt to show off his body, engaging in what Diaz and friends referred to as a thirst trap. The most startling thing for the teenager was not necessarily the clothes (she did not judge) but the fact that in middle school Ramos would have made fun of someone dressed that way. "That's what shocked me. So much that I remember sending it to my friends and they were like, 'Whoa, what has happened?'"

Months later, Ariana, then a senior, came across one of Ramos's Instagram pages and noticed that he was "being more edgy, maybe wilding." She told me her thoughts were that COVID-19 might have pushed her classmate into even more antisocial behavior.

The pandemic hit hard for all students, stripping them of the social interaction they craved—and needed for development. Of course, many had access to social media, which helped maintain communications, but that was no substitute for the spontaneous fun that comes only face to face. The forced isolation could not have helped the troubled Ramos. He normally shunned interaction, but by the fall of 2021 he had more time to dwell in an online world that grew increasingly violent. Years of dysfunctional parenting, poverty, and relentless bullying had finally hollowed out the shy boy with a speech impediment and replaced him with a hate-filled seventeen-year-old who yearned to be noticed.

On October 28, 2021, the school district officially gave up on the young man, citing poor academic performance and lack of attendance for his "involuntary withdrawal." By that point, Ramos had accumulated enough credits to complete only ninth grade. Even though he was considered at risk, there is no record that he received special education services or speech therapy, which someone in the family had reportedly requested. At the same time, save for a case of "mutual combat" in a hallway with another student in late 2018, he had no record of disciplinary infractions.

Perhaps Ramos could not have cared less that he had been expelled—he obviously felt little need for school—but it marked an accelerating descent into darkness. According to the Texas House Investigative Committee report, notes on Ramos's phone suggested that he had self-image issues. He had expressed an interest in weight and fitness that may have resulted in an eating disorder. An ex-boyfriend of Adriana Reyes told investigators that Ramos "had become a loner who punched holes in the walls of his room after arguments with her."

People who may have provided some comfort began to slip away. Ramos's older sister had graduated and left home, and a person that investigators described as his best friend had moved to San Antonio. By mid-2021, his relationship with his girlfriend had also ended. She told the FBI that he "was lonely and depressed and constantly teased by friends on social media who called him a 'school shooter.'" He is said to have told her that he would not live past eighteen because he would commit suicide or just "wouldn't make it much farther."

The house report said Ramos began to show an interest online in gore and violent sex. He sometimes shared images of beheadings and suicides. Playing online games fed his growing anger, leading him to threaten others, especially when he lost to a female. In private, he lamented his inability to connect with others or to even care about them. He had delusions about his lack of humanity and labeled others as "humans" as an apparent insult. That internal conflict led to searches about the meaning of "sociopath" that resulted in online solicitations for treatment of sociopathy.

Ramos began to promote his TikTok and YouTube channels in texts with online friends in the belief that the social media posts would make him famous. A recent Netflix series, *Don't F**K with Cats: Hunting an Internet Killer*, about an animal abuser and murderer who was hunted down by amateur online sleuths, caught his attention. In late 2021, he shared a video online of him riding around with "someone he met on the internet" holding a clear bag containing a cat. Ramos flung the cat into the street and spat on it while the driver laughed. The teenager is next seen wearing a tactical plate carrier and dry-firing BB guns at people. The episode ends with footage of emergency vehicles responding to a serious accident that Ramos claimed was caused by his driver.

Around this same time, the teenager accepted a job at Whataburger. He was fired a month later for threatening a female co-worker. His next employment, at Wendy's, also proved to be a dead end. A co-worker described him as "not a good person" and "troubled," someone who "put himself in a box and would not talk or associate with anyone he worked with."

Investigators noted an exception, however. Ramos attempted to talk about guns with a fellow employee, who did not approve. Ramos's response was to challenge him to a fight.

Two months before the shooting, Ramos and his mother had an explosive argument that was live streamed on Instagram. The Texas house report did not specify who posted it. However, the *Washington Post* reported that Ramos put up an Instagram story in which he screamed at his mother, who, according to a high school classmate, said she was trying to kick him out of their home. The fact that she was successful marked another turning point for the teenager, who moved into his grandmother's house at 552 Diaz Street, only three blocks from Robb Elementary.

Sixty-six-year-old Celia "Sally" Gonzales had served the Uvalde school district for twenty-seven years before deciding to retire. Her last job had been as a teacher's aide in the computer lab at Robb. She was self-confident and devoted to her Catholic faith and had served as a maternal role model to her children's offspring, several of whom were already living with her. A granddaughter, Aubrey Salazar (Ramos's cousin), and her son, a third grader at Robb, occupied one bedroom and she the other. Ramos was forced to sleep on the floor in the living room.

The arrangement was far from ideal for either party. Gonzales was constantly prodding, questioning her grandson's cell phone use (he was on her plan) and suggesting that the teenager find a way to continue his education. The bright side for Ramos was that it allowed him to continue to hoard money. After his brief employment in the fast-food industry ended, his only income came from jobs he did for an uncle in the air-conditioning business. The teenager was paid in cash. He also assisted his grandfather, Rolando Reyes, with his work as a self-employed air-conditioning technician.

Well before his eighteenth birthday in May, he asked at least two people, including his sister, to help him buy guns. They refused. In November 2021 and again in February 2022, Ramos went online to acquire firearm-related accessories. His purchases included rifle slings, a military carrier vest, and a snap-on trigger system (called Hellfire) that is designed to turn a semiautomatic into an almost fully automatic weapon, approximating a machine gun.

His internet searches reveal that he had developed a fascination with school shootings. The comments he made about them and his threats of violence and rape soon earned him the nickname "Yubo's school shooter" on the French social networking app of that name. People he played games with online apparently taunted him with the nickname, as did others he knew personally in chat rooms. Regrettably, none of his online behavior was ever reported to law enforcement, and investigators did not find evidence that any social media platform attempted to restrict his access or report him to authorities as a threat.

He celebrated his eighteenth birthday on May 16 with the purchase of a DDM4 V7 (an AR-style gun manufactured by Daniel Defense) and 1,740 rounds of .223-caliber ammunition. The next day he made a second large purchase, a Smith & Wesson M&P15, also an AR-style weapon. The following day, he bought an additional 375 rounds of the same caliber, spending $4,896 for all of the purchases.

The rifle from Daniel Defense was ordered online and delivered to Oasis Outback in Uvalde, an authorized gun dealer. Ramos completed the required paperwork and background check before Oasis handed over the weapon. Much of the process is perfunctory: attest that you have never been convicted of a felony and are in good standing with the authorities and off you go. The second rifle was purchased directly from the store, accompanied by the same paperwork and background check. All of this was carried out according to state and federal laws.

Ramos did not possess a driver's license, so his uncle drove him to the gun store. Oasis Outback also houses a popular lunch spot and the uncle assumed his nephew wanted a ride because he planned to eat there. When the teenager returned to the car with a long cardboard box, it was evident he had purchased a firearm. Investigators did not learn who drove him to the store on May 18, but the uncle returned to Oasis with Ramos two days later. Again the teenager came back to the car with an oblong package. The uncle claimed not to know what it contained. Investigators later verified it was the more expensive weapon from Daniel Defense.

The bulk of the ammunition, the first 1,740 rounds, was purchased online and shipped directly to the Diaz Street address, arriving on the afternoon of May 23. The second purchase was made at Oasis.

Questions have arisen as to why the back-to-back acquisition of assault-style rifles on the day a man turned eighteen—and on the next day—did not flash a warning sign. Store owner Randy Klein told authorities that the young man "appeared to be an average customer with no 'red flags' or suspicious conditions" and was seemingly alone and quiet. Klein remembered asking Ramos how an eighteen-year-old could afford such purchases and Ramos simply said that "he had saved up." Store patrons who saw the teenager told a different story to the FBI in interviews following the tragedy. They described him as "very nervous looking" and said that he "appeared odd and looked like one of those school shooters." Another described his all-black clothing as giving off "bad vibes."

Not surprisingly, the eighteen-year-old had no criminal record. After all, he had just turned eighteen on May 16, the day he bought the first weapon. Prior to that, he was considered a juvenile, and the law does not allow those records to be examined. In hindsight, a red flag law might have made a difference, as there were more flags whipping around Ramos than the Uvalde Coyotes drill team wielded. He had begun to post pictures of his weapons and to spell out plans that indicated an obvious act of violence.

Two months before the attack, a student told Ramos in a group Instagram conversation that "people at school talk shit about you and call you a school shooter." On April 2, Ramos asked in a direct message on the same platform, "Are you still gonna remember me in 50 something days?" Someone answered "probably not," and he replied, "Hmmm alright we'll see in May." Investigators found that many of those with whom he chatted felt the cryptic deadline spelled violence. To underscore that, in a message on May 14, the eighteen-year-old simply wrote "10 more days."

After the mass shooting in a Buffalo, New York, supermarket on May 19, Ramos read stories and other information about the mass murder. He also plied his cousin's son, who attended third grade at Robb, for information about his schedule and how lunch periods were handled. On May 23, the teenager reached out in a Snapchat exchange with a German girl he had befriended: "I got a little secret." When she showed interest, he told her it was "impossible for today" because he was still waiting for something "being delivered Monday, May 23 by 7 p.m." His online order of 1,740 hollow-point bullets arrived later that day.

In the aftermath, some in the community speculated that the killer had originally planned to attack participants in the senior walk the day before, since they were long-time classmates he may have blamed for his status as an outcast.

On the afternoon of May 24, when Diaz and her friends discovered that their former classmate may have been the shooter, they immediately looked him up on Instagram and were horrified to see that Ramos had been posting weapons. It was not that they were close, but the teenagers felt that they could have seen it as a major red flag. "So it was kind of just like a moment—I don't want to say disappointment, but we didn't follow him. So there would have been no way of seeing this red flag," one former classmate said.

CHAPTER 5

552 Diaz Street

In the aftermath of the shooting, I drove past Diaz Street on numerous occasions, slowing down in front of 552, trying to imagine the day and its impact on the neighborhood. Although the house was well kept and perhaps occupied, it did not appear receptive to visitors, which it was not, largely because its owner was hospitalized in San Antonio.

The house across the street, however, proved more welcoming. A riot of flowers bloomed in the beds, and when I knocked at the door an elderly man answered. I knew him to be a longtime *Leader-News* subscriber named Gilbert Gallegos. I identified myself and my aim, which was to learn what happened to his across-the-street neighbor on May 24.

Gilbert, who at eighty-two was exceedingly thin and had a raspy voice, let himself out the door and stood on the front porch. He said he and his wife, Maria, had left the house early for their usual morning walk that day. It had been warmer than normal for spring, and they had returned, eaten a leisurely breakfast, and then slipped back outside to water plants and perform other chores before the heat became too much.

By that point, Maria had positioned herself so she could talk though the screen— or at least listen. The couple told me that they had lived at 555 Diaz Street for decades and had known their across-the-street neighbor Celia half as long. Diaz Street was a quiet, two-block street sandwiched between the higher traffic of South Grove and South Evans. A mere three blocks from Robb Elementary, the location made for a quick commute during the years Celia Gonzales worked in the school's computer lab as a teacher's aide.

The houses on Diaz Street, like the neighbors, were close. Gilbert recounted that he had been standing in the shade beneath a tree in the front yard on that fateful day when he was startled by the unmistakable explosion of gunfire inside the structure less than seventy-five feet away. He had immediately called to his wife, who was toward the back of the house, saying "Something's wrong, something's really wrong. Something bad has happened over there."

Minutes later, the couple said, they had watched, hidden from view, as a young man they knew to be Gonzales's grandson Salvador Ramos, dressed in all black, exited the house carrying some kind of a soft-sided bag.

"He got in the truck, but he didn't know how to drive," Gilbert said, describing the eighteen-year-old's efforts to steal his grandmother's 2008 Ford F-150. "He couldn't get it out of park . . . but then he did and it took off." Gilbert, who died on October 31, 2022, after a battle with lung cancer, made the sound of spinning tires.

Within a handful of minutes, the sixty-six-year-old Gonzales managed to pick herself up from the floor and exit the house. Maria said their neighbor walked across the street, holding her face, and stood beneath a tree. "She said, 'Look what he did to me.'"

Gilbert remembered that he hurried inside to retrieve a towel to staunch the heavy bleeding, while his wife guided Gonzales to the back of the house. Maria, seventy-seven, said that she had not wanted to see the damage done to her neighbor's face, which was extensive. A hollow-point bullet had torn away a large part of her lower jaw, nicking an artery. The fact that she was still alive, much less able to speak, seemed miraculous to the Gallegoses.

"I told her to go to the back, because I was afraid that he [Ramos] would come back and shoot her and shoot me," Maria related. Both husband and wife heard sporadic gunfire coming from Robb. Later reports would show that Ramos fired almost two dozen times outside the school.

Maria said she called 911 but it took two times to get help. The first time she called, no one responded to the scene. The second time "it rang and rang and finally they picked up. I said, 'My neighbor's been shot in the face.'"

The Uvalde Police Department recorded no 911 calls from the Gallegoses' number. However, records supplied to me by Mr. Gallegos show two 911 calls made 2 minutes apart. The first was placed at 10:33 a.m. and another at 10:35. The Gallegoses' cellular provider attributed the one hour-time discrepancy to the time the call was stamped by the reporting equipment, which was located in a different time zone.

The first announcement of a 911 call for Diaz Street came at 11:36 a.m., as heard on a body camera worn by Sgt. Daniel Coronado of the Uvalde Police Department (UPD).

Uvalde County sheriff Ruben Nolasco testified in Austin to the Texas House Investigative Committee (he had declined to speak to them in Uvalde) that he was responding to the Robb shooting when he was flagged down in the street by a motorist who reported a woman had been shot on Diaz Street. Mr. Gallegos told me that the sheriff and a Texas Ranger were the first to arrive. They went through the house to the back but did not interact with the victim. The UPD also responded, as did Uvalde EMS, which transported Gonzales to Uvalde Memorial Hospital. After being stabilized, Celia Gonzales was airlifted to Methodist Hospital in San Antonio, where she would spend a month and undergo multiple surgeries. The Gallegoses' memory as to the exact time of the shooting was fuzzy, but according to the House Investigative Committee report, Ramos sent a private text to a girl in Germany at 11:21 a.m. saying, "I just shot my grandma in her head. Ima go shoot up a elementary school rn [right now]." The time-line places the stolen vehicle and the short drive to Robb as having occurred between 11:22 and 11:27 a.m.

Video footage from Hillcrest Funeral Home at the corner of Geraldine and Perez Streets revealed that at 11:28 a.m. Ramos lost control of his grandmother's pickup while trying to turn left off South Grove, where it dead ended into Geraldine. Instead of completing the turn, which would have taken him directly to the school half a block away, he hurtled straight ahead through a wooden barricade and down the steep embankment of a concrete drainage ditch. The F-150 came to rest right side up after a hard impact.

Office manager Claudia Perez told us that she heard a loud crash from inside the funeral home and felt a threat to the business and its employees. She checked the exterior security cameras and did not spot the source of the noise, but when she looked out her office window, which faced the school playground, the top of a vehicle was clearly visible in the bottom of the ditch. She shouted to fellow employees Gilbert Limones and Cody Briseño, who were nearby in the lobby, that there had been an accident and to call 911.

The three flew out the door. Perez remained behind in the driveway, while the men hurried across Geraldine toward the ditch. Limones, in an emotional interview Melissa Federspill and I conducted with five Hillcrest employees, said he was dialing 911, look-ing at his phone as he walked and did not see the driver struggling to get out, first through the driver's door and then through the passenger door. Finally Salvador Ramos stuck his feet out the passenger window and wriggled free of the pickup.

As the men drew within several dozen feet, Briseño said he kept repeating, "Are you okay? Do you need help?" Briseño said that he thought the man was "dazed or something from the hit" because he would not answer. The driver stared at them and then reached inside the vehicle. Briseño shouted, "He has a gun, he has a rifle!" Both men pivoted to run, but not before Briseño noticed that the driver was trying to insert a clip into an AR-15. Those precious seconds bought the would-be rescuers time to reach the road. By then the gunman had chambered rounds and fired three times, missing the men entirely.

Perez, who was standing less than 100 feet away, screamed when Briseño tripped on the curb and crashed into the asphalt. She thought her co-worker had been shot, but the short, solidly built man who performed many duties at Hillcrest, including grave preparation, scrambled to his feet. Perez yelled at them "begging them to get down, stay down," but fueled by adrenaline, the men continued running wildly until they dove through the open door of the funeral home.

Limones, the soft-spoken pastor at Casa El Shaddai in Uvalde, told us that he immediately composed himself, picked up his cell phone, and dialed 911 a second time. "I'm standing at this window watching, I'm reporting at this point what just happened, and I'm screaming at them, 'Please send cops quick,' and I'm watching him and he walks up the trail from the ditch, and I see him throw the duffle bag over the fence, and I tell them 'He's walking toward the school! Please hurry!'" The time was 11:32.

Video from the Hillcrest security camera captured in grainy detail what the pastor described in his plaintive report to police. A thin, long-haired figure clad in black carries a long gun and a duffle bag toward the school. His gait is neither hurried nor nervous—almost casual—as if he only needs to keep moving forward to fulfill an awful destiny.

CHAPTER 6

"Shut It Down"

Robb coach Yvette Silva watched in horror as a man scaled Robb Elementary's perimeter fence, raised a long gun, and began firing toward the school and a playground full of students. Silva told investigators that she ran from the field, keying her radio to report the intruder. "Coach Silva to office, somebody just jumped over the fence and he's shooting," she wrote. She then raced toward a group of third grade students on the playground, instructing them to lock down.

Silva expected to hear the announcement of a general school lockdown, but none was forthcoming. Instead, the intruder continued toward the fourth grade teachers' parking lot, firing his gun randomly toward the school.

Principal Mandy Gutierrez had returned to her office after one of many awards ceremonies when she heard Silva's warning. The first-year principal attempted to initiate a lockdown on the school's Raptor app but was hindered by an intermittent Wi-Fi signal. She chose not to communicate the lockdown over the school intercom for fear of alerting the intruder. Instead, she called school district police chief Pete Arredondo, who moments before had heard "shots fired" over the radio in his office at Uvalde High School.

Gutierrez reported to the Texas House Investigative Committee that the chief told her, "Shut it down, Mandy, shut it down." That order would have triggered the standard lockdown procedure practiced throughout the district, which called for teachers to lock their doors, move students to prearranged hiding places away from doors and windows, and turn out the lights. However, Arredondo told investigators he had no recollection of speaking to Gutierrez.

Minutes earlier, teacher's aide Emilia Marin had propped open the west outside door with a rock so she could retrieve items from her car in the nearby teachers' parking

24

lot. This was a common practice for school staff, particularly on special occasions like today's end-of-year party. Marin's Room 132 was immediately adjacent to the exterior door, and when she returned inside, she heard the crash of a vehicle outside. The teacher called 911, thinking someone was hurt.

"I walked out and then they yelled 'He has a gun!' . . . I ran back in. I ran back to the building and I closed the door," she said. "I am telling the operator that he is shooting. I could hear the kids screaming."

Marin told ABC News that children were outside on the playground, running for their lives. "I could hear the kids screaming. I closed the door. I went in and knocked on the teacher's door across from me. I was banging," she continued. "She opened it. She said 'What is going on?' I said, 'There is a shooter on campus.'"

Still on the phone with emergency operators, Marin decided to hide as she heard more gunshots. "There was shooting and it wouldn't stop. He just kept shooting and shooting," she said. "I looked around and I hid under the counter. The whole time I am asking the operator, 'Where are the cops? Where are the cops?'"

Teacher Sasha Martinez and her students had left Classroom 110 for recess a little before schedule. She told investigators the class was approaching the playground when they heard Coach Silva yelling and pointing toward the roof, imploring them to run. Hearing gunshots, some of the students began racing for the cafeteria, while others followed Martinez back toward their classroom in the west wing. For some reason, Martinez decided to take her class to an open classroom in another building. That simple decision more than likely saved lives.

Meanwhile, the gunman had reached the school's south entrance and the first of the classrooms on the west side, Room 102. Special education teacher Nicole Ogburn heard a scraping noise and walked to the window to investigate, where she was startled by a figure dressed in black who was pointing a gun toward the outdoor pavilion and shooting at students who were playing there.

The thirty-eight-year-old said she pivoted to the class and shouted at her students, "Get down, he has a gun!" She and co-teacher Patricia Albarado herded the children toward their prescribed hiding places beneath the built-in computer table that was a feature in all the fourth grade classrooms. Ogburn said the shooter reversed direction and began firing into their window. She crawled with the children to get out the line of sight with the window. Because of the angle, bullets hit the ceiling, showering debris on the two teachers and their fifteen students.

Ogburn lay on the floor beneath the table and a little boy crawled on top of her and began rubbing her arm. The teacher said she was shaking so badly that she could not make her fingers hit the right buttons on her Apple Watch. "But he was on me saying 'It's okay. It's okay. It's okay.'"

She dialed 911 three times. On the first attempt she got a call failed message; the second time an operator answered and then clicked off. She called a third time and somebody answered. "I was so scared that he was going to hear me and come into my classroom that I just said 'I'm a teacher in the fourth grade building at Robb Elementary. There is an active shooter in the building. Please get somebody here now.'"

When Ogburn first spotted the gunman, he was walking toward the south entrance, which would have put him in front of her classroom. Her door was not locked because the class had just returned from the cafeteria and children were coming in and out to use the restroom. She wanted to get up and lock the door, which must be done with a key from the outside, but feared the gunman would confront her in front of an open door with children inside.

But either the south door was locked or the attacker changed his mind, because he began walking north, pouring gunfire into windows of the four remaining classrooms on the west side. Moments later, at 11:33 a.m., he entered the west door, which under normal conditions, like the day before when high school seniors had attempted to gain access, would have been locked.

Surveillance video shows that once he got inside the building, the gunman rounded the corner into the northwest hallway and then turned left, where he shot into Classrooms 111 and 112. It is not clear from the footage which classroom he entered first. Investigators believe that since the lock to Room 111 was faulty (the tongue would not release into the strike plate without being jiggled), that door most likely was the point of entry.

Teacher Arnulfo Reyes told me he did not get the Raptor alert on his phone. His only warning was the sound of gunfire coming from Classroom 112, accompanied by pieces of Sheetrock flying from the walls. He believed the killer had already shot co-teachers Garcia and Mireles and many of their students before he walked through the closed (but unlocked) door that joined the rooms.

One of the students who survived in Room 112 said that Garcia attempted to lock the door, but when she stepped into the hallway, Ramos was already there. The child said the attacker shot out the small window in the door and pushed his way in, shooting the teacher and others.

What is undisputed is that within the first two and one-half minutes of entering the classrooms, Ramos fired more than 100 rounds of .223-caliber ammunition. Investigators later recovered 142 shell casings of the same caliber from the hallway and two classrooms.

Uvalde Police Department sergeant Eduardo "Eddie" Canales, who commanded the SWAT team, had been at Robb an hour earlier for his son's awards ceremony. Now back in his office on the city's west side, he noted the sudden commotion as officers began racing down the police department hallway. Canales told investigators he climbed into his patrol car and followed the acting chief, Lt. Mariano Pargas, to Robb, parking at a spot on Geraldine Street. Cars were stopped along the road and Canales immediately saw a man firing a weapon. The officer retrieved his AR-15 rifle, slapped in a magazine, and grabbed an extra. People at the funeral home just across the street were pointing at the school and Canales heard someone say the attacker was in or near the building.

Lt. Javier Martinez had also reached the scene, and the two officers met inside an open gate on the west side of the campus. Martinez carried his service weapon, a .40-caliber Glock 22, and wore a vest but without the armor plates.

Around the same time, an officer drove into the teachers' parking lot and, noticing a suspicious person dressed in black, sped forward. Unfortunately, the officer passed within yards of the attacker, who was hunkered down between parked cars, one of which belonged to Ogburn. The suspicious person turned out to be another coach, Abraham Gonzales.

Students in Room 111 were watching *The Addams Family* on Netflix when gunfire startled them. Reyes directed the children to "go to their places, close their eyes, and play like they were asleep." Ramos appeared suddenly, shot the teacher, and then turned the AR-15 on the students. Reyes told us they were crouched, "like sitting ducks," beneath a computer table that stretched across one side of the classroom.

Uvalde County justice of the peace Lalo Diaz, who would be called on that afternoon to identify the nineteen children and two teachers who were shot, told me in an interview that it looked as though the killer had swept his rifle back and forth under the table in Room 111 as if he were directing a water hose. Dozens of bullet holes and blood and tissue traced the path against the bare wall.

In describing the devastation in Room 112, Diaz recounted that Garcia, who was shot eleven times, had fallen forward with seven of the children fanned out behind her, as if she were holding out her arms to protect them.

Reyes said he did not know what the teachers and children could have done differently. The sudden, violent nature of the attack was simply overwhelming.

CHAPTER 7

77 Minutes

Gunfire echoed from within the building, as UPD officers Canales and Martinez followed the intruder's path through the west entrance and into the brightly painted blue-and-green fourth grade hallway. They described smoke and debris from bullet holes blasted in the Sheetrock walls. Sgt. Louis Landry soon joined the men as they positioned themselves to engage the shooter. Acting UPD chief Pargas also entered the hallway but remained behind cover with Landry.

School district police chief Pete Arredondo and Officer Adrian Gonzales with the school district police had been joined by UPD sergeants Donald Page and Daniel Coronado at the south entrance. They, too, had heard steady gunfire and upon entering the building encountered a cloud of debris and multiple brass shell casings on the floor. None of the initial responders recalled hearing screams or "having any contemporaneous understanding, as they arrived at the building, that teachers and students just then had been shot inside the classrooms," according to the Texas House Investigative Committee report.

School surveillance video showed that the officers moving north from the south entrance were the first to reach the vicinity of Classrooms 111 and 112. They found the rooms to be dark and the hallway quiet with no additional gunfire. An officer could be heard commenting on Coronado's body camera footage that the shooter's weapon was an AR-15. The officers also tried to use their radios, which worked only sporadically inside the building. In fact, the only radios that functioned consistently in the fourth grade wing on May 24 turned out to be those carried by agents with the US Border Patrol.

At the same time, Martinez and Canales were working their way south from the west entrance. Martinez approached along the east wall as Canales followed on the west wall, as the recording from Canales's body camera and school surveillance video show.

At approximately 11:37 a.m., the officers converged from both sides of the hallway on Rooms 111 and 112. Martinez peered into the vestibule for the two rooms and drew immediate gunfire. Fragments of building material torn away by the high-velocity bullets grazed the top of his head. Canales received a similar grazing wound to his ear. The officers, who had not returned fire, retreated and exited the building on the west side.

"He is in the class!" Canales spoke excitedly into his radio after stepping outside. "I've got shots fired! We're going to be in the building—the west side." At 11:38 a.m. Canales told other officers, "Dude, we gotta get in there! He's gonna keep shooting! We gotta get in there!"

After an officer on police radio asked dispatchers to activate SWAT, Canales, who headed the UPD SWAT team, again stepped outside and made a phone call, asking for help. "The guy's fucking shooting," he said. "He's in the classroom actually shooting. Robb School. Just givin' you a heads-up. The more the better." Canales and Martinez would later tell other officers that they did not return fire when Ramos shot through the door because the classroom was dark and they did not want to hit students.

From that moment, fear sucked the wind from active shooter protocol. The realization that the attacker commanded a weapon capable of piercing regulation body armor at the rate of almost 100 rounds a minute paralyzed officers and their commanders.

The mantra since Columbine, "Stop the shooting, stop the killing" was replaced by a maddening series of delays underpinned by mindless rationalization. The first occurred immediately after the officers received fire. Arredondo noticed that the light was on in Room 110, which was immediately south of Room 111. The room's teacher, Sasha Martinez, had been on the playground with her students when the attacker appeared. Instead of returning to Room 110, she herded the kids to a different building.

Arredondo decided that there could be a threat to Room 110, so he entered to clear it, noticing holes in the walls. The room was empty, and the chief told the House Investigative Committee weeks later: "There's no babies in there. It's awards day." He testified that he prayed that if Room 110 was empty, the children might be gone from the rooms the attacker occupied as well. However, the day after the shooting Arredondo acknowledged in an interview with a Texas Ranger and FBI investigators that he thought everyone might already have been killed, and he did not want to risk more deaths among students or teachers in nearby classrooms or police officers.

Adopting either line of reasoning led officers away from stopping the killing to containing the killer as a barricaded suspect in what was either an empty classroom or one filled with dead and wounded victims.

The chief's decision was a colossal mistake, especially given what was happening inside. In Room 111, teacher Arnulfo Reyes lay on his shredded arm, a fact that might have saved his life as the compression slowed the bleeding. But the shooter was not finished. After terrorizing Room 112, he returned to the wounded teacher. Reyes's memory is muddled as to when he was shot the second time—in the back as he lay on the floor. But he distinctly remembers the killer going to great lengths to discover any signs of life.

Ramos took an insulated cup from Reyes's desk and dribbled cold water on his back. Eliciting no response, the teenager knelt in front of the 47-year-old educator and "touched, tapped" the blood pooled beneath him. "He then flicked it in my face. He was looking for anything to make me flinch, but I was in so much pain that I couldn't respond." In a final act of cruelty, Ramos picked up the teacher's cell phone, which had been ringing and chirping steadily as family and friends tried desperately to make contact, and dropped it on his back. "He did that like four times. It kept ringing, and I thought 'He is going to get angry and shoot the phone.' I kept praying, 'Please don't shoot, please don't shoot.'"

Teacher Eva Mireles, clinging to life in Room 112, had managed to tie a plastic bag around her wounded arm and called (or texted) her husband, Uvalde Consolidated Independent School District police officer Ruben Ruiz, to say she had been shot. Ruiz is pictured on body camera video in the hallway yards from his wife's classroom. The time stamp is 11:48 a.m. The camera records the officer holding up his cell phone as if in supplication. "My wife says she has been shot," he said before being led away by Uvalde County constable Johnny Field.

In Room 109, teacher Elsa Avila had also suffered a life-threatening wound. She had been struck by a round fired when Ramos began shooting in Rooms 111 and 112. The .223-caliber bullet passed through both Sheetrock walls of Room 110 and struck Avila in the right side of her chest, lodging in her colon. A piece of that same bullet or separate fragments also hit student Leann Garcia, tearing a small hole in her nose. Had the high-velocity projectile not been slowed by the drywall, the teacher probably would not have survived.

Avila told me she fell to the ground in front of her students, losing her cell phone, which skittered across the floor and beneath a desk. She crawled after it and managed to send a text, although she sent it to a family group instead of the teacher group she intended. "I am shot and bleeding," she texted. The time was 11:35 a.m., two minutes after the gunman first entered the building. After texting Vice Principal Shawna Wolbert, who was away from the campus that day, Avila reached out at 11:50 a.m. to her close friend in Room 106, Mercedes Salas, a teacher "who gets things done." Salas had taught fourth grade at Robb for sixteen years and Avila had been there for Salas from day one as her mentor. Now the mentor was in trouble.

Salas, who agreed to be interviewed in support of Avila, said "As soon as I got her message, I texted immediately, and [Robb principal Mandy] Gutierrez responded. She asked where she was, and I said 'She's in in her room, and I need you to help her.' She was like 'Okay.'"

Not hearing anything more from the principal, Salas tried her wounded friend. "Amiga, are you okay?" she texted. After getting no response, Salas said she began to panic. "I was almost in tears, but I couldn't be in tears because I had my kids, and I had to stay calm for them."

Salas's Room 106 was directly across the hall from Room 112, where gunfire had been heard before any Raptor alert from the principal. Salas and her students crouched in the darkened classroom as bullets ripped through the walls inches above their heads. One of her students, Ivan Cerillo, whose sister Miah was in Room 112, remembered lots of smoke in the room from Sheetrock dust. Salas said the gunfire never stopped but continued sporadically during the 45 minutes that she and her sixteen students waited for police to pull them from the windows.

Officers' supposition that Robb students had gone home early because of awards day flew in the face of logic. Children had been evacuated from the second and third grade rooms early on. A simple phone call or question to the principal, who was locked down in the cafeteria, would have confirmed that the fourth grade classrooms were nearly full. Police knew by 11:48 a.m. that an officer's wife, Eva Mireles, had been shot in Room 112. Five minutes earlier, 13 minutes after the shooter entered the building, school district officer Adrian Gonzales said over police radio that the suspect was in a classroom. "The classroom should be in session right now," he said. "The class should be in session . . . Mrs. Eva Mireles."

Coronado's response, saying under his breath "Oh, no, oh no," is captured in recording from the body camera he wore that day. The officer did not realize that his ten-year-old cousin, Xavier Lopez, was inside, fighting for his life from multiple gunshot wounds.

Texas Ranger Christopher Ryan Kindell, who was stationed in Uvalde, arrived around noon. He was the highest-ranking Department of Public Safety officer at the scene. He told investigators that he immediately concluded that someone needed to take charge and began organizing officers positioned outside. And yet despite more gunfire and calls confirming that children were inside, the ranger did nothing to challenge the idea that the shooter was a barricaded suspect.

Body camera footage recorded by UPD officer Justin Mendoza at 12:12 p.m. relays a 911 call from a student in Room 112 saying that there were victims in the classroom. Mendoza had walked outside of the building and was standing next to Acting Chief Pargas and Detective Jose "Jrod" Rodriguez. Kindred was also walking nearby, and Canales and Field were in earshot when the information was shared loudly. "They say they just got a 911 call and there are victims in the classroom," Rodriguez said.

"Victims?" Pargas repeated. Four minutes later, at 12:16 p.m., the acting chief telephoned dispatch and asked about the 911 call. "The calls you got from . . . from one of the students, what did they say?"

"Okay, Khloie's [Torres] going to be in Room 112, Mariano, 112."

"So how many are still alive?" Pargas asked.

"Eight to nine are still alive. She's not too sure. . . . She's not too sure how many are actually DOA or possibly injured . . ."

Pargas responded with "Okay, okay, thanks," and disconnected.

At 12:18 p.m. Pargas talked to Kindell about organizing the flow of information. And then the sixty-five-year-old acting chief walked away. Video footage does not show him returning to the hallway until the shooter had been killed.

Information about the 911 call was quickly shared with Paul Guerrero, acting commander of the Border Patrol's elite tactical unit known as BORTAC. Around the same time, a US marshal carried a rifle shield into the hallway. Another 40 minutes passed before Guerrero's team breached the classroom, according to a *Washington Post* review of available videos and interviews.

The 911 call from Khloie Torres at 12:10 p.m. was not the first from Room 112. Khloie's best friend Amerie Jo Garza was dialing 911 when the gunman killed her and her teacher Irma Garcia, who was trying to protect them. "She [Ms. Garcia] ran over to us, sat down and started covering my friend. She started saying 'No!" because he [Ramos] said 'You will die' and he shot my friend with the phone and he shot my teachers Ms. Garcia and Ms. Mireles." Khloie described Mireles "screaming and crying and calling for her daughter."

Khloie said she got up to turn her friend's phone off, afraid it would attract more attention, and when she did, Ramos tried to shoot her. She ran and was struck by shrapnel. Khloie used slain teacher Eva Mireles's phone, at great personal risk, to call 911 a total of four times, pleading with police to save them.

One of the first calls from a trapped student came at 12:03 p.m. It was barely audible. "There's a school . . ." the muffled voice says, breaking up in the recording, "at Robb

Elementary." The call lasted 84 seconds. The child remained silent as the dispatcher asked their name and room number.

During Khloie's initial call, she told the dispatcher "There's a lot of bodies," the *New York Times* reported. The child added that her teacher had been shot but was still alive.

Khloie remained on the line for more than 17 minutes. While she spoke, another dispatcher answered a call from the Department of Public Safety and erroneously reported that Arredondo was in the room with the shooter.

At 12:19 p.m., Miah Cerillo used the same cell phone to call 911. "Hi, can you please send help?"

"There's a school shooting," Khloie said in another call at 12:36 p.m.

"Yes, I'm aware," the dispatcher responded. "I was talking to you earlier. You're still in your room? You're still in Room 112?"

"Yeah," Khloie replied.

"Ok. You stay on the line with me. Do not disconnect," the dispatcher said.

"Can you tell the police to come to my room?" Khloie whispered.

The dispatcher said: "I've already told them to go to the room."

A survivor in Room 112, Noah Orona, lay bleeding from a back wound. His parents told me that Noah heard a boy whispering to him "Hide with us." The friend, Jordan Olivarez, was concealed with Jaydien Canizales beneath a computer table with a long black curtain. Noah, who is big for his age, said he could barely move and was afraid that if he made it to the table his legs would stick out and "the man would find them." He lay still, listening to a stricken girl nearby who was struggling to breathe.

Jordan pulled his cousin, Kendall Olivarez, from under their slain teacher and toward the hiding place, but he only had room to get the wounded girl's legs behind the curtain.

Asked if Classroom 112 had grown quiet, Jaydien said no "because a little girl was crying." The nine-year-old boy said he thought police were telling children to call out if they needed help. One girl did, catching the attention of the attacker, who then shot her dead. Jaydien suffered hearing loss in his left ear, the result of gunshots fired so close to his head.

Khloie recalled that it was actually the attacker calling out from Room 111 who mimicked police, causing her classmate to call out for help.

Hallway video recorded four shots fired inside the classroom at 12:21 p.m., further evidence that the shooter had not stopped the shooting or the killing. Still, officers took no direct action other than to wait. They waited for ballistic shields, more firepower, and even keys to unlock a door that in all probability was not locked. Surveillance video shows four different ballistic shields arriving on the scene between 11:52 and 12:21. The last shield, furnished by the US marshal, was rifle rated to withstand rounds from the rifle the attacker carried.

The search for a master key absorbed more than 40 minutes, a vast amount of time given the casualties. Arredondo tried more than thirty keys, many of them on the door to Room 109, behind which Avila and her students cowered in fear. When Avila watched the hallway video footage after being released from University Hospital, she told me it was disturbing to see Arredondo standing with a wad of keys in front of her door. "That is my classroom. We are in there. All he had to do was tell us it was the police, and we would have let him in."

There is no evidence that Arredondo sought the master key from the principal or the head custodian, Jaime Perez, who had also taken cover in the school cafeteria. Officers eventually asked school district maintenance supervisor Jacob Kubish, the stepfather of Makenna Elrod, to produce keys for Classrooms 111 and 112. But by then the rampage had ended.

While Arredondo fumbled for a way to get at the shooter, other officers began evacuating students from classrooms on the west side of the building. Nicole Ogburn's Classroom 102 was among the first to be rescued. The teacher said police came to her door shortly after noon and advised they would be taking the class out through the windows.

Ogburn and co-teacher Patricia Albarado pushed the shelves of the classroom's library out of the way and positioned a chair next to the window. Terrified students climbed through the opening, aided by law enforcement outside, and ran in the direction of the crowds that had formed in front of the funeral home. The process was repeated for the four remaining rooms on the east side of the building. In some cases, teachers opened windows and in other instances officers used tools to break out the thick glass.

Monica Saiz-Martinez, who worked at Hillcrest, did not remember what time she got to the west gate to the playground, but it was open, "always open," and kids were running in her direction. Martinez looked back at the funeral home and locked eyes with Claudia Perez, who was watching from the front door. "I really feel at that moment that our motherly instinct kicked in, and I just said 'Run toward the funeral home!'" Anxious parents crowded the police cordon, blocking the fleeing children, and Martinez remembered yelling "Come on, Uvalde, come on, work together, get out of the way!"

Inside the fourth grade hallway, around 12:30 p.m., the BORTAC team finally moved into position. Their movements were directed by SWAT team leader Paul Guerrero without any apparent coordination from District Chief Arredondo. And the BORTAC team also waited, for another 20 minutes. Finally, at 12:50 p.m., four BORTAC members and two deputy sheriffs, one from Uvalde and another, Joe Vasquez, from nearby Zavala County, entered Room 111.

Ramos immediately opened fire from his position in front of a closet but was overwhelmed by a hail of gunfire. Justice of the Peace Diaz estimated that the attacker was struck by as many as twenty-five bullets. "He was lying face down, but his body was facing up, as though he had been completely broken in the middle."

The officers who breached the darkened classroom in a "stack" and immediately fanned out, described the sickening feeling of stumbling over the bodies of dead children. The classroom's teacher, Arnulfo Reyes, lay face down in his own blood, eyes clenched tight, waiting for the gunfire to end.

When the barrage finally stopped, Reyes said a Border Patrol agent advised him to get up and leave the room. The teacher responded that he could not move. The next thing he remembered was being dragged into the hallways by his pants leg.

CHAPTER 8

"Let Us Go In"

Kindergarten teacher Veronica Mata was in her Dalton School office finishing end-of-year paperwork when staff relayed a message that Robb was in lockdown. Her reaction was the same as virtually everyone in the city that day: "Just another bailout." Still, she texted her daughter's teacher, Irma Garcia. When she got no response, she called her husband, Jerry, who worked as an aviation mechanic at Garner Field Airport. He also was skeptical but decided to check the Uvalde Police Department Facebook page, where incidents were routinely posted. The message that popped up said that there had been a shooting at Robb. Jerry's co-workers at X-Air Flight Support offered that it was probably just "people shooting at each other," but the father of two girls later said that "something told me to go."

When Jerry Mata reached the school around noon, he was submerged in pandemonium. He said it felt like a combat zone. Children were running toward safety at Hillcrest Memorial Funeral Home, while parents were fighting with police to get inside the school or to extricate their kids from the funeral home. Police appeared to be running everywhere at once and were as "scared as the parents."

"What are they doing trying to fight with us?" Mata later said he wondered. "Get in there. You guys are all suited up and everything, get in there."

Mata grew up in Uvalde, the son of a soft-spoken house painter named Raymundo Mata who taught his son to be respectful, to give people the benefit of the doubt. Jerry said he wanted to believe that law enforcement was doing the best it could, even though the chaos of the scene suggested otherwise.

When a little girl ran from the school with a bloodied face, the crowd's mood turned even more frantic. Jerry told me later that at that point, things began to happen in slow motion for him and all of the sounds—shouts, sirens, helicopters—became muted, leaving only voices.

When Pete Luna captured images of the girl with the bloodied face, his reaction was that she must have fallen and broken her nose. That kind of injury—or any facial cut—produces excessive bleeding but did not necessarily equate to a shooting. That perception changed when other children began to emerge with more blood. At that point, Pete accepted the awful possibility that an active shooter might be targeting students.

He texted Kimberly Mata-Rubio to ask if she were coming to Robb, adding that he would check for Lexi Rubio among the children sheltering inside the funeral home. Pete did not remember the time, but Kimberly appeared soon after and then almost as quickly was gone, headed to the civic center.

Meanwhile, Pete had officially put aside his cameras and assumed the role of devoted friend. If Lexi was inside the funeral home, he would find her.

Pete Luna, who had five older brothers and one little sister, had grown up in the tiny farming and ranching community of Batesville 20 miles southeast of Uvalde. He had discovered early on how to leverage his resourceful mind and positive attitude to open virtually any door. He and his brothers had found ways to access ample hunting and fishing on the properties where their father worked. Later in life, if Pete and his friends obtained tickets to sporting or music events, they inevitably ended up in the best seats thanks to Pete's smooth talking. When a new tire store had opened in Uvalde, the business offered a cash prize to anyone who could roll a tire between two markers about 100 feet away. Pete had walked away with $1,000, quipping that he had been rolling stolen tires in Batesville since grade school.

The "stolen" tires was meant as a joke but there was no doubt that the pithy bear of a man was a quick study. He explained that it was just a matter of discovering the trick, like at carnivals where he could always toss the ball in the correct hole or shoot down the required number of targets to claim a prize. When you grow up hunting with a single-shot .22 and a handful of cartridges, you need every advantage.

Pete's father worked for area landowners who grew an assortment of winter garden vegetables. As the youngest son, Pete found that his older brothers attracted the most attention from their hardworking father, who was highly valued for his dependability and skill with machinery. Consequently, the number five son, a self-avowed "brat," identified more with his mother. Not only did she join the family in the field harvesting onions, cabbages, and cantaloupes when necessary, she also worked in the Batesville school cafeteria, a job she held for many years. Pete admired the way she used her mind to make life easier. For him, that was the key to escaping the brutal sun and backbreaking field work that he loathed.

Before joining the *Leader-News* in 2006 as a typesetter (he would become circulation manger two years later and general manager in 2021), Pete had transitioned to indoor jobs, including as a convenience store clerk, troubleshooter for an internet company, and medical clinic assistant. Those experiences had taught him to spot fraud or a cheat a mile away. In the end, his mind, his street smarts, and his radar for people counted more than a BA from any university. All of those assets more than qualified him to help guide our newspaper.

———————

At the funeral home, Pete Luna said that Lexi was the daughter of a dear friend and that her father was a deputy sheriff and pleaded to be let in. Maybe not to Luna's surprise, but to the astonishment of other parents clamoring to enter, a staff member opened the door. Luna quickly pulled the door closed behind him against shouted profanities and more banging and jerking. A search of the rooms failed to produce Lexi, only children huddled next to their teachers on the floor, looking up with fearful eyes and hoping that the big man looking down at them was their father.

Finally, Pete walked outside and called Meghann. "I just told her 'This is not good . . . this is not good. I can't find Lexi.'" With that, he ended the call and wept.

Hearing from his wife about a shooter at Robb, Miguel Cerillo implored his co-worker at the Continental Tire testing facility to either loan him his truck or take him to the school. Cerillo told me he had sold his "crotch rocket" motorcycle the day before and needed help finding his daughter Miah. The friend replied that his girlfriend had children at Robb and he would drive. The men covered the seven miles to the city within minutes.

Like Mata, Cerillo entered a world of confusion, where hundreds of law enforcement officers had been neutralized by the perception (or order) that "other personnel" were handling the situation. For a large number of parents, it was insupportable, and yet not all reacted in the same way.

Ten years earlier, Cerillo had moved to Uvalde from a different world, what he called a "Houston ghetto," where a man's word was only as impactful as his fists. What he saw at Robb were "cowards and pussies," hundreds of officers who refused to do the job they had sworn to do, to serve and protect.

"I told them to let me go in there. . . . I don't know whose class it is, but I need my baby out," Cerillo described his confrontation with officers. When they pointed an "AR and a Taser at my body," the thirty-four-year-old father challenged the officers to "either shoot me or let me go in."

Cerillo said he was standing next to a group of fathers who were legally armed—wearing pistols on their hips—who also insisted on going inside to rescue their children. The men said, "If y'all can't go in there and do nothing for the kids, let us go in."

Virginia Vela's first reaction to the shooting was to check in with Uvalde EMS and offer her help. The young mother of two had joined the emergency services provider six months earlier but did not have a shift on May 24. She learned in a call with co-workers that units were staging at a convenience store near Robb, since EMS could not enter a shooting scene until it was considered secure.

By the time Vela and husband Bobby Olivarez reached Robb, children had been freed from most of the classrooms and were safe in the funeral home. Cody Briseño, the funeral home worker who had been fired on by the attacker, knew Virginia and allowed her inside to look for her son Jordan. A quick search failed to locate the boy or any of his classmates, so Vela applied her basic EMT knowledge to treat kids with minor cuts and scrapes suffered as they crawled through broken windows.

When Vela emerged from Hillcrest, she learned that medics had been requested at the scene. A couple of ambulances had been moved into position in front of the elementary school, and Vela "jumped on a crew" and began assembling triage tags (basic information such as name, age, vital signs, etc.). With news spreading that the shooter had been "apprehended," Vela and a partner grabbed a stretcher and pushed it toward the back door of the fourth-grade wing.

"Honestly, I don't know how I was doing it. I mean my faith . . . I almost was already thinking my son was gone, because I didn't see him running. It was his building. I didn't know what I was going to walk into," Vela remembered with obvious emotion.

Suddenly shots rang out inside the building and the medics scrambled for cover. Vela told me that she couldn't remember how many shots, but they were "back and forth." She was stunned by the fact that the gunman had not been subdued until that moment. "This whole time I'm standing outside the building, and he's shooting my son . . . he's killing all of these kids. And we're just standing here?"

Almost immediately officers began running from the building with wounded children. Vela described one of the first victims as being "not suitable" for treatment because the child had suffered a disfiguring head wound and was clearly deceased. At first she thought it was Jordan, but after a quick look at the clothing, she realized it was another child. "We covered the head so no one could see him—or her—I don't know."

Vela expressed outrage that officers had brought the child out in such condition. "Why would you do that? Why wouldn't they bring me somebody that we could save? They brought someone I could do nothing for, not even a surgeon."

Virginia Vela moved from truck to truck helping treat kids and a teacher, cleaning away blood, providing oxygen, taking vitals. On three different occasions when no victims were coming, Vela climbed into an empty ambulance—Uvalde, Alamo, or Sabinal EMS, whatever was available—got on her knees and prayed "for my son to still be there . . . for God to give me the strength to pull through and for my co-workers . . . for God to just work through us."

Two students smeared with blood were brought to the back of the ambulance and Vela and her partner began checking their injuries. A third student entered through the side door, and the young EMT assessed him as well. In the process it dawned on her that all three children were her son's classmates. She finally asked if they knew where Jordan was. The kids told her he was in the classroom, but they did not know his condition.

Determining that her crew needed more help, Vela asked the supervisor for an additional EMT, but the new person was already walking toward their unit with yet another student. Vela helped the child into the ambulance and when she turned around, Jordan was running from the school alongside an officer who was carrying another student over his shoulder.

Javier Cazares was having lunch at his sister-in-law's house when he learned about an active shooter. He sped to Robb, parked his pickup on a side street with the motor still running, and charged toward the school. The stout 1997 Uvalde High School graduate got within 40 feet of the west wing before hitting police resistance.

"I have a picture where you see how close I was . . . and just hoping my daughter would come out, but that never happened," Cazares said. As time dragged on and children stopped exiting from the windows and there was no news from family waiting at the civic center, Cazares grew more alarmed. Then Khloie Torres was carried from her classroom covered in blood, and "things turned really ugly."

Amerie Jo Garza's stepfather, Angel, asked Khloie if she needed help. Not knowing who the man was, she responded that it was not her blood but that of her best friend, Amerie Jo. "Angel went crazy, and they tackled him," Cazares said of the scene.

Javier Cazares and his wife, Gloria, then spotted a little girl who looked like their daughter Jackie receiving CPR on the sidewalk. It turned out not to be their daughter. A message from a niece at Uvalde Memorial Hospital reported that Jackie had just been carried in on a gurney.

Khloie's father, Ruben Torres, was at work with a SwiftWater crew installing a water pump near Sutherland Springs south of San Antonio when he learned that his daughter had been wounded at Robb. The former Marine called his boss to explain why he was leaving. His next call was to 911 to alert law enforcement that he was in a government vehicle headed to Uvalde in response to a school shooting. He described the car and gave the dispatcher his name and driver's license number. "I'm not going to be stopping for your police officers. I'm just giving you a heads up," he told them.

Veronica Luevanos was "waiting and waiting" for her daughter Jailah to appear among the students, but there was no sign of her. Finally, a boy from her classroom, Room 112, Gilberto Mata, came to her and said "I'm sorry I couldn't save Jailah. I tried, but I couldn't." Luevanos knew Gilberto as the son of a co-worker at Church's Texas Chicken.

"So I lost my dad the week before on Tuesday and then the next week I lost Jailah and Jayce [Luevanos, a nephew in Room 111]. It was a double whammy for us," Luevanos told me.

Miguel Cerillo watched as Miah appeared with other students who were being shepherded toward waiting buses. He began running for his daughter, shouting her name, but police officers tackled him and pinned him to the ground.

Azeneth Rodriguez said she chased her son Jaydien, who was being directed toward the buses, but once again officers intervened, insisting that parents would have to pick their children up at the hospital. Once he got inside the bus, the ten-year-old put his hands against the window and cried for his mother. Rodriguez hurried to her car and fell in directly behind bus no. 19 as it covered the two-mile trip to the hospital. She never lost sight of Jaydien, who had moved to the back of the bright-yellow vehicle and pressed his face against the glass to maintain sight of his mother.

The driver, Silvia Uriegas, had been directed to report to Robb just before noon. Because of the congestion, she parked in the side entrance to Hillcrest off Perez Street and waited. Over the next hour, the Uvalde native, said she occupied a catbird seat to a show that seemed more suited to a B movie horror film than to reality. Finally Uriegas learned she had been handed a mission for which no Uvalde school bus driver had ever been trained. Bus no. 19, without benefit of any medical supplies other than Band-Aids, was to transport wounded children to the hospital.

Uriegas watched in horror as BORTAC agents ran toward her carrying children, all of whom were smeared with blood. The officers loaded six kids in quick succession, but then decided to shift two—who were more severely wounded—to awaiting ambulances. That left four students on board until one little boy, Gilberto Mata, was pulled from a window by his father. After that, Uriegas maneuvered her bus through the crazy maze of randomly parked civilian vehicles and squad cars and headed to the hospital. Two Border Patrol officers remained on board to assist the children, one of whom was bleeding profusely from a leg wound.

"They were crying, like 'Mom . . . mom.!' I mean, they kept yelling for their mom. The whole ride," Uriegas said.

Once the students were taken into the hospital, the fifty-eight-year-old driver, who operates her own denture fabrication business, sat in the driver's seat and cried, wondering "What just happened?" The two officers returned and requested a ride back to Robb.

The handsome bus driver with perfect white teeth wanted to offer the agents something to clean the blood from their hands, but all she had were wipes. The agents declined the offer.

Pete Luna had resumed taking photographs and recording video, including images of Kimberly darting in front of the lens after she spied a familiar-looking child in the distance. The photographer zoomed in, revealing a little boy who had been shot through the shoulder, followed by a girl gripping her bloody arm who also appeared to have a gunshot wound to the leg. "And these kids are running . . . with gunshot wounds. It's unbelievable." Pete recalled.

Eventually, the pace of evacuations slowed because there were no more children to be saved. The majority of parents had melted away, headed for the hospital or back to the civic center. Those who remained had terrible thoughts to contemplate. Word circulated that teacher Arnulfo Reyes had been killed, which meant children in his Classroom 111, like Lexi and Jackie, may have shared the same fate. The same was feared for those students in 112 who had not been seen leaving the school.

The parents of the still-missing children, including Kimberly, stood out for Pete. He knew many of the adults from years of photographing community events and watched as they stared at the empty Robb doorway in the growing silence. "It was just a void. You could see it in their eyes, in their body language. They were just defeated."

When Pete returned to the newspaper around 2 p.m., it was clear that he had been immersed in trauma. Always upbeat and unflappable, he looked deflated, as though the killer's rampage had taken part of his life as well.

We talked shop for some minutes, about what he had seen and about possible photographs he had captured. He described the panicked parents and students running for their lives. Those images seemed to stick with him most: the absolute terror on children's faces as they ran from a killer who was murdering their fourth grade classmates. The juxtaposition of those tragic faces with the happy ones of children running to score in the myriad sports photos Luna had taken in the last decade was devastating.

Certainly his initial supposition about a simple act of domestic violence had been exploded. There was no doubt that an active shooter had killed students. No one in authority had proffered casualty numbers, but Pete felt certain that the toll would not be small. Even more haunting to him was the fact that he had been unable to help Kimberly find Lexi. Through the long minutes of documenting the attack, that had been his most fervent wish: not to take emotion-charged photographs of children running to safety but to text Kimberly with the message "I found her."

CHAPTER 9

Asylum

As the only adequate structure near Robb, Hillcrest Memorial Funeral Home was the logical place to shelter refugees. And yet it was a singular irony. Funeral homes are meant to dispatch the dead with quiet efficiency and offer grieving families a measure of compassion. No one in that line of work, including Hillcrest employees, ever expected to pivot 180 degrees into the business of saving lives.

But there they were, opening the doors to wild-eyed students being pursued by even more hysterical parents. Hillcrest owner Leroy Briones was racing back to Uvalde from Port Aransas on the Gulf Coast (he would be pulled over four times for speeding and sent on his way, as the shooting news had spread statewide) after being apprised of shots fired at his employees. He issued orders to Claudia Perez for everyone to remain inside the building and lock the doors. It was a prudent reaction for a manager whose foremost obligation was to protect his employees and his business.

But Briones, the father of six, would not arrive for another hour and in the meantime his employees ignored the directive, turning the small funeral home into a sanctuary for one hundred students and many of their teachers. Once inside, they filled the two small chapels designed for a couple of dozen mourners. The refugees spilled into the hallways and assorted offices.

The thing that stuck in Perez's memory was the sound of the children's crying. "They were scared. They wanted mommy and daddy. That's all they wanted."

And parents wanted their children. Once the adults spied kids racing toward the funeral home, they charged. At that point it turned into a siege. Employees worked desperately to calm the terrified children, who thought that the parents banging and pulling on doors were the shooter trying to get at them. At first the staff was on its own, but gradually law enforcement began to offer security, and once the shooter had been killed, the Department of Public Safety set up a command post inside the facility. Among their instructions were not to release any children from the premises.

Teachers Nicole Ogburn and Patricia Albarado were among the first to reach the funeral home. They gathered their students on the pews in one of the chapels and Albarado sent out a group text to parents saying "We are okay and our class is safe."

"The people at the funeral home were amazing. They were guarding doors, they were yelling at people outside: 'We're trying to keep these kids safe and make them feel safe,'" Ogburn said. "And then one of the funeral directors came up there and he was like 'Quit banging on the doors. There's children and you're scaring them to death.'"

Ogburn worked to soothe her students as well as those from Elsa Avila's class, since the teacher had been transported to the hospital. "The children were saying 'My teacher, my teacher, my teacher' . . . they were so worried about her." Ogburn began calling the children's parents, trying her best to relieve them of their worry.

The girl who had fled the school with a bloody face was ushered into one of the chapels where Perez asked if she could clean her up. The girl agreed, saying it was her friend's blood, but Perez felt there was too much blood. She helped Leann Garcia into the bathroom to wash, partly to keep her from scaring the other children. That's when Perez noticed a BB-size hole in the girl's nose.

Uvalde Memorial Hospital ER doctor Gilberto Arbelaez, who treated Leann less than an hour later, said the fragment pierced her right nostril and lodged in the upper left part of her nose, causing minimal fractures. "Millimeters in another direction and it could have killed her," he said of one of the few body scans he looked at that day with a happy outcome for the patient.

Leann's mother, Angelica Rodriguez, gained entrance to Hillcrest after convincing a deputy sheriff that her daughter was the one with the facial wound. Seeing her daughter relatively unhurt flooded Rodriguez with relief. The feeling doubled when she discovered that her fourth grade son, Ivan, was also safe inside. In a panic to find her injured daughter, she had temporarily forgotten Ivan.

Another father who came looking for his child was admitted to the building because he was known to the staff. Alfred Garza III, an automobile salesman at Cecil Atkission Motors, a local business, pitched in to comfort kids despite the fact that his only child, Amerie Jo, was still inside her classroom.

Garza arrived at Robb around noon, as police had begun pushing parents away from the school toward the parking lot at Hillcrest. The buzz in the crowd was that students would be released from the back door of the funeral home, so families congregated there. Garza joined them, but when kids were not forthcoming, families moved on. Left alone by the back door, he decided to try it.

"I don't know why I thought of it, but I turned the knob to the back door and it opened, so I went in." A maintenance worker intercepted Garza and asked him to leave, but Claudia Perez came to the rescue, telling the anxious father he could stay but to lock the door behind him.

The scene inside the smaller chapel was chaotic. Some children were crying uncontrollably. One little girl told Garza that she was going to have an asthma attack. He assured the children that they were safe and said that if they knew their parents' phone numbers, he would try to call them. Garza, who graduated from Uvalde High School in 2005, next moved to the larger chapel, where he joined the staff in trying to organize the students according to their classroom and their names.

Monica Saiz-Martinez said Garza assisted boys who needed to use the restroom, hugged children who were crying, and helped with other tasks. "Alfred was in there, and he was so calm. Not knowing . . . I think maybe it was just the unbelief. Like there's no way. 'I'm just waiting for my daughter. She's somewhere,' because what else can you do? I didn't see him cry or anything. He was just helping."

Somewhere in the middle of that work, the thirty-four-year-old received a message that his daughter had been injured. He departed immediately for Uvalde Memorial Hospital.

Funeral home employees knew many of the children in the close-knit community, either directly or by connecting their features with those of acquaintances.

"I remember looking at kids and trying to see who I recognized," said Martinez. "Whose kid is that? Oh, gosh, I call the sister at the church: 'Your granddaughter's in here.' I called another: 'Sir, your grandson is here.'"

School district buses had already transported second and third graders to the Willie de Leon Civic Center, where they were reunited with parents. By around 2 p.m., the buses had returned to transport fourth graders from the funeral home to the civic center. As soon as that operation began, parents shifted their attention to the city facility downtown. There they traded one chaotic scene for another.

CHAPTER 10

Medical Emergency

U valde Memorial Hospital emergency room physician Gilberto Arbelaez had just treated a patient for a life-threatening pulmonary edema when he heard "gunshots fired" over the radio of a nearby security guard. Texts and phone calls followed in quick succession, advising that an active shooter was at Robb Elementary and that someone was being airlifted to San Antonio after being shot in the face. The confusing reports flew through the community, but with each iteration the scope of the catastrophe grew into sharper focus.

Arbelaez, who is trained in Level 1 trauma care, geared up his small ER team. The first order of business was to return the emergency department to its optimal setup. Floors that had been improperly finished months earlier in the new hospital were being redone that morning, and crews had relocated the ER to a space nearby. Arbelaez's staffers, which included a physician assistant and a few nurses, worked quickly to reassemble the department, while others sought to discharge non-emergent patients. The team gathered extra beds, intubation trays, chest tubes, and tourniquets—and then they waited.

Adam Apolinar, the hospital's chief operations officer at the time, said the hospital learned of the shooting from employees rather than through official channels. Apolinar telephoned CEO Tom Nordwick, who had gone home for lunch, to tell him that there was an apparent shooting and directed the hospital's head of security to contact UPD for clarification. The initial response from the police department was there had been a shooting at a school. "But we weren't told that it was a mass shooting. . . . We anticipate one, two, maybe three victims . . . so we were more than prepared for that."

Apolinar immediately activated the incident command center in the conference room on the second floor. In the disaster drill that the staff practiced two or three times a year, the commander assigned tasks to a dozen individuals, ranging from nursing and deploying physicians to procuring supplies, including whole blood, and handling the press. Longtime employees Karla Radicke and Sheri Rutledge had recently resigned from public relations and marketing, respectively, so Nordwick volunteered to deal with the press and to handle communications.

Dr. Roy Guerrero, a Uvalde native who was the community's only pediatrician, was having lunch at Oasis Outback on the city's far east side near the hospital when he received a text message from a colleague at a San Antonio trauma center: "Hey, Guerrero, why is every single pediatric surgeon and anesthesiologist on call for a mass shooting in Uvalde?" The doctor replied that he had no idea. He returned staff members, who had joined him for lunch, to his clinic and sped to the hospital.

"It seemed like it took forever," Arbelaez said of the long wait for casualties in a story that appeared in *ACEP Now*, a publication of the American College of Emergency Physicians—long minutes ticking by in the "golden hour" of trauma treatment. Finally the team got the call from EMS that the first patient was inbound.

"Everybody was gowned and gloved. Lines were primed [IV lines cleared of air], everything was ready," Arbelaez said. "We were waiting for the ambulances to arrive in the emergency entrance when all of the sudden we heard shouting from the lobby. For some reason the ambulances decided to bring the patients through the main doors."

The confusion stemmed from the fact that the new hospital had been open for less than two months and signs designating various entrances, including for ambulances, were still not in place.

Arbelaez and general surgeon Dr. Sandra Boenig looked down the hallway to see two young girls being pushed toward them on gurneys. The first child was virtually lifeless and when Boenig performed a cut as part of a pericardial window (an opening to release fluids from around the heart), there was no bleeding from the child's skin. "She was completely exsanguinated by the time she got to us," Arbelaez said in the publication.

The next child was treated for gunshots in the shoulder and buttocks. Doctors then turned to fourth grade teacher Arnulfo Reyes. The forty-seven-year-old teacher had lain on his classroom floor for over an hour with gunshot wounds in the arm and back. By the time he was airlifted to Brooke Army Medical Center in San Antonio, he had lost 70 percent of his blood. Another young girl, who had been shot in the chest, arm, and hand, received emergency treatment. Then came a little boy covered with a white sheet. He was taken to the only space available for the deceased—the hospital chapel.

When Roy Guerrero walked into the hospital around 12:30 p.m., he was greeted by the shouting of frantic parents, some of who called his name, pleading with the doctor to find their children. Right away, he spotted Miah Cerillo, the patient he had seen that morning.

"She was sitting in the hallway. Her face was still, she was clearly in shock, but her whole body was shaking from the adrenaline coursing through it," Guerrero testified on June 8 before the US House Judiciary Crime, Terrorism and Homeland Security Subcommittee in Washington.

Miah had sustained a number of shrapnel wounds, but although she was covered with blood, she was largely unhurt. Most of the blood belonged to her best friend, a little girl who had been lying next to her. Miah had reached over to get her friend's Apple Watch to summon police and realized that Makenna Elrod was gone. Miah later recalled that it was Khloie Torres who had urged her to use Makenna's blood to play dead.

Tom Nordwick, a trim CrossFit practitioner in his early sixties who had turned the struggling hospital into a cash machine through an arrangement that provided quality control to nursing homes (the new $85 million hospital was paid for in the first year), later said that the ER was already busy when the shooting occurred. Those patients who were stable were quickly moved to other areas, including the cafeteria on the second floor.

"The first two patients to arrive were DOA and they were not identifiable, which was very, very hard for the staff and doctors to deal with . . . because there was nothing they could do," Adam Apolinar told me. The health care executive, a former ER nurse at the Bexar County Hospital in San Antonio, possessed an intimate knowledge of trauma care.

As the arrival of wounded children accelerated, hospital officials summoned local physicians, who closed their offices and sped to the facility. Those doctors managed the ER patients now being triaged in the cafeteria area. Meanwhile, Gilberto Arbelaez and Sandra Boenig and a couple of other doctors remained downstairs in the ER dealing with the kids and teachers who continued to arrive. "It was just about as chaotic and hectic as it could be," Apolinar said of the scene.

Apolinar said the staff was fortunate to be in the new two-story facility with nineteen beds in the emergency department; there had been only eight in the old hospital. "Had we been in the old facility, we would have been triaging those poor kids in the parking lot. It would have been a circus."

The many physicians who offered their services were extremely helpful, but Apolinar said the hero of the day was the hospital's general surgeon, Dr. Boenig. "She is retired military and all that military training just kicked in for her. So between her and Dr. Arbelaez, they were just fantastic."

The medical response from across the region proved invaluable. The South Texas Regional Advisory Council loaded a helicopter with blood in San Antonio and dispatched the life-saving fluid to Uvalde Memorial Hospital within forty-eight minutes. Ten ambulances from Del Rio, Eagle Pass, Dimmitt County, and other neighboring communities raced to the scene, and four helicopters and their crews remained on standby. Apolinar said the hospital utilized two helicopter pads that day after he petitioned the Federal Aviation Administration to grant emergency use for the newly completed but yet-to-be-approved new pad.

Three of the more seriously injured patients, Mayah Zamora, Noah Orona, and Arnulfo Reyes, were airlifted to San Antonio. Another patient, ten-year-old Xavier Lopez, was en route to San Antonio via ambulance when he began to fail. The transport team attempted to divert to Medina Regional Hospital in Hondo, but the boy did not survive.

Mayah suffered the worst injuries of those who lived. She arrived at University Hospital, San Antonio's premier civilian trauma care center, with what doctors later described as only minutes to live. That she survived at all was largely attributable to programs put in place in the aftermath of the 2017 Sutherland Springs shooting just south of San Antonio. Mayah had received a whole blood transfusion in Uvalde, an option that would not have been possible before the earlier tragedy.

Trauma surgeon Dr. Lillian Liao, who also served as the pediatric trauma medical director at University Hospital, received notification of a school shooting in Uvalde at 11:52 a.m. That was far earlier than even Uvalde Memorial Hospital, which had to rely on employees and social media to learn what was happening.

Liao said that the damage inflicted on small bodies by high-velocity rifle bullets was horrible to see and more difficult to repair. Children like Mayah, who suffered wounds to her chest, legs, arms, and hands, could only tolerate so much surgery at a time. Surgeons and other staff had to take numerous steps to first clean and sterilize the wounds and then gradually replace missing tissue through multiple surgeries performed over weeks and even months.

Even with the additional space, Uvalde Memorial Hospital was "busting at the seams with just people." Apolinar said that the staff had practiced diligently for a mass casualty event, but the one thing they had not prepared for was "mass people." Those were the families and their children who piled into the facility, looking for missing students—waiting to hear, waiting to see them.

In hindsight, Nordwick, whose daughter Shawna Wolbert served as the assistant principal at Robb, wished there had been better coordination with school officials, as they could have expedited the process of matching children with their parents. As it was, hospital staff worked to identify patients who were there as part of the mass casualty event and not for other reasons. The CEO felt that far too many parents were directed to the hospital unnecessarily.

Rev. Mike Marsh, the rector at St. Philip's Episcopal Church, was driving home from San Antonio when he began to be overtaken by first responders—"police cars, unmarked cars, all sorts of people"—flying west on US Route 90 East. Shortly after reaching his house, the reverend received an urgent call that he was needed at the hospital.

Marsh found himself in the facility's chapel on the second floor with a group of families, but no information was forthcoming. "Then it just got more and more crowded and more and more chaotic . . . questions and no answers." He asked about a list of students and was told [the hospital staff] were working on it. "Parents are crying, screaming, some were getting mad and then the place just got covered up. It was just packed upstairs and downstairs with people wandering around crying." The soft-spoken priest in his early sixties, a longtime friend of our family, later said that law enforcement was maintaining order but parents and relatives kept coming, saying they had been told that the children were being taken to the hospital.

The minister was approached by a social worker who wanted his help in identifying a body. He was asked to accompany a mother, two nurses, and armed Border Patrol agents. They took the elevator to the first floor, where they were directed to a room where a body lay covered with a sheet. The mom held back, saying she did not want to go in. When she finally relented and they pulled back the sheet, she thanked Jesus that it was not her girl. Tragically, the woman would soon discover that her daughter had also died in the shooting.

But the mother identified the child who lay on the table, and Marsh knew the parents. In fact, he had spent much of his time at the hospital with the couple. Now he made the long trip back upstairs and "waded into the crowd to find them."

Gloria and Javier Cazares reached Uvalde Memorial Hospital shortly after 1 p.m. in search of their daughter, Jackie. However, officials knew of nobody by that name. Their niece, who had seen her cousin carried in, said that the little girl had to be there. Javier told me hospital staff debated with them for almost two and a half hours "before they finally even had pictures [supplied by family members] and they still couldn't find her."

Internist Dr. Issac Sosa, for whom Gloria had worked, attempted to intervene with no better luck. The excruciating search came to an end when it was determined that emergency doctors had been unable to save Jackie and had placed her in an unused surgery room. It was there that the grieving couple were finally taken to identify their daughter's body.

They were escorted to the second floor by a couple of nurses, Border Patrol officers, and Rev. Marsh. Before they got to the room, one of the nurses asked to see Jackie's picture again, and Gloria said "Just tell me if she is alive or not."

Marsh said no one spoke, and he finally said "No, she is not." Gloria collapsed to the floor and initially refused to proceed. Still, the couple needed to be sure, and they continued to the room. Javier described seeing "his little princess" on the table as the worst thing any parent could be called to do. Somehow he summoned the courage to examine her wounds, finding a piece of gauze on one side of her chest and a piece of clear tape on the other. A small incision closed by staples marked the front of the girl's chest where surgeons had made a cut in a desperate attempt to relieve pressure on Jackie's heart. As devastating as that last view of Jackie must have been, it was a final goodbye that the majority of victims' families would not experience.

Apolinar said that the scene described above repeated itself throughout the early afternoon. "I don't know how many sets of families we went through to try to identify, because all we had . . . was pretty much their clothes. There was very little facial recognition at all, on either one of [the DOAs]."

George Rodriguez, Jose Flores's step-grandfather, picked up Pedro Flores, the boy's maternal grandfather, at his home on Oak Street and drove to the hospital after receiving a text from another family member that they had found Jose. George told me that following a frantic trip to Robb when the shooting began, he had searched in all the usual places for the boy he had helped raise from a baby—the funeral home, the civic center, and finally the hospital.

George's spirits had soared when he was directed to the hospital, but when he got there, he learned that Jose had not survived. The seventy-three-year-old had been so overjoyed by the text that he had failed to read to the conclusion. The two old men held each other in the hospital's crowded lobby and cried for Josecito.

"How could he make it?" George wept. "That big of a bullet. His body was riddled to pieces."

When Ruben Torres finally reached the hospital in search of Khloie, he met resistance from officials who wanted proof that he was the parent. The blunt-spoken combat veteran was in no mood to quibble. He replied that his sister-in-law was in the room with his daughter, so it was going to be a simple swap. "She gets out and I go in . . . and why? Because I'm the father."

Once inside, a nurse explained that Khloie had a small piece of shrapnel in her left eye and fragments in her forehead above the eye. Doctors removed the metal pieces and after a series of X-rays to confirm there were no more serious wounds, the child was released to her parents. It had been 5 hours.

Oscar and Jessica Orona were also among the lucky ones whose child had indeed made it to the hospital and was very much alive. Noah had played dead for more than an hour in Room 112 after being shot through the back. The Oronas told me they found the ten-year-old propped up on a bed in the emergency department with what doctors initially thought was a flesh wound. The little boy bravely refused to cry, expressing more concern about his bloody clothes and missing eyeglasses than his wounds. He was airlifted to Methodist Hospital in San Antonio for treatment and released six days later, after extensive surgery.

Alfred Garza looked for Amerie Jo at Uvalde Memorial. Staff told him that they did not know the names of the children there or "could not release them because of privacy concerns." They also told him that they had the bodies of two students who had not been identified.

The young father hurried to Rushing-Estes-Knowles funeral home, where he again failed to find Amerie. He then returned to Hillcrest and finally to Robb. He was told that none of the kids were at the school, that "everybody's wherever they should be."

Someone suggested the hospital again or one of the hospitals in San Antonio or Hondo because some of the injured had been flown there. "So we're calling all of these hospitals, and we just don't know." Garza said they finally ended up at the civic center. "And it was the longest 10 hours of my life. It was like 10 hours before we knew what happened."

CHAPTER 11

Reunification

B y noon, the Willie de Leon Civic Center, a modern, tastefully landscaped facility on East Main Street just blocks from downtown, had been designated as the school district's reunification center. It was here that parents of Robb students were meant to regain possession of their children. Of course, in the beginning there was little organization anywhere. The entire city had been knocked to its knees and was scrambling to regain some semblance of balance.

Early observers, including *Leader-News* reporter Melissa Federspill, described a scene of uneven chaos. When buses began arriving from the besieged school, the passengers were second and third graders. They came from classrooms in separate wings from the fourth grade classrooms, and their rooms were largely unscathed by direct violence. Of course, no student escaped the trauma that had enveloped the entire campus. Federspill was struck by the incongruous sight of a school counselor sipping a drink as though she were leading a field trip to the San Antonio Zoo instead of directing children fleeing from violence.

Susan Rios, director of Main Street Uvalde, a nonprofit that works for the revitalization of the city, had responded from her office adjacent to the civic center. She saw hundreds of people crying and screaming, not knowing if their child was there. "You saw children coming off the buses, mixed emotions from the kids. Some of them were really calm . . . it was just normal. Some were just crying. You'd seen that some of the children had wet themselves because they had been so terrified by the experience."

Federspill had retrieved *Leader-News* managing editor Meghann Garcia from her home and delivered her to the newspaper. The women now conferred by text, especially after an angry parent questioned the identity of our reporter and what business she had at the civic center. Meghann responded unequivocally that Melissa should return to the office to avoid getting between people and their grief.

That message spelled out in a handful of words the gulf that lay between our reporting ethic as a community newspaper and the take-no-prisoners approach the national media later practiced. Melissa retreated to the *Leader-News*, where she and the rest of the staff worked to obtain the unfolding facts and at the same time support reporter Kimberly Mata-Rubio in her search for Lexi.

The wild scene at the civic center was further complicated by the fact that the facility served as an official polling place and voters had begun queuing that morning to cast ballots in a runoff election for Uvalde County justice of the peace for Precinct 6. The incumbent, fifty-year-old Roland Sanchez, had arrived before the polls opened at 7 a.m. He began hearing sirens around 11:30 and half an hour later caught sight of Assistant City Manager Joe Cardenas signaling to him from across the crowded walkway. The city official told Sanchez that school buses with students from Robb—second and third graders—were set to begin arriving at any minute and that help was needed to unload them. Cardenas added that school district officials were not yet on the scene but were expected soon.

As a Uvalde native and a former school board member (Sanchez had resigned from the board when he had been appointed to fill the unexpired term of the former Precinct 6 justice of the peace), Sanchez's desire to help was a natural response. His wife, Mikka, was an administrative assistant to District Superintendent Hal Harrell, which further cemented Sanchez's relationship with the school system.

The plan school officials had developed on the fly was to organize the children in the main auditorium, the Live Oak Room, into groups according to classroom. No events had been scheduled that day, so the space that could easily accommodate 400 people was devoid of tables and chairs. As the buses unloaded, teachers sat on the floor and by dint of years of training and instinct, directed their students to gather around them for a head count.

Outside the civic center, parents were instructed to form lines and be prepared to show some form of identification. Many pushed back. They had bolted from their homes or places of employment without purses or wallets to secure their children.

By then, Susan Rios had retrieved a portable PA system and a large whiteboard from her office and had positioned them outside to help inform parents about the status of the students. "We would say 'Okay, Ms. so and so's class,' and if you were the parent you could come up and show your ID and that would get you in to pick up your child and leave."

The adults entered through the glass front doors and exited with their children out the back of the building to avoid the growing media presence that was fighting to film anybody and everybody. At one point, a broadcast reporter even attempted to interview our education reporter, Melissa Federspill. "I know it's a story and it's important, but grief—grief and time and place and what becomes a spectacle and what doesn't," Rios lamented.

Rios told me that about 1:30 p.m., many of the buses had arrived and "You started seeing who's missing, who's missing and parents going 'Where's Mr. Reyes's class, where's Ms. Garcia's class?' And nobody had any answers yet, not even central [school district's administrative] staff."

Kimberly Mata-Rubio's father, Ruben Mata, had gathered her son Julian from the civic center and taken him to relatives. That freed the young mother and her husband to focus entirely on finding Lexi. They joined the throng of parents at the civic center who watched desperately as buses unloaded without any sign of their daughter or her classmates.

If things were not fraught enough, another disturbance soon roiled the civic center. Ramos's girlfriend was rumored to be on her way there to continue shooting. Officials ordered a lockdown of the facility, and a desperate effort followed to move the large crowd inside. Rios said that officials were gripped by panic because "we don't know if we're letting in this other person. . . . We didn't know what she looked like, we didn't have videos yet." Rios said that once pictures of the girlfriend were made available, they began a desperate scan of the crowd to make sure the potential attacker was not already inside.

Rios, who had long taught a concealed handgun course with her husband, David, a biologist with the Texas Parks & Wildlife Department, remembered that an off-duty Zavala County sheriff's deputy showed up in support, followed by a criminal investigation unit from the Texas Department of Public Safety. "They were great and really took care of us, and then one police officer was sent over."

An unfortunate response to the imagined girlfriend threat included helicopters circling low overhead, which horrified the children. "It was just a matter of staying calm and really having to kind of compartmentalize your own emotions . . . because you have all of these kids and these parents."

Rios said that by early afternoon the civic center had received all the kids who were going to come. For parents who had not been reunited, that ending launched a more frenzied circle of searching that included Uvalde Memorial Hospital, hospitals in San

Antonio, Robb Elementary, the local funeral homes, and ultimately back to the civic center, which would be the place of ultimate reckoning for many.

Melissa Federspill revisited the civic center after receiving a text from school district Director of Communications Anne Marie Espinoza about a press conference scheduled for 3:30 p.m. She recalled sitting at a table at the center next to Judge Sanchez, who got up to talk to a man who was "obviously law enforcement." When the judge sat back down, he turned to Melissa and said, "One of the deceased is someone you know."

"Lexi?" Melissa said, and Sanchez nodded. She reported the news to Meghann in a phone call just after 3 p.m., and the managing editor fell apart. After composing herself, Meghann shared the information in the newsroom, and the rest of us either broke into tears or slinked off to cry on our own. Meghann steeled herself for the two-block walk to the civic center to console her dear friend.

Sometime between 3:30 p.m. and the beginning of the press conference, which was delayed until 4:16 p.m., Meghann and Melissa picked out Kimberly through the large glass windows of the building's vestibule. They watched as a group of people led her away from the crowd, where she sank to her knees. Her co-workers thought she had been told of Lexi's death, but her reaction was to the news that no more buses—or children—were expected from Robb.

Meghann went to her friend, who had been gathered up by family and was exiting the building, and offered love and support. None of us was prepared to share the news imparted by Judge Sanchez, since it had not come from official channels.

Kimberly later remembered that by then it seemed apparent that either Lexi was being treated at the hospital or she was gone. The trip to Uvalde Memorial Hospital took at least another hour, where Kimberly was met by the same forlorn result—no news of Lexi's whereabouts. The last resort was a trip to Rushing-Estes-Knowles Mortuary to look for a body. Funeral director June Ybarra told the Rubios that none of the funeral homes had received victims.

With nowhere left to turn, Kimberly was drawn to Robb Elementary. If Lexi was still in her classroom, she needed her mother to be nearby. The young woman slipped off the flimsy sandals she had worn to awards day and ran a mile over scorching pavement. Her husband Felix and their daughter Kalisa, a high school senior, followed close behind. When they got there, they encountered Kimberly's aunt, whose parents lived across the street from the school. She supplied them with badly needed water.

"I'm obviously upset and still I have questions . . . and we don't know for sure. But I felt something telling me I was in the right place. I want to be with her. So I'm in the

right place." The Rubios stayed at Robb until the sun began to set. Finally officials suggested they return to the civic center yet again. A San Antonio firefighter named Mario
Carrillo offered to drive them.

The final tally of casualties was still unknown, but when 38th Judicial District
Attorney Christina Mitchell arrived at the civic center with two Texas Rangers, the
atmosphere changed. Rios and a handful of others had been advised of what was coming because they needed to rearrange the facility. "So now it went from being a reunification to a notification," Rios said.

CHAPTER 12

Job from Hell

Lalo Diaz, Uvalde High School class of 1991, was not prepared for the job that landed in his lap on May 24, 2022. As a justice of the peace for the last eight years, the worst he had seen was a grisly car accident two years earlier near Garner State Park. A small SUV loaded with family had turned left off of Ranch to Market Road No. 1050 into the path of an 18-wheeler headed north on US Route 83. Judge Diaz had identified the mangled bodies of three adults and a child and had signed the death certificates. A fifth passenger had died later in a San Antonio hospital.

Now he had "gotten the call"—his family's code for response to a death scene— that he was needed at Robb Elementary to identify two or three victims of a school shooting. That was the rumor circulating in the city when Diaz met District Attorney Christina Mitchell at the school around 2:20 p.m. The first thing Diaz noticed was that the local officers who had responded initially were gone, replaced by members of the Texas Rangers. He also learned that sixteen or seventeen children and two teachers lay dead. The ranger in charge, Jose Sanchez, suggested that Diaz might want to request help from a medical examiner.

Uvalde County, like most rural counties in Texas, has no coroner or medical examiner. The job of investigating unattended deaths—those that occur outside hospitals, nursing homes, or hospice care—falls to the justices of the peace. They are charged with determining the identity of the deceased and the manner and cause of death. But processing the sheer number of victims at Robb presented a challenge that few justices of the peace were prepared to tackle.

Diaz found the phone number for Bexar County medical examiner, Dr. Kimberley Molina, in his contact list, and she answered the call. She said she would be available to help if Diaz would send an email authorizing her to work in Uvalde County. It was done, and Diaz chose to wait the hour and a half it would take for the doctor to drive from San Antonio rather than enter the school alone. The burly justice of the peace, who has salt-and-pepper hair and expressive brown eyes, drove across the street to the parking lot of Hillcrest Memorial Funeral Home to "sit and think about what I was about to do—about to see."

In the meantime, fellow justice of the peace Steven Kennedy showed up to assist, but when he learned that there were sixteen victims, he said apologetically: "I can't do it. I am sorry, but I can't."

The last busload of students had left Hillcrest almost an hour earlier, and yet parents continued to probe the facility in search of missing children. A couple appeared on such a mission but were refused entry by the horde of state police that had occupied the building. Diaz heard the parents arguing with the strange officers. The couple wanted to know what was going on and wondering why they didn't recognize anyone. Diaz stood up and offered to help. "We know who you are," the mother told him. "I thought you might have our child in here and no one has told me."

Diaz explained that the Robb crime scene was still active and that there were victims inside. He told them that the identities of the victims had not been confirmed but that he was going in soon and would find out. "I ask that you please go back to the civic center, take pictures, whatever you can, but wait for the news there. I am waiting for the medical examiner to show up and then we are going in."

"I tell people that's the thing about this whole ordeal we've lived. . . . Early on, families wanted to hear from their local people, people they elected, people they could trust. Trusting a stranger is hard."

The chaos of the response to the shooting seemed to have spilled over into the crime scene, or at least that was the way it struck Diaz. As soon as he and Molina entered from the south entrance—rather than the west door the shooter had used—they encountered victims. But they were in the wrong classrooms. The killing had taken place in Rooms 111 and 112 and yet many of the bodies now rested in Rooms 102 and 103.

Diaz said he was initially confused, thinking that perhaps students in other rooms had also been shot. Crime scene protocol dictates that bodies remain where they are discovered until investigators have gathered their evidence. The judge suspected that in this case, officers had frantically dragged children from the two classrooms into the hallway in an attempt at triage.

Diaz and Molina worked the classrooms, numbering bodies, noting their condition, and placing small identification cones next to the deceased. Diaz said only Molina actually touched the victims. The goal was to send bodies that night to the Bexar

County Medical Examiner facility in San Antonio, get them cleaned up, and then send back a picture. "We wanted to make sure we sent back pictures with a clean face for comparison. It was a bloody mess. The whole building."

After finishing with the initial work, Diaz and Molina walked down the blood-drenched hallway and entered Room 112. It had been four years since the father of three had had a child at Robb, so he was unfamiliar with which rooms belonged to which teachers. It wasn't until he walked behind Irma Garcia's desk and looked back and saw the framed pictures of *familia* that he realized that the teacher lying face down was Garcia.

"It was at that point that I said 'I know who someone is.' Later on, of course, I find out I know more people. But that day it was Irma [who had been a year behind Diaz at Uvalde High School]. And I knew Eva [Mireles] was there somewhere, but I hadn't gotten to her yet."

Diaz said that Garcia was not actually holding any students, but she "had huddled them all here. . . . She fell, and they were all around her," the official said, gesturing with outstretched arms.

Over the years, the judge had trained himself to look objectively at violent death without focusing on the grisly details. But in the Robb classroom, it was the ringing of phones that challenged his emotions. "The phones just nonstop ringing in the backpacks and on [Irma Garcia's] desk."

The investigators moved into Room 111 through the interconnecting door and immediately encountered the shooter. Diaz said the eighteen-year-old was lying face down and yet his body was facing up.

"Now that you hear more, three Border Patrol agents probably unloaded their clips on him. I won't know until the autopsy report comes in but anywhere from 20 to 40 shots," Diez estimated.

More disturbing was the lettering that Diaz discovered on the classroom's whiteboard. The killer had used the blood of his victims to spell out in large letters "LOL."

The wall behind the long computer table under which all eleven of Reyes's students had died while attempting to hide was riddled with holes. "That's why Arnulfo said 'they were sitting ducks,' because he [killer] just went da, da, da, da, right down the wall. You could see body tissue, all kinds of stuff under there. I see the spray that was in the walls. And the holes where he shot at the cops. This guy was evil. For him to sit there and write and have the time to do the things he did. Later on your mind thinks, imagines things as survivors tell stories."

The officials worked well into the evening marking bodies and placing them in body bags for transport to San Antonio. They also waited for school district police chief

Pete Arredondo to retrieve pictures of the students from the school. By 9 p.m., two buses sent by emergency management were backed up to the far south door off Old Carrizo Road and the victims were placed on board. The shooter remained in Room 111, marked with an "S."

Diaz said he was not able to say with certainty who everyone was. Some of the head wounds were terribly disfiguring. Diaz ordered blanket autopsies, something he had never done, leaving a blank space on the form for the name.

The judge, worried about how quickly the bodies could be returned to their parents, said it normally takes 24 to 48 hours. The day after the shooting, nine bodies were released to Rushing-Estes-Knowles Mortuary, and by the day after that, all of the bodies had been made available. Still, the deceased were not all returned to Uvalde because there was no place to keep them.

"The funeral home [Rushing-Estes-Knowles, which held the contract as the county morgue] didn't want to put up a refrigerated truck out of respect. So they were held somewhere else, at the Schertz [suburb of San Antonio] location, unless [funerals] were going to be done by Hillcrest," Diaz said.

A Texas law that Gov. Abbott had signed in 2017 ensured that parents could see their dead children before autopsies were performed. Prior to that, the fear was that human contact could contaminate the evidence and parents had to seek permission from a justice of the peace.

If the parents do not get to spend time with their deceased children, by the time the body returns from the morgue "they've lost what is called the 'essence of life.' So they should have a chance. I feel so bad they could not have this opportunity to even hold them, even though they were hurt. But we couldn't. I couldn't," Diaz said with obvious emotion. "The scene by the time we got done, it was as if someone had dropped a fifty-gallon barrel of oil down the hallway. That clean hallway you see [on surveillance cameras] is red. The whole scene, just blood everywhere, where they [officers] were moving children."

At around 10 p.m., the exhausted official returned to his home, where his wife, Patricia, and his daughter, Ariana, were waiting. After finally climbing into bed at 1:30 a.m., Diaz found it impossible to sleep. His phone rang at 2 a.m., and by 5 a.m. he was wide awake. He said his "mind was racing . . . I imagine the families being in my office wanting to know where their child is, because I'm the one who sent them [away]."

CHAPTER 13

Notification

The majority of the nineteen young victims could be identified by their facial features or their clothing. A few were unrecognizable and required a DNA match with their parents. That process mandated a new configuration at the civic center, where by 4 p.m. officials had shifted into a notification-of-death mode.

Barriers in the three meeting rooms were removed, creating one large space. Volunteers set up tables to accommodate Texas Rangers, who would collect DNA swabs for transport to the crime lab in San Antonio. Local school officials as well as those from the Texas Education Agency Region 20 office in San Antonio were also located in the room to monitor social media and process the information required for identification.

According to 38th Judicial District Attorney Christina Mitchell, the decision to take samples from all parents still waiting for notification was rooted in a desire to shield the few who truly required a DNA test. Mitchell later said that officials hoped to spare families being left alone in the spotlight with their grief.

Susan Rios remembered being horrified by the process because everyone was in one big room together and if you were being swabbed the outcome was pretty obvious. "And so being right there with them, when they're told that their child essentially is deceased and not coming back. That was so heart-wrenching."

Jerry and Veronica Mata had been bounced around like other victims' families, visiting the civic center and being told nothing except to check the hospital. At the hospital, they had been advised to leave one person there and have the other family members return to the civic center. At the civic center, Jerry finally had had enough around 3 p.m., when he was asked to give his daughter's name to the same school official for the third time in as many visits. "Get away from me. You're from the central office, so tell me what's going on," he demanded.

Instead, the Matas ended up in the big room, where they produced a DNA swab and then sat down for yet more waiting. When their daughter Faith arrived around 6 p.m. from Texas State University in San Marcos, she asked her father if Tess was going to be okay. Jerry replied that he did not think she was coming back. He recounted that head custodian Jacob Kubish, Makenna Elrod Seiler's stepdad and a friend of Matas's family, had told him that the shooter had been in Tess and Makenna's classroom.

Jerry said that the room was made more uncomfortable by the way school employees he knew stared at him and then dropped their heads when he looked back. He got the same treatment from Robb principal Mandy Gutierrez, who was sitting with friends. "I looked at her and she just put her head down. All of them. They just put their head down. You know? By that time, you know, I don't want to cause a scene 'cause I'm a bigger . . . bigger man than that. So my dad taught me well, and I just kept my cool," Jerry remembered.

More unnecessary grief landed inside the facility when DA Mitchell announced: "The reason for the swab is because we are trying to identify the dead bodies." The Matas knew Mitchell well because Faith had played softball with the prosecutor's daughter. The parents were stunned by the insensitivity of the statement. "She's said dumb things before but that took the cake," Jerry said, describing the impact on the room, where people fell to the floor, as if bludgeoned by the weight of the revelation.

Much later, District Superintendent Hal Harrell would tell Jerry that the school knew the names of children who had died by 3 p.m. "but because of lawyers and blah, blah, blah no one was being forthright. I mean he knows my family real good, too. . . . Couldn't you just say 'I'm sorry, Jerry?'"

Instead, the Matas and many others would not get official notification until almost midnight.

Chris Seiler, the man Makenna Elrod had called "daddy" since the age of two, described the same shattering impact from the DA's blunt remark. Makenna's mother, April, had provided a DNA swab, and they had been waiting for hours without any information. "They just dropped it on us. There was no compassion. It was just the DA came on 'You gave DNA samples because your babies are gone.' This hit me like a ton of bricks," Seiler said.

Families waited for the results, while relatives, clergy, grief counselors, school board members—anyone who could provide support—crowded the hallways. Texas Rangers, who were sitting behind computer screens, announced a family's name as a name confirming a child's death came up. The parents were then escorted to one of the smaller, private spaces that Rios had helped set up for sharing the awful news. Only two family members were allowed to enter, accompanied by grief counselors, clergy, and a Texas Ranger, who was there to take a statement. In many cases that left dozens of extended family members outside crying in anguish.

"You knew what the result was—so much mourning, so much grief," Rios told me. She distinctly remembered seeing Seiler "in his cowboy attire curled up in a corner and just bawling . . . there's just something about watching a man cry that's different than watching a woman."

Uvalde County Attorney John Dodson arrived at the civic center as the notification process was just getting under way. His role was to serve as a liaison among the various state agencies, including a Department of Public Safety Crime Victim Services unit. He said the Texas Rangers and DA Mitchell were essentially trying to avoid sharing the wrong facts with families. "You have one chance to get the information out right when it comes to something that tragic."

When Kimberly Mata-Rubio reached the civic center for the third time that day, she gave Anne Marie Espinoza, the school district communications director, another description of Lexi. Seated next to Espinoza was a Texas Department of Public Safety officer taking down the details, but he already had a picture of the little girl. The Rubios were directed to a table for more waiting.

Rios recalled Kim and Felix sitting there. She offered them a heartfelt embrace and water, encouraging them to stay hydrated, which struck her as "completely asinine," but she was at a loss for words. She said Felix was "looking at the water bottle and crying, and he said 'My baby loves water. Honey, wasn't that her favorite drink in cans?' like she loved water. And he said 'Who's giving my baby water now? She's thirsty, she needs water. I need to take her this water.'"

Kimberly had once sat on the board of the Uvalde Chamber of Commerce and had reported on many of the city events Rios was involved in. That relationship intensified the impact of Kimberly's suffering. The scene of the Rubios wrestling with what appeared to be inevitable heartbreak tore at Rios when she finally got home around 10:30 p.m. and "had the really ugly cry."

Eventually, the Rubios were joined by Felix's fellow officer and friend, Chief Deputy Brandon McCutchen, and another man, who offered to take them "somewhere quiet."

"Felix got up immediately. But I kind of knew that they're not moving us just to do that. So I kind of . . . I don't know who I turned to. I think it might have been Susan Rios. I said 'I don't want to go. I don't want to follow them,'" Kimberly recalled.

She had lost one of her sandals and her feet had been rubbed raw by the hot pavement and gravel. She managed to collect herself, and they crossed the street to Dodson's office on East Nopal Street. She and Felix sat at a conference table with several people Kimberly did not know, and McCutchen told them Lexi was among the victims.

"I heard this chair just fly back. . . . [Felix] like stands up. I don't know what he says, though I know he's freaking out. And I look at the woman, and I just tell her 'I don't think I understand.' So twice. 'I don't think I understand.' And then I look at Felix, and I stand up with him because he's crying, and I'm starting to try to process what they've just told us."

In a few minutes, they all walked back outside, and Felix said they needed a ride to Kimberly's mother's house on Fourth Street. Kimberly had different plans. She got in the sheriff's patrol vehicle and asked Deputy J. J. Vera, who was driving, to take her back to Robb. She suggested that he leave Felix and McCutchen, who were still outside the vehicle, and drive her there alone.

"'I'll behave. I'm not going to do anything . . . to go past anywhere. I just want to sit right there back on the curb,'" she told Vera. "He can't even look at me. But he obviously can't do that."

Once the other men entered the car and it got under way, McCutchen asked if there was anyone Kimberly wanted to text. She named Meghann Garcia. Kimberly said that after that things became muddled. The arrival at her mother Cindy's house, going into a back bedroom, Cindy asking her to post something because names were being announced . . . and then rain—heavy rain. By the next morning, gauges across the city brimmed with almost 1.5 inches, the hardest rainfall of the year.

CHAPTER 14

Invasion

Telephones signaled the start of the invasion. They began ringing before the shooter lay dead in Room 111. The ravenous, all-devouring world media landed with practiced ferocity and we—the local press—were about to be reminded why our profession ranked closer to car salesmen and member of Congress than the family doctor.

"Hello, this is KSAT in San Antonio, KNX in Los Angeles, or ABC Australia—can you give us a couple of minutes to explain what you are seeing?" CTV News Channel in Canada wanted comments, as did *Good Morning Britain*, MSNBC, the *Daily Beast*, and *BBC World News*. And of course, FOX, CBS News, NPR, and CNN clamored for a bite of their own. Talk shows also plied us with offers to get the word out.

Longtime classified manager and recently appointed gatekeeper Norma Ybarra performed her duties heroically. Meghann Garcia had asked Ybarra to wave off any calls for interviews, and her precision in deflecting requests rivaled the performance of a World Cup goalie. There were some, however, who simply pushed through the unguarded front door. Once inside, they greeted us as if we were fraternity brothers, except that many could not get the name of our paper straight. No, it was not the *Uvalde News-Leader*. We were the *Leader-News*, as we had been for eight decades.

For Ybarra, deflecting the press was far easier than dealing with the hundreds of irate Americans who jammed our phone lines. Callers typically began by offering condolences and prayers for the community and then shifted into a full-throated attack on law enforcement, the city, the school, and even the newspaper for not insisting that the whole lot of them be fired posthaste. In some instances, we were even accused of being part of a cover-up to protect police officers and the school district. So angry were our fellow Americans that they could easily have turned to vigilante justice if they had not lived five states away.

Ybarra defended us vigorously, pointing out that their criticisms should be directed to those responsible. The callers countered that the police and others refused to take phone calls. When the hecklers declined to hang up, Ybarra handed them off to the general manager Pete Luna, who happily served as enforcer.

It was astounding how blindingly fast news of the tragedy circled the globe and more unsettling how soon the big rigs sprouted with antennas squeezed into the narrow streets surrounding Robb Elementary. It was as if these media outlets had mastered the science of teleportation. All that was missing as evidence was the talking head of a housefly planted on the shoulders of Anderson Cooper in a twisted version of *The Fly* (1986 horror film). But the media were real and they were crowding our space.

The *New York Times*, the *Washington Post*, the *Los Angeles Times*, Reuters—everyone wanted Pete Luna's photos: indelible, gut-wrenching images of children fleeing the carnage. We wanted them to be seen, but how to manage it? Who should get them and would we charge? We leaned toward fixing a price and donating the money to the victims but finally decided to release select photographs free to only the most credible outlets. Everything was happening so fast that deciding how to manage the photographs meant that there was one less thing to worry about. There was no time to engage an attorney to draw up a license agreement. We were clearly out of our depth.

Finally, the *Daily Mail* in London wondered, ever so politely, if one of our reporters could "just jump on the phone with us." The requests were the same as the ones that pinged from every corner of the English-speaking world. What the callers did not know—or could not have cared less if they did—is that there were exactly four of us who wrote the news, we were up to our asses in grief, we were on deadline for the Thursday (May 26) paper, and there were people just like them at our front door. We were drowning and could ill afford to give another news agency its next sound bite.

Even in the throes of disaster, there was humor. How could we not snort at the unmitigated gall? Hello, from Madrid, speaking only Spanish to our West Coast–born circulation manager, who passed the call to Luna. Later, he said the caller wanted to talk to him about the scene. When he declined, the Spaniard asked for anyone in journalism who had been at the school. Pete replied he had been the only one, and he was not talking. In desperation, the reporter requested any Spanish speaker, adding that he worked for the second most popular radio station in Spain. Pete told him, in Spanish of course, to call back when they were number one.

The national media pressed hard, propelled by the knowledge that the globe's voracious appetite for our horror would soon be sated. Or rather replaced by a tastier, newer entree. It is that fickleness that allowed many of them to be so casual, so careless with people's emotions. Like novice campers in the backcountry who figure they will never return, much of the world's media could not be bothered with the mantra "leave no trace."

Hospital chief operating officer Adam Apolinar faced the media bulldozer immediately after the shooting. Camera operators and reporters pushed against the hospital's front entrance, jockeying to film stricken parents and other family members in search of the wounded. The mob scene presented an obstacle for the ambulance crews who were mistakenly delivering victims to the front instead of the emergency entrance located on the west side of the newly opened facility.

The administrator finally drew the line, sending the media to the other side of the sidewalk and then another 100 yards away, to the Kate Marmion Regional Cancer Medical Center. On the next day, Apolinar ordered journalists to vacate the campus altogether. Hospital security helped put teeth in the final directive.

A similar scene unfolded outside the civic center, where news crews had positioned themselves to capture the reaction from frantic parents. One journalist stuck a microphone in our reporter's face, asking if she had found her children. Federspill replied that she worked for the local paper. Undeterred, they attempted to extract a comment on how our staff was dealing with the coverage. Once again a police presence was required to keep order.

The neighborhood around Robb Elementary remained in turmoil as the media prowled the streets, knocking on random doors in hopes that someone—almost anyone—would open up, both literally and figuratively. Bus driver Silvia Uriegas found herself a virtual prisoner in her house a block from the school. Her bus no. 19 had become a makeshift ambulance as she transported wounded children to the hospital. Now her worst fear was that reporters would discover her role in the trauma and never leave her alone. They came close. The school district employs another woman named Silvia Uriegas, and the media had sniffed her out. She denied knowing how to drive anything larger than her car, and the bus-driving Silvia Uriegas remained anonymous—for the time being.

My introduction to the national media—outside the walls of our newspaper—came on May 26 in front of Robb. State police southern region director Victor Escalon stood tight-lipped before a lectern planted in the intersection of Geraldine Street and Old Carrizo Road. He was flanked by a platoon of starched uniforms, there to buck him up or carry him away if he faltered.

A virtual sea of cameras bristled in front of the officer as he delivered a timeline of the events of May 24. Nothing the trooper uttered was startling, but what he left out was noticeable. From dozens of lips with many accents the same question erupted: What happened during the 60 minutes when officers apparently did nothing? Escalon looked startled, paused, and said that he had no answers but would get the information and circle back. I concluded that "circle back" was taught in Department of Public Safety training for public speakers as the equivalent of an ejection seat. The maneuver failed to mollify the bloody crowd, and their response was withering.

I knew at once why it was me standing there instead of another member of our editorial staff. They had already stuck their toes into the press conference maelstrom, fought for balance, and realized that watching it live from our newsroom was far safer and even more productive. Besides, our questions never would have been heard over the din of the invaders' louder, more artful voices.

The first funeral on May 31 marked a new low for media coverage. Leroy Briones, whose Hillcrest Memorial Funeral Home was handling arrangements, estimated that 150 cameras had been assembled along the street in front of Sacred Heart Catholic Church as mourners gathered to bury Amerie Jo Garza. The intrusion proved too much for Briones, and he summoned the Uvalde Volunteer Fire Department to block the view with a curtain of fire equipment.

"They were trying to follow the funerals from the funeral home to the church and the cemetery," Briones told me. Law enforcement took up positions at the cemetery to prevent the press from invading the gravesite.

Soon afterward, signs sprang up at the cemetery that read "No Media." Motorcycle clubs like the Bandidos also rolled into town, their sole purpose to create space for families to bury their children. The motorcycle clubs were our new self-appointed guardians and were not entirely unwelcome, given the now-violent mistrust of local law enforcement.

Meanwhile, Pete Luna's heart-pounding images of children being rescued from Robb Elementary School flew around the world. But he wanted no part of being painted with the same brush as the world media. "When I carry my camera, I now try to hide it. I don't want people to think that I am one of them," he said.

CHAPTER 15

"It Could Have Been Worse"

The day after the shooting, Gov. Greg Abbott took the stage at Uvalde High School's John H. Harrell Auditorium. His entourage featured the state's brightest lights, including US senators John Cornyn and Ted Cruz. Seated at the table to the left and right of the two-term Republican governor were District Superintendent Hal Harrell (the facility bore his father's name), Lt. Gov. Dan Patrick, Speaker of the House Dade Phelan, and Department of Public Safety director Col. Steve McCraw, perhaps the person the crowd wanted most to hear from.

Standing at various degrees of attention behind the table were the two US senators, state senator Roland Gutierrez, whose district included Uvalde, and others who were not cleared to speak unless called upon, including Texas attorney general Ken Paxton.

Abbott opened with a practiced tone of sorrow and support, not unlike speeches delivered in the wake of mass shootings in Sutherland Springs, Santa Fe, Midland-Odessa, and El Paso. "To begin with, let me point out the obvious. Evil so swept across Uvalde yesterday. Anyone who shoots his grandmother in the face has to have evil in his heart. But it is far more evil for someone to gun down little kids. It is intolerable. And it is unacceptable for us to have in the state anybody who would kill little kids in our schools."

The governor called on all Texans to come together and support the families who had been affected by the horrific tragedy. He followed with "what they need now more than ever is our love."

Perhaps overcome by his own histrionics and a larger need to command the room—from a stage, no less—he then uttered a line that would have choked even the most resolute Shakespearean actor. "The reality is [that] as horrible as what happened

[is], it could have been worse. The reason it was not worse is because law enforcement officers did what they do. They showed amazing courage by running toward gunfire for the single purpose of trying to save lives."

Lt. Gov. Dan Patrick was beginning to speak when Abbott's Democratic challenger in the upcoming midterm election, Beto O'Rourke, strode toward the stage. He had no microphone, but his accusations were audible in the live video feed. The response, especially from Uvalde mayor Don McLaughlin Jr., was loud and instantaneous. As the lanky O'Rourke wagged his finger at Abbott, blaming his lack of leadership for the mass murder at Robb, McLaughlin yelled for the former member of Congress to get out.

"You're a sick son of a bitch coming in here trying to make a political deal out of this tragedy," McLaughlin declared. The mayor had been raised by a former NFL lineman whose response to confrontation was engines all ahead full. The city's top official was joined by others, and Beto was soon escorted to the exit.

Once outside, media recorded O'Rourke shouting—over repeated questions from reporters—that the largest mental health facility in the state was the Harris County jail in Houston. "He [Abbott] has refused to support red flag laws This kid just turned 18, bought an AR-15 and took it into an elementary school and shot kids in the face and killed them."

The former presidential candidate continued to hammer on Abbott's failures. "He has refused to expand Medicaid, refused to support safe storage laws, refused to support a ban on AR-15s. Why are we letting this happen in this country? Why is this happening in this state, city after city, year after year? This is on all of us if we don't do something, and I am going to do something, and I am not alone. The people of Texas are with us."

Still on the stage, the governor picked up the conversation, saying there were family members at that very moment with broken hearts and no one could shout words that would do anything. "Every Texan, every American has a responsibility not to focus on us and our personal agendas but the healing and hope for those who have suffered unbearable pain."

Patrick soon resumed his stab at compassion, following the governor's lead but trending toward a more religious theme. "Evil will always walk among us. And in times like this, I've seen it. The governor has seen it, the speaker is seeing it, the senators have seen it, the attorney general [has] seen it in these other shootings, Sutherland Springs, El Paso, Odessa, Santa Fe."

Patrick said it was God that brings a community together, heals a community and a shattered and broken heart. "And if we don't turn back as a nation to understanding what we were founded upon, and what we were taught by our parents and what we believe in, then the situations will only get worse," he sermonized.

Of course, Patrick was taking liberties with American history, as so often happens when politicians are given free rein in times of grief. The country may have been founded by certain men who believed the gospel that Patrick was espousing, but the majority had been unequivocal in their demand for a clear separation in the Constitution. Conflating church with state was a nonstarter and a direct path to demagoguery. Not to mention a cop-out. How convenient to blame the massacre solely on pure evil, i.e. the devil, when the state had failed to provide accessible behavioral health care and laws that promote responsible gun ownership.

Patrick called for more security in the state's schools—a hardening that would result in a single entrance for visitors—an echo from comments he had made following the Santa Fe High School shooting four years earlier. That tragedy had resulted in Senate Bill 11, which appropriated $100 million to the Texas Education Agency to provide funding for improvements to school safety. The package included implementation of a School Marshal Plan or a School Safety Training (Guardian) program that would arm teachers, enact threat assessment protocols, and make physical upgrades. One hundred million dollars sounds impressive but it shrinks to a pittance when you consider that it had to be divided among the state's 1,022 public school districts. Uvalde Consolidated Independent School District had received a paltry $69,000 from Senate Bill 11. Ironically, part of the funds was used to install security cameras, including those in Robb Elementary School hallways. Meanwhile, the district still had doors that would not lock, five-foot security fences that a child could scale, and a Raptor Alert system that had proved unreliable due to poor internet service.

In 2021, Abbott had signed into law legislation that made firearms even more accessible. At the stroke of his pen, Texans gained the right to openly carry a pistol without having to pass a concealed handgun course. The governor argued that none of those laws would have changed the outcome of the Robb massacre. But what about others that were yet to happen?

When it finally came time for McCraw to speak, he delivered a timeline that included the prompt arrival of city and school police officers, who "immediately breached because we know as officers [that] every second is a life." As he continued with the halting—almost stumbling—narrative, it seemed as though he was trying to convince himself that his account was believable. "They breached it, engaged the active shooter and continued to keep him pinned down in that location."

Breached it? The police breached nothing for an hour and 17 minutes. In fact, evidence that surfaced ten months after the shooting showed that officers were frozen by fear of what they described on body camera video as a "battle weapon."

After a question from the media about exactly how much time all of that intense activity consumed, McCraw estimated it was going to be "within 40 minutes or an hour." He declined to give a particular timeline but said the bottom line was that law enforcement arrived quickly. "They did engage immediately. They did contain him in the classroom, and they put the tactical stack together, you know, in a very orderly way and of course breached and assaulted the individual."

Javier and Gloria Cazares were among the only parents of slain children present at the governor's press conference. In fact, few Uvaldeans attended the event, which was dominated by media. When it ended, reporters from two Spanish-language television stations corralled the Cazareses for their reaction. Javier said that Abbott's narrative was "complete bullshit. I was there. They didn't go in swiftly, they didn't take the guy out. You heard them say it took 45 minutes—or something—to respond."

The governor learned of the couple's criticism, and the Cazareses were pulled aside to speak with him privately. Javier recounted to me in an interview that he told Abbott the same thing he had said to the cameras. "Everything you said and the DPS said was bullshit. I was there and none of that happened." He said it was his information that led the governor two days later to walk back his assertions about the textbook police response.

Abbott's schooling from Cazares apparently failed to reach those who most needed to be forewarned before a press conference scheduled the next morning in front of Robb Elementary. Acting UPD chief Mariano Pargas was meant to lead the session, but the sixty-four-year-old veteran officer passed out minutes before the scheduled start. Victor Escalon, head of the Department of Public Safety Southern Region, picked up the fallen blue standard and marched into an enfilade. It was exceedingly warm for late May, and the world's press was in no mood for dissembling. The starched and booted commander attempted to advance the heroic law enforcement narrative the governor and McCraw had begun, but the math refused to cooperate. Dozens of reporters and camera operators, who stood three and four deep in front of the intersection, demanded to know what officers were doing between the time the shooter entered the school at 11:33 a.m. and his death more than an hour later at 12:50 p.m. Escalon stiffened (if that was even possible), a deer frozen in the spotlight.

On the afternoon of May 27, Abbott, flanked by Mayor McLaughlin and District Attorney Mitchell, returned to the Uvalde High School stage to announce a host of services available for anyone impacted by the tragedy. The governor promised a one-stop family assistance center at the Uvalde County Fairplex a few miles west of the city, where residents could obtain mental health care in person. Alternately, they could get help by calling a 24/7 hotline. Money was also available for traditional health care; airfare, lodging, and meals to bring family members to Uvalde; food, gas, or other essentials; child care; unemployment benefits; and small business relief. He compared the humanitarian response to Uvalde with the OneStar Foundation program that had pumped $200 million into the Houston area after Hurricane Harvey.

Reporters chafed at the mundane discussion about the state's laundry list of services and several attempted to refocus on the elephant in the room. Abbott held them off as long as he could, and finally—when no follow-up questions ensued regarding services—called on a reporter who had attempted to question Abbott's characterization of the law enforcement response as being prompt, even heroic.

His voice rising, the governor said that he had been misled. "I am livid about what happened. I was on this very stage two days ago. And I was telling the public information that had been told to me in a room, just a few yards behind where we're located right now."

Abbott described writing down notes in sequential order based on the information he had been fed. What he then presented to the public was a recitation of the briefing in the room behind the stage, whether it came from law enforcement or other officials. "And as everybody has learned, that the information that I was given, turned out, in part, to be inaccurate."

Going forward, Abbott called for the law enforcement leaders heading the investigation—from the Texas Rangers and the FBI—to get to the bottom of every fact with absolute certainty and 100 percent accuracy. He insisted that the information would be shared with the public and the victims.

Earlier the same day, McCraw had conducted a press conference in front of Robb Elementary. The director had come out rolling and jabbing—at local police. The head trooper declared that officers at the scene, especially school district police chief Pete Arredondo, who was considered incident commander, had made the wrong decision not to force their way into the classrooms at once, despite the likelihood of casualties. "From the benefit of hindsight where I'm sitting now, of course it was not the right decision. It was the wrong decision, period."

Few were prepared to argue with that conclusion, but the director made no mention of the fact that his agency had three times as many troopers on the scene—with more equipment and more training—than the Uvalde Police Department and school district police combined.

Mayor McLaughlin had arrived at Robb within 10 minutes of the emergency. The mayor's son, Mac, served as a member of the Uvalde Volunteer Fire Department, and it was his radio that gave warning. McLaughlin had parked on the Old Eagle Pass Road, and although he was using a walker due to recent hip replacement surgery, he had made his way to the nearest squad car for an update. He was directed to the funeral home across the street. From that vantage point, the sixty-year-old had watched, along with hundreds of others, as police maintained a perimeter while the shooter continued to menace and kill as a barricaded suspect.

The mayor's description of the scene as chaotic echoed other accounts. "I fault [acting UPD chief] Mariano [Pargas] for not taking more of a leadership role, but also there were numerous lieutenants and captains with the DPS that didn't assume the role either," McLaughlin said in a later interview. He added that while "two wrongs don't make a right," it was his opinion that the more experienced members of the Department of Public Safety should have brought order to the response. Instead, they did not bother to set up a command post in the funeral home until minutes before law enforcement breached the classrooms.

The mayor, who was born and raised in Uvalde, also took exception to early Department of Public Safety statements that their troopers did not arrive until later. "They were like ants. They were everywhere." What's more, within the first 30 minutes, McLaughlin saw the badges of the FBI, the Drug Enforcement Administration, the US Marshals Service, and the Border Patrol.

The mayor tended to the conservative side but had no affinity for the governor (he had endorsed Abbott's opponent Don Huffines in that spring's Republican primary). State senator Roland Gutierrez, a Democrat whose District 19 included Uvalde, was an unlikely ally, but the men's growing disdain for Col. McCraw supplanted politics. Their position was that if the Uvalde Police Department and school police had failed to end the slaughter at Robb, state police had the same blood on their hands.

Sen. Gutierrez had rushed to Uvalde in the wake of the shooting and had spent most of the night at the civic center with victims' families. Initially, he sought to know the identities of the nineteen officers who had waited in the Robb hallway for 77 minutes before breaching the door.

"I want to know where the cops were in that room. I want to know how many of my cops were in there, how many state troopers were there? I want to know how many state troopers were outside," the senator declared in a news conference on the Uvalde Downtown Plaza, which had become the site of a memorial for victims.

Within days of the shooting, as the narrative from the Department of Public Safety and Gov. Abbott continued to shift, Mayor McLaughlin requested that the United States Department of Justice conduct a critical incident review of the law enforcement response. In blunt language, he said that he wanted families and the community to have answers. "If mistakes were made, as tragic and sad as it is—if I could change it [from ever happening], I would—we have to know the truth."

Just over three weeks later, during a presentation to the Texas Senate Special Committee meeting in Austin, Col. McCraw doubled down on his criticism of local law enforcement. "We have compelling evidence that the law enforcement response to the attack at Robb Elementary was an abject failure and antithetical to everything we have learned in the last two decades since the Columbine massacre." The pugnacious Department of Public Safety director, who had grown up poor and had been threatened with expulsion from school for habitual fighting, deflected questions as to why his own force had not taken control of the scene, saying, "It would have been dangerous."

The lines were drawn in blood, and in the coming weeks and months, a bitter back-and-forth battle would play out over which agency bore the greatest responsibility for the most damning law enforcement response to a mass shooting in US history. There never was going to be a winner, only losers all around.

CHAPTER 16

"Make It Black"

On May 24, our reporting staff fought to process the enormity of what had happened and at the same time begin piecing together a Thursday edition. There had been no time to come up with a brilliant blueprint for coverage. We never gathered in the conference room for a staff meeting. Tuesday had landed on the city like some wayward asteroid, and our entire staff was struggling to make sense of it. The human instinct was to recoil in disbelief (and tears), not to prod people to give up information. For all of Tuesday and into Wednesday, it felt as if we were paralyzed bystanders, watching the tragedy unfold on television as the national media flew about the business of reporting with the cool detachment of a bomb disposal team.

Our reporters could not have done it. We could not have asked a grieving family to comment on the loss of their child within hours of their death. We could not have knocked on the front door of parents who had just lost a child and walked inside their home to take pictures and record their cries of anguish. Not a single one of us could have done those things, much less have attended the funeral for a child we did not know (which other news agencies would do within a week) while the family recognized us as being with the local newspaper.

It was not that we had no experience covering tragedy. Gang shootings; flash floods that frequently roared down the narrow canyon walls of the Hill Country, carrying away people and animals; and the deadly 2017 pickup/bus crash that had killed thirteen senior members of the New Braunfels First Baptist Church on a hilly stretch of road north of the city came to mind. (Kimberly won first place in news writing from the Texas Press Association for her coverage of the latter tragedy.)

But the May 26, 2022, edition would be like none in the previous 140 years. Nothing could approximate the death of nineteen fourth graders and two teachers. Or the fact that a little girl named Lexi belonged to one of us. That fact changed everything for our staff, particularly for Meghann and reporters Julye Keeble and Melissa Federspill.

Meghann and Julye had grown up in the small town of Sabinal 20 miles east on US Route 90. Both women were only children who had received homeschooling for their junior high and high school years. Meghann's father was a popular mechanic who had operated a garage for decades, and her mother had worked for a period of time as a truck driver, often taking her daughter on cross-country trips. Julye's mother had been a waitress and her father had delivered the *Uvalde Leader-News* and the *San Antonio Express-News* in his retirement years. He had died when Julye was eighteen.

Even though their families knew each other, the young women did not become friends until they took a creative writing course together at Southwest Texas Junior College. Meghann, who was nineteen at the time (six years younger than Julye), completed an associate's degree and moved to the University of Texas at Austin. Julye earned an associate's degree in management and entered the workforce.

Years later, when a reporting position opened at our newspaper, Meghann encouraged her friend to apply. Julye demurred, but Meghann was insistent. By the time Julye had come around, Kimberly had decided to accept the post. In that moment, Julye, another voracious reader, became our new receptionist. "I have been following Kim for years," she observed of her subsequent move to Kimberly's reporting job.

Melissa was new to Uvalde when we hired her in January 2019. Like Kimberly and Julye, she had no reporting experience but lots of practice in technical writing as part of earning a master of science degree in urban planning from the University of Texas at San Antonio. The forty-four-year-old also came from a background that was bound to instill empathy. As a second grader, Melissa had lived in the family's car with her parents as they struggled financially. Three years later, the financial picture had brightened enough for the family to purchase a sailboat, which became their new home.

In 2009, one of Melissa's closest friends, Dana Clair Edwards, was murdered by her boyfriend in a crime that rocked San Antonio's Alamo Heights community. The boyfriend was finally convicted four years later, but Melissa felt betrayed by media that used her trial testimony against her wishes. She was visited by further trauma at the age of forty-one when a diagnosis of uterine cancer resulted in a hysterectomy.

The deadline to send digital files to the printing plant in San Antonio was Wednesday at 3 p.m. We missed that mark by hours that week. The challenge was not just tracking down accurate information, particularly from law enforcement, but willing ourselves to change gears. Long years of a twice-weekly production schedule had become so ingrained that we found it challenging to post breaking news about the shooting on our Facebook page or our website at uvaldeleadernews.com. In the back of our minds, each time we handed over our reporting to social media, we sacrificed the print edition to the endlessly hungry consumers of free news. It was irrational, especially given the plummeting trajectory of print journalism and the fact that the world media now lived on our doorstep. Every minute of every hour there seemed to be a new posting about the tragedy, more evidence that the *Leader-News* had apparently become irrelevant.

We entertained zero illusions about being able to match the reporting of the *New York Times*, ABC, or CNN, who appeared to have more boots on the ground than we had subscribers. If we had a spoken plan—and we did not—it would have been something akin to the fable of the tortoise and the hare. Let the world media run themselves ragged with their 24/7 news cycle, scooping up all the headlines and sound bites they could, but in the end, when they packed up, we would be here to finish the story. One member of a national media outlet who had befriended us acknowledged how difficult it must have been in the beginning to watch the headlines go to outsiders. However, she affirmed that at the end of the day the story always belonged to the local paper.

The first official—albeit unofficial—announcement of the dead came Tuesday afternoon from Gov. Abbott, who put the number at fourteen (another swing and a miss for him). That number accounted only for the victims who were left in the school until Judge Diaz and the Bexar County medical examiner identified them. In the chaos of triage, one child left the scene without a heartbeat and two others were barely alive. Teacher Eva Mireles made it as far as a waiting ambulance that never left the school. Two children would arrive at Uvalde Memorial Hospital as dead on arrival and a third boy succumbed in an ambulance en route to San Antonio.

By Wednesday afternoon we had regained enough balance to seriously contemplate a Thursday edition. Plenty of routine stories were already written, including the results of the runoff election that had been held the day of the attack. But Julye, the quintessential community newspaper reporter, struggled with the shooting story. The combination of her amazing smarts (she did tax returns for friends because she liked helping) and a bottomless well of human kindness had yielded a contact list that made the rest of us look like recent arrivals. She enjoyed excellent relations with all the agencies—UPD, the sheriff's department, and the school district police—but now calls and texts went unanswered. Whatever window we had to access our sources closed almost immediately, thanks largely to the Department of Public Safety and the Texas

Rangers. They controlled the investigation from the moment the shooter was gunned down, and it was their narrative that would be spoon-fed publicly or leaked through media sources for months to come.

Melissa faced similar obstacles, as school district administrators refused to comment. No statements were forthcoming regarding the number of students in each classroom, much less how many had actually died or been wounded. Nor was there definitive information about the shooter or what his motives might have been. The school district's only organized response came on Tuesday afternoon during a two-minute press conference at the civic center that was preceded by a statement from the district's director of communications, Anne Marie Espinoza, that there would be no follow-up questions. That unfortunate barrier, no doubt inspired by advice from the district's legal team in San Antonio, would remain in place in the coming weeks and months, much to the detriment of public trust in the school as an institution.

Beginning at exactly 4:16 p.m., just over three hours after the attacker had been killed, school district police chief Pete Arredondo stood before a portable lectern and delivered a terse statement: "At approximately 11:32 a.m. this morning there was a mass casualty at Robb Elementary School in Uvalde, Texas. . . . I can confirm right now that we have several injuries—adults and students—and we do have some deaths." The chief went on to say that the suspect, who "was deceased," was believed to have acted alone. "DPS is assisting with the investigation."

Of course, Arredondo was crawfishing. He and other law enforcement knew full well that "some deaths" was a gross understatement, a prevarication designed to buy time. At that moment, sixteen children and one of their teachers lay dead in Rooms 111 and 112. Another slain teacher rested in an ambulance parked outside the school. As the day wore on, the big networks began reporting those numbers, quoting each other and then changing their number, which the original sources then cited. It was a merry-go-round of shifting information.

Our reporting the next day included the official number of nineteen dead students and two teachers. No names were made public, even though all the families had been notified by midnight Tuesday. We identified the killer and the fact that he was an eighteen-year-old Uvalde High School dropout. There was no picture of him, a position that Pete had insisted on from the beginning and with which we all agreed. It was pretty bare bones. What we did have were startling photographs of fourth graders running to safety after being freed from their classrooms.

By early afternoon, with the staff's best efforts to describe the devastation sitting in the computer server's Thursday folder, I touched base with Meghann on plans for the front page. I envisioned one of Pete's pictures dominating the layout, accompanied by the lead story beneath a 72-point banner headline. The rest of the page would carry copy the staff had assembled describing donations of money and blood as well as the fact that high school graduation ceremonies had been postponed.

Meghann said the staff had other ideas: Melissa felt strongly that the page should be black and Meghann agreed. They said it would best reflect the darkness of the day and the community's grief and avoid the pain that a large photograph might inflict. The women feared that pictures of children fleeing the fourth grade wing would tear at the families whose students had not escaped the killer. That possibility was very real, as we had been accused of insensitivity for previous images involving fatal vehicle crashes, none of which had ever shown bodies.

The idea of a black page caught me completely off guard. Such a response to a mass shooing seemed like a dereliction of our responsibility to feature our best reporting. Meghann and I talked back and forth. After a few minutes, I heard former editor Willie Edwards, a close friend, in the front office talking with a woman whom I presumed was a writer for the *New Yorker* magazine. Edwards had called earlier to see if he could introduce Rachel Monroe, a friend of a friend, who wanted to do a piece on how we were covering the tragedy. The staff bristled at the fact that an outside reporter had gained access to the newsroom. Along with Norma Ybarra, all of us had taken turns declining requests to speak on camera or in Zoom meetings. I told Rachel that our deadline had flown by and we had no time to talk. Edwards wept when he learned that Lexi had died in the shooting.

I returned to Meghann's office and closed the door. Once again, I suggested Pete's compelling images accompanied by our best stories, but Meghann held firm that we "make it black." As did the staff. And the more we talked, the more sense it made. No pictures, no words, no matter how excellent, could capture how we and the community felt. If pictures spoke a thousand words, a black page spoke one: devastation. It expressed crushing sadness and a desire to cradle the intimacy of what had been lost, at least for now. I agreed to the page and it felt exactly right. My only request was that we include the date of the shooting in white lettering across the top. And thus we went to press with the most sorrowful news a community newspaper could ever be asked to deliver.

The next day Kimberly texted me with a request: could she write Lexi's obituary and might she include two pictures? I responded that she could have a full page. Her reply was heartbreaking and impossible to answer: "Why would anyone want to hurt my baby, Craig?"

CHAPTER 17

"Look What They Did"

The White House press office contacted the *Leader-News* just after 2 p.m. on May 26, advising that we would soon receive a news release announcing Pres. Joe Biden's plans to visit the city. Dhara Nayyar, regional communications director for the White House, explained that the release was not to be posted to our social media a moment before 3:30 p.m. After that, the message would be shared with the world.

The statement read: "On Sunday, May 29, the President and First Lady will travel to Uvalde, Texas, to grieve with the community that lost twenty-one lives in the horrific elementary school shooting. This trip will be pooled press. Additional details to follow."

I responded that we would gladly follow the White House's wishes but hoped our newspaper would be permitted to cover the event. We received no reply, which was disappointing. We had no desire for ego stroking, only to be allowed to record what was meant to be an historic visit by a man whose words of support were in great demand— at least by much of the community. Plus, this was our town, our tragedy, and our job to report it.

None of that mattered when it came to the president's security, which was exceptionally tight. Marine One, escorted by three V-22 Osprey tiltrotor aircraft touched down at Uvalde's Garner Field Airport around 11 a.m. and the entourage sped to Robb elementary, where the president and First Lady were immersed in a scene of despair that had been building for days. Oversize photographs of the nineteen fourth graders and their two teachers stood in front of the school. Each picture, outlined with white roses, bore the name of the child or adult. Nearby, twenty-one white crosses had been planted in the earth. Each bore the painted name of a victim.

Getting close to the scene at Robb proved daunting, as security checkpoints allowed no one to enter with a camera unless it had been preapproved. Pete and

Meghann arrived without benefit of the preapproval protocol (all local knowledge was useless). Nevertheless, the two were allowed access, and Pete managed to take pictures with his cell phone that ultimately ended up on our front page.

They watched as the first couple stood in silence, reading the names and reaching out to touch each photograph. The president had lashed out in his condemnation of gun violence following the mass shooting of ten black people in a Buffalo grocery store on February 17 and immediately after the shooting at Robb. Now he held his tongue, absorbing the tragedy with reverence and concern for those afflicted.

The Bidens were joined by District Superintendent Hal Harrell, Principal Mandy Gutierrez, US representative Tony Gonzales, and Mayor McLaughlin. When Gov. Abbott appeared, some members of the audience booed, chanting "Vote him out!" The White House had also invited Cornyn and Cruz. The senators elected to stay away.

Following the short stay at Robb, the Bidens traveled across town to Sacred Heart Catholic Church for a celebration of Mass conducted by Archbishop Gustavo García-Siller of San Antonio. As the Bidens made their way from the sanctuary to the front pew, the First Lady touched the hands of several people seated along the aisle. A violinist played "Ave Maria" before the service began.

Archbishop García-Siller announced to the approximately 600 mourners that "our hearts are broken." He then invited the children to the front of the church, where they sat on the floor. The priest told them they were the ones who would help the community to heal.

When the service ended, the Bidens moved quickly to awaiting vehicles. A group of spectators had gathered to watch them. One of them shouted "Do something!" Biden, who had reached the open door of the presidential limousine, turned and without hesitation replied: "We will!"

Meanwhile, Felix and Kimberly had been waiting for several hours with other family members at the Fairplex. In a meeting the day after, which was the first time I had seen Kimberly in person since the shooting, she told me that the president and First Lady had seemed genuinely concerned as they moved among the tables of families. She recounted giving the president a picture of Lexi after he stopped at their table. She said that in return the president presented her with a photograph of his son Beau Biden, who died of brain cancer in 2015. "It was a really old picture that he pulled from his wallet," Kimberly said. "It was kind of a prayer card."

She and Felix introduced the Bidens to all of their kids, and Jill Biden was especially good with them, Kimberley said. The couple's blended family include Isaiah Rodriguez, David Falcon III, Julian Rubio, Kalisa Barboza, and Jahleela Rubio.

Our visit took place at Kimberly's mother's house on Fourth Street. The couple sat in the middle of a king size bed, while I perched on the edge. It was here that they had sought refuge after absorbing the devastating news that Lexi had been killed. The sadness in both of their faces seemed just as fresh as it had on that day.

On top of the pain of losing Lexi, Felix was wrestling with what he had seen at Robb. While Kimberly waited outside the yellow police line with hundreds of other frantic parents, the off-duty sheriff's deputy had entered the fourth grade hallway around 12:20 p.m. As much as he wanted to save his daughter, Felix knew that he would be stopped because he could possibly distract officers from the job that needed to be done. The fact that his fellow officers had failed to take action weighed on him.

"You do not wait, you do not wait," Felix told me with tears in his eyes. "That is why you put on the uniform. If you have to take a bullet, that is what you do."

We welcomed the president's journey to stand by the victims' families, even if he had to slip into the city beneath a veil of secrecy and an umbrella of attack aircraft. It was the world we lived in—a jarring juxtaposition with the previous visit to Uvalde by a sitting president.

In November 1942, a train bearing Pres. Franklin D. Roosevelt had pulled into the station in North Uvalde for the sole purpose of touching base with a man who had served two terms as his vice president. John Nance "Cactus Jack" Garner still commanded enormous influence, and Roosevelt had not traveled thousands of miles to enjoy the Southwest Texas view; he had done so because it was politically expedient.

Garner had split with Roosevelt in 1940 over the president's thinly veiled plan to pack the US Supreme Court. The Uvaldean had then launched his own campaign for the presidency. When it failed and Garner left Washington in 1942, he vowed never again to cross the Potomac. The fact that he still wielded power within the party was borne out by Roosevelt's visit.

Garner continued to exert an influence on national politics far beyond his tenure in the White House. His ninetieth birthday on November 22, 1958, summoned a trio of luminaries. Former president Harry S. Truman, Senate Majority Leader Lyndon Baines Johnson, and Speaker of the House Sam Rayburn traveled to Uvalde for the occasion. Five years later, on his ninety-fifth birthday, Cactus Jack received another presidential salutation. This time it came from John F. Kennedy, calling from Dallas. A photograph of Garner taking the call appeared on the front page of the *Leader-News*. It was Kennedy's last phone call.

In an interview months after the Robb tragedy, Uvalde native George Rodriguez shared the pain of losing Josecito in the shooting. The longtime partner of the boy's grandmother, George had helped raise the child from a baby. In the course of our hour-long conversation, the seventy-two-year-old reflected on Biden's recent visit and remembered another connection with the White House.

As a boy, George and his family had worked for Garner, harvesting pecans in the orchard behind the old man's stately house on North Park Street. One of George's other duties was to assist the former vice president with his televisions. That is plural because Garner owned two sets, which allowed him to watch baseball games that were being broadcast during the same time slot. The nine-year-old's job was to make sure the volume was adjusted to his employer's satisfaction. Former *Leader-News* editor Willie Edwards jokingly referred to George as the first television remote control in Uvalde. Eventually George became a driver for Garner's son, Tully, who paid for the teenager's driver's education course. "I was like driving Mr. Daisy," he said with a pained smile.

When Garner died at the age of ninety-nine on November 7, 1967, George had a front-row seat to the proceedings, including the dignitaries who paraded into the city. He remembered waiting to greet Vice President Spiro T. Agnew and reporting to his history teacher at Uvalde High School that he had "seen the vice president."

At that point in our interview, George paused, forcing himself back to the present, which filled his eyes with fresh tears for Josecito. "And I said look what these kids are doing . . . look what they did. They brought the president of the United States to Uvalde for the wrong reason. Wish it would not be what happened. But, no, the president came."

CHAPTER 18

Outpouring

I t was as if the nation and the world had turned a fire hose of love and support on Uvalde. A town of 15,000 in the far reaches of Southwest Texas that was best known for its deer hunting and sparkling, spring-fed rivers, had become the newest ground zero for tragedy. Suddenly, we were the next Sandy Hook or Parkland. A place in America where yet another disturbed young man with an assault-style rifle had cut down helpless children and their teachers.

Uvaldeans responded immediately, stepping up to cook meals, care for children, feed pets, serve as drivers, monitor the sick and injured, and donate money—no need was too great. In fact, so many were offering their services that they could scarcely fit in one community.

Uvalde resident Cujo Rodriguez worked late into the night of May 25 to construct twenty-one handmade wooden crosses for the front of Robb Elementary. His team, which included his wife, Chelie; their children; and his sister-in-law, Kristi Nicole Montoya, completed the project at around 10:30 p.m. Each cross, festooned with flowers, bore the name of a deceased child or teacher. They were positioned in front of the monument-style sign in front of Robb Elementary School that said "Welcome" and "Bienvenidos." Almost immediately the crosses became magnets for photographs, stuffed animals, sports paraphernalia—anything that was a favorite of the deceased. That memorabilia continued to grow until it soon connected with the school's chain-link fence, which accrued its own distinct characteristics.

Within days, the downtown plaza acquired a similar mantel of mourning. By the end of the first month, tokens of remembrance stood waist deep around crosses that encircled the plaza's central fountain. For months, family members, friends, and visitors made pilgrimages to the site, walking slowly around the fountain pool, heads bowed as they paused before each cross to absorb the loss. Most strangers found it impossible to visit the shrine without leaving a piece of their own heart.

The *Leader-News* received hundreds of emails decrying the massacre. The messages lamented the wanton nature of the crime and offered prayers and love for the victims' families. Some resorted to poetry for the "fallen angels," stretching the boundary between maudlin creativity and genuine concern. Still, the vast majority were deeply sincere expressions of compassion. We made space in our Sunday opinion section for as many of the "letters to the editor" as we could accommodate: almost a page and a half in the May 29 edition and another two pages the following Sunday.

A tsunami of material objects also washed over the city. Psychologists refer to the response as "helpers high," acts of altruism carried out because the act itself makes people feel good. Evidently the world felt pretty rotten because the volume of "stuff" was staggering. Hundreds of flower arrangements, bicycles, backpacks, children's books, laminated photographs of the victims, Christmas ornaments, hand-painted rocks, and assorted school supplies coursed through the city and the school system.

Our newspaper was asked to receive a shipment from The Comfort Cub nonprofit, which put us on high alert. Following the mass shooting at Sandy Hook Elementary School on December 14, 2012, the city of Newtown, Connecticut, took delivery of 60,000 teddy bears, the equivalent of two animals for every resident of the city. The avalanche forced officials to rent an 80,000-square-foot warehouse to store the stuffed animals and the thousands of Christmas toys delivered en masse to the grieving community. It was too much, and most of the items were regifted. A large volume of other donated material was later incinerated and buried as part of a memorial to the tragedy.

As it turned out, our fears were unfounded. The Comfort Cub, located in Encinitas, California, delivered 1,000 of its four-pound stuffed bear cubs to families of victims and children who had survived the shooting. Of that number, the newspaper received about 300 by FedEx and the remainder were flown courtesy of United Airlines to San Antonio, along with founder Marcella Johnson. She and other volunteers delivered the amazingly comforting creations the last 70 miles to Uvalde.

A man in the tiny Georgia town of Eastman felt compelled to build handcrafted benches for each victim. Sean Peacock, owner of Jass Graphix, told Melissa that Georgia was hot and humid but everything was also sweeter, including the watermelon and corn. Peacock and his team proved it by building the bespoke benches and delivering them to Uvalde in record time. Carved out of South Georgia pine with a butterfly design, each bench featured a laser-engraved photo of the victim in the backrest and a personalized inscription on the seat. Peacock raised $20,000 from a local GoFundMe effort to help underwrite the $1,800 price tag for each bench.

Perhaps the most distant expression of support found its way to Uvalde from a group of school children in the Kenyan mountain town of Loitokitok. The African children did not have many details about those who had died—what their voices sounded like, the clothes they wore, or who they admired. What they did know is that—like themselves—their American counterparts brimmed with life, love for their parents and siblings, and ambitions to fill many important roles.

A former educator from Quebec named Irving Rother reached out by email to say that students at Entonet Primary School in Loitokitok wanted to plant twenty-one saplings in honor of the Robb victims. After many emails back and forth, Rother announced that the project had been completed. He sent pictures of the children, dressed in their bright blue-and-green school uniforms (the same colors as the Robb fourth grade hallway), digging in the town's rich volcanic soil. It was easy to imagine the trees growing tall and strong in the mountain air, nourished by frequent rains that swirl around Mount Kilimanjaro. Africa's tallest peak at 19,341 feet watches over Loitokitok from just across the border in Tanzania.

As we soon learned, mass shootings attract a fair number of opportunists, not unlike the scads of roofing companies that routinely fell on the city following brutal hailstorms. When the *Leader-News* began running advertisements placed by out-of-town law firms, the grumbling grew audible. A longtime friend came to visit about a project to construct a new softball field. He envisioned the formation of a nonprofit entity to solicit donations. We enjoyed a productive talk, and then he offered that people wondered why the paper was running the "lawyer ads." I replied that there were two reasons: families needed representation and our newspaper needed the revenue.

And then there was Nathan Baller, a man whose original intentions may have been well placed, but who became swept up in the grandiosity of a mission that he could never have delivered. Nathan Kouamou, which was his legal name, arrived in the city soon after the shooting. The self-proclaimed former pro soccer player with the Houston Dynamo spent months telling families of shooting victims that the super-sized music festival he was planning—Balling for Uvalde World Weekend—would generate up to $50 million, much of which would flow to them. He threw out names like Drake, Justin Bieber, Bad Bunny, and LeBron James. None of the celebrities had committed, but

Baller assured Uvaldeans that the event scheduled for February 4 and 5, 2023, would be a blowout success.

"LeBron James, I'm calling you out. What are you gonna do, right? Drake, can we get a recording session with Drake? Can we auction it off?" he crowed to families during a dinner in October 2022.

Uvalde mayor Don McLaughlin said that Baller approached him about the city setting up a bank account for Baller Academy to hold funds for the event. Baller wanted access to the account, but the mayor declined, saying the city alone would have to be accountable to the public. The mayor added that alleged headliners for the event had never heard of Baller. The final straw was a contract presented to families with terms city officials described as "horrible." The agreement would give Baller the use of the victims' "image, likeness, signature, voice, photographs, names . . . in perpetuity and royalty-free for any purpose."

Amerie Jo's step-grandmother, Berlinda Arreola, said they ran the contract by lawyers and were cautioned not to sign it. "You're gonna put yourself into a situation that he's gonna walk away with millions and y'all are gonna walk away owing and paying everything outta your pocket, basically," she said.

At that point, in November 2022, a cease-and-desist letter was sent to Baller, signed by twenty families saying they were terminating any agreements made with him and demanding a halt to fund-raising.

Jesse Rizo, whose niece Jackie Cazares was a Robb victim, said that Baller continued to try to meet with the families. But when they demanded answers about the event, Baller declined to answer them. Rizo said that a few weeks later, "he just vanished." Families never saw a penny of the money. Although no one knows exactly how much was raised, Mayor McLaughlin said that Baller had told him he had sold 4,500 tickets.

In the meantime, far more practical help arrived. Dozens of florists poured into the city to assist local shops that had been slammed by unprecedented demand. Yolanda Moreno at Country Gardens & Seed said people from Pearland, Winnsboro, San Antonio, El Paso, Odessa, LaCoste, and other Texas cities volunteered their services. "People just started reaching out to us, calling and seeing if we needed any help. And the flower growers were also calling, saying they were willing to donate the product, anything we needed," Moreno said.

Liza Marquez, a florist with Flowers by Liza in El Paso, responded to Uvalde with a rotating crew of volunteers who remained for thirteen days. Marquez had experienced the aftermath of the August 3, 2019, shooting at an El Paso Walmart, where a gunman killed twenty-three and wounded two dozen others. She knew what was coming. Her shop, along with the other fifty florists in town, had been overwhelmed with orders.

"I told my husband, people don't understand. . . . I said they're going to be swamped by a nation, a country, different countries calling, different states. I remember when I would look at my phone and it would ring after our massacre, I'd see Alaska and I'm like 'Oh my God, just spam, more spam.' And then I started answering them, because I knew it wasn't spam, they were people sending flowers to try to reach out," Marquez said.

For most Americans, the easiest, and most impactful, way to show support was with a monetary gift. Their generosity exceeded anything donated to victims of a mass school shooting in the last decade. By the time the Uvalde Together We Rise Fund was distributed six months after the tragedy, it contained $22.3 million donated by 13,000 individuals and organizations. The scope of the donations ranged from onetime gifts of hundreds of thousands of dollars to $32 collected in a penny drive conducted by an elementary school, the Liberty Lions, located in the high desert area of Southern California.

A fourteen-year-old girl in Wisconsin sold $8 handmade bracelets to generate $3,000 for Robb victims. The teenager's desire to help, as described by her mother, reflected the sentiments of much of the world. "As much as she wanted to help the families and community, this helped her, too. It made it feel like in some small way, she was acting. She was doing something. We think of Uvalde every day."

The sheer creativity of the fund-raising had also been singular. Reagan Allen of San Antonio, a student at Emerson College in Boston, re-created the design of an Emerson College shirt worn by a character in the television show *Stranger Things*. Sales of the shirts raised $38,819, which became a donation. And an online global nonprofit Star Wars appreciation group called the Mando Mercs Costume Club donated $2,000.

A group of elementary school students in Richmond, Virginia, opened a lemonade stand, raising $200, with the message, "With love from our families and children to yours, we are praying and holding you in our hearts."

With so much money pouring into the community (there were seven different funds), it was imperative to create a single entity to manage the largesse. Community leaders including Mayor McLaughlin, County Judge Bill Mitchell, and County Attorney John Dodson conducted a series of meetings to create a steering committee. Local attorney Mickey Gerdes, a 1994 Uvalde High School graduate who had experience with probate and heirship, was asked to chair the ten-person group.

The Texas Department of Emergency Management steered the group to Kevin Feinberg, who had headed the $200 million September 11th Victim Compensation Fund. Feinberg responded that he was "no longer in the game" but recommended the National Compassion Fund (NCF) for guidance.

That contact proved to be enormously valuable, as the NCF had been involved in twenty-three previous tragedies that involved disbursing money to victims of mass casualty crimes. The organization, which is a subsidiary of the National Center for Victims of Crime, was formed after shootings at a theater in Aurora, Colorado, and at Sandy Hook. Families from those two tragedies came together in search of a better way to distribute money that had been donated specifically to victims. The process after the rampage at Sandy Hook had been particularly fraught, as it was administered by the United Way, which apparently deposited donations in its general fund and then disbursed a percentage to families.

Jeff Dion, executive director of the NCF, traveled to Uvalde with other members of his team to discuss what their help might look like. Gerdes said the committee studied the response to shootings at Virginia Tech, the Pulse nightclub in Orlando, the Walmart in El Paso, and others to create protocols for applying for funding. Part of that process included conducting a series of town hall meetings to gather input from potential applicants for funds and other community members. Prior to the public meetings, the steering committee met privately on a Sunday afternoon with families of those who had been killed as well as the injured.

Gerdes said the tiers for applicants established for the Uvalde Together We Rise fund did not line up exactly with those for other mass shootings, but the concept was similar. Heirs of the deceased received the largest percentage, followed by those with physical injuries and those who had been physically present but were not injured. Within the injured tier, a distinction was drawn between levels of injury because some were far worse than others. A similar differentiation was made in the tier for those who were physically present.

"We tiered within the physically present [at Robb Elementary], because we knew that the epicenter had all happened around these two classrooms and in that West building. Those kids that were not injured in that building itself still heard it all, smelled it all, were connected to the same HVAC system and probably tasted it all for an hour or more. And so we wanted to make sure that that building was singled out . . . and then dealt with everybody else on the campus in a separate way," Gerdes explained.

The number of fund applicants that were receiving public assistance caught NCF officials by surprise. The same was not true for locals on the committee, but the fact served to complicate the distribution process. "We were very upfront before the first community meeting in June. I had a conversation with Legal Aid, saying 'there's going to be 70 to 80 percent of these people that are on some form of public benefits that will need to be dealt with or vetted through the process,'" Gerdes said.

The attorney allowed that if he had to do it over again, he would have appealed early on to legislators to seek waivers for counting the donated money as income for purposes of public benefits. By June 2022 it was too late, and Legal Aid struggled to vet each case. In the meantime, the committee reached out to US representative Tony Gonzales, state representative Tracy King, state senator Roland Gutierrez, and the Texas Health and Human Services in search of a solution.

Gerdes acknowledged that the conflict with public assistance slowed the process, but even worse, it added stress to families. "We didn't want to hand a chunk of money over to somebody that disqualified them for six years for SSI or Social Security," he said. He added that it was possible to roll on and off programs like the Children's Health Insurance Program or the National School Lunch Program, but the other programs are not as flexible. "So . . . we really wanted to make an effort to make sure that when we handed over this money to these folks, we weren't going to put them in a worse situation than they were before just because they got this gift."

Some community members and those on the steering committee feared that fund recipients would become targets of fraud or simple grift. Still, Gerdes said it was not their place to tell people how they were supposed to spend money that had come from generous donors with no strings attached.

The committee lined up resources for financial planning. Frost Bank in San Antonio and offices of Edward Jones and Raymond James in Uvalde made advisers available, and some recipients availed themselves of the advice. For others, it was not a priority. The process was complicated further when the money was earmarked for children who had survived the shooting. To ensure that the funds went to the kids, the Uniform Transfers to Minors Act required families to set up minor child or minor children trusts.

The companies that offered financial planning volunteered to serve as third-party trustees, until the first $1 billion lawsuit was filed. After that, the institutions feared the liability of advising families to limit spending only for things that benefited the child—education, general welfare, and maintenance—which precluded purchasing a $70,000 car for everyone in the family.

Gerdes said the committee received complaints about the time it was taking to distribute the money, but when he explained that time quite literally was money—because the fund continued to grow—people backed off. Of course, once the distribution took place on November 14, 2022, some groused about not getting a fair deal. "I did not hear a lot of complaints from the families of category A, the kids and teachers that were killed. I got a lot of pushback in category B. And then I got a little bit of pushback further on down . . . mostly because they were like, 'Well, I thought I was going to get more.'"

A simple question usually ended the conversation: "Which group of people should we have taken money away from in order to give to another group? 'Okay, I get it. If I get more money, the deceased families get less or the wounded families. Somebody's got to have less in order for me to get more.' And that sort of took care of that."

Divvying up money brings out the worst in people; just ask any probate attorney. People filed false applications that claimed they were on the Robb campus that day when they were nowhere close. And then there were those who felt that some families of victims should have gotten less because they received money from other sources, like GoFundMe accounts.

"I'm like, 'They will never have their daughter back, and your child is still alive. I understand there is trauma, but we have resources available in town for that that need to be taken advantage of. Your child may never be the same again but your child is here.'" Gerdes said the fund could have contained $100 million and there still would have been applicants who felt they deserved more—all the way down to those who received a check for their physical presence but had been on the other side of the campus.

At the end of the day, Uvalde Together We Rise contained more money than any fund previously organized by the NCF. What Gerdes reluctantly referred to as the "highest death pay" on record showed the incredible generosity that flowed to the victims.

The money will "never make the survivors whole," but they should derive comfort from the fact that "so many wanted to give something to help them in whatever way possible," Gerdes said of the fund.

Asked if he would take on the difficult job again, Gerdes grew emotional. "Never in a million years would I have thought that I would have to tell my fourth grader last year that her two softball teammates were killed. And then to see Lexi in her casket—with [my daughter] Pippa standing there—never in a million years. I mean, there was a need, and I had the capacity to fill a role. And that's all I did."

CHAPTER 19

Never-Ending Funeral

W ithin days of the shooting, families confronted the most soul-rending task a parent can contemplate: burying a child. And not as the result of a car accident or some awful disease but because of mass murder in a schoolroom. The savagery of that act increased the pain beyond description. Parents could barely lift themselves from their beds to eat and bathe, much less make funeral arrangements. In many cases, family and friends shouldered the burden, but when the deceased is a child, the sadness consumes everyone in the family's orbit.

Picking a funeral home may have been the easiest decision, because in Uvalde there were exactly two options: Rushing-Estes-Knowles Mortuary and Hillcrest Memorial Funeral Home. Rushing-Estes-Knowles, which was home grown but in recent years had been purchased by a large corporation, dispensed its services with practiced efficiency and compassion. Hillcrest, on the other hand, was a small startup that became part of the Robb story the moment Salvador Ramos crashed his grandmother's pickup across the street and fired at two Hillcrest employees. Thirty minutes later, children raced to asylum inside the funeral home after being freed from their fourth grade classrooms.

In the days after the shooting, representatives from the two funeral homes were summoned to the Uvalde County Fairplex, where the state had established a grief command post. Later it would become the Family Resiliency Center, which was funded by a $5 million grant from the governor's office. Initially, the FBI Victim Services Division operated there. Ongoing services included counseling, financial assistance, and funeral service planning.

"They basically put us in a room with Rushing-Estes-Knowles, and we were supposed to sell ourselves, which is not something we were prepared to do," Hillcrest owner Leroy Briones said of the arrangement. "It was like this is the competitor, this is us, who do you want to go with? It was horrible, just horrible."

Briones said they participated for about an hour and then declined to continue. He was uncertain who had orchestrated the fiasco but said it felt like "David versus Goliath," especially since Rushing-Estes-Knowles had the contract to serve as the county morgue. In that sense, they controlled the initial disposition of bodies. In the end, Rushing-Estes-Knowles handled sixteen of the funerals (including the funeral of Joe Garcia), leaving five for Hillcrest. The feeling of frustration was heightened by the fact that Hillcrest had the capacity to handle many more services, while Rushing-Estes-Knowles was challenged by the sheer volume to meet families' immediate needs.

Hillcrest had been the first to post on social media that there would be no charge for the funerals of Robb victims, a move that Rushing-Estes-Knowles quickly followed. At the same time, the OneStar Foundation received $170,000 from NFL star Bo Jackson to cover funeral costs. The city of Uvalde also gathered about $300,000 from multiple anonymous and community donors to pay for funeral-related expenses such as plots and headstones.

A story that appeared in the *Leader-News* on September 18, 2022, reported that Rushing-Estes-Knowles had received $152,000 and that Hillcrest had received $17,800 from donated funds for funeral services.

Another donor stepped up to provide caskets for the nineteen slain children. Tony Ganem, owner of SoulShine Industries in Edna, Texas, was contacted by the Texas Funeral Directors Association about fabricating the caskets with themes ranging from softball to Spider-Man. Ganem met with the victims' families to learn how to best represent each child. "The purpose is to let your loved one's life shine through our designs," SoulShine said in a Facebook post. An anonymous ranch owner in Kinney County covered the cost of the caskets, which ranged from $3,400 to $3,800 apiece.

Both funeral homes received spontaneous support from fellow colleagues and others in the community. "A lot of my buddies from mortuary school instantly took up on the call of help and came the next day," Briones said. He added that US Customs and Border Patrol sent volunteers who helped with behind-the-scenes work such as picking up trash, opening doors, and helping with repairs.

Father Eduardo Morales, the lone priest of the only Catholic parish in the city, Sacred Heart, faced his own awful challenge. He was called on to celebrate Mass of Christian

Burial for ten children and two teachers. The magnitude of loss was unprecedented, even for a man who had spent the last two years consoling dozens of parishioners who had lost parents and grandparents in the pandemic. COVID-19 swept through Uvalde County with special lethality, carrying away 144 people. A disproportionate number were older Hispanics, people who often lacked adequate health care to begin with. Many of them had been faithful parishioners of Sacred Heart.

In August 2020, as the church curtailed operations due to social distancing, Father Morales posted on the church-affiliated Facebook page that he had conducted a funeral Mass nearly every day for the last several weeks. That had disrupted routine daily services. "Once again, thank you for being patient and understanding as life events have happened," he wrote.

Now the priest told reporters that the aftermath of Robb felt like "one huge funeral that is not ending." He also lamented that burying the victims was a particularly daunting task, as "everyone here knows someone who was killed. I'm burying parishioners, but it's people I've known all my life—and that's what makes it difficult."

Father Morales, or Father Eddy, as he was affectionately known to his congregants, may have been better prepared to offer comfort than most priests. Born in Uvalde in 1960, he was raised with ten siblings in a house just two blocks from the church. Many of the worshippers at Sacred Heart were his childhood friends and neighbors. And some of the nine- and ten-year-olds he would bury had received their First Communion from his hands only a few years earlier. Ties to the community were further strengthened through his mother, Genoveva Morales, the same woman who had won the class action lawsuit against the school district for discrimination.

The Morales family's political activism did not extend to Father Eddy. The unassuming priest was guided entirely by faith—cultivating it in his parishioners and employing it to deliver comfort at times like these. It had been tested often and early. In June 1996, as family members were driving back from San Antonio after watching him celebrate his first Mass, his sister, Michelle Contreras, who was twenty-nine, had been killed in an automobile accident just west of Sabinal. The driver of the vehicle Contreras was riding in had lost control after swerving to miss a deer.

Genoveva Morales had been less than thrilled when her son announced his intention to join the priesthood. In a story that appeared in the *Austin American-Statesman* in 1996, Father Eddy recounted his mother saying, "They're going to lock you up, and we won't see you for years. And you'll only come home to tell me they're going to send you to Africa or South America." When the priest moved back to Uvalde in 2016, he lived down the street from his elderly mother.

On May 24, Morales was on vacation in Boston when he received an urgent call from San Antonio archbishop Gustavo García-Siller. Father Eddy packed his suitcase and arrived in Uvalde by late Wednesday. The following day brought more devastating news. Joe Garcia, husband of slain fourth grade teacher Irma Garcia and a long-time parishioner, had died. Joe had traveled to Robb on Thursday morning to lay flowers on his wife's memorial cross, which stood with twenty others. Upon returning to the family house, the fifty-year-old had sat down on the couch and suffered a massive heart attack. The couple's four surviving children, ranging in ages from thirteen to twenty-three, rightly called the cause of death a broken heart.

Area priests offered to share the crushing burden that Morales had been called to carry. The priest declined, saying he would see to the services himself.

The first funerals, for Amerie Jo Garza and Maite Rodriguez, were held on Tuesday, May 31, exactly one week after they were killed in Classroom 112. Amerie's service began at 2 p.m. at Sacred Heart, with Father Eddy officiating.

The small, almost austere church was packed with family and friends of the "sassy" ten-year-old who was attempting to call 911 when she was killed. The mourners also included hundreds of Girl Scouts from across the region. Amerie was posthumously awarded the Bronze Cross by the Girl Scouts of the United States, one of the highest honors in Girl Scouting. "On May 24, 2022, Amerie did all she could to save the lives of her classmates and teachers. It was our honor as Amerie's council to present the Bronze Star to her family," read a statement.

The priest described Amerie's love of creativity and her desire to become an art teacher. He then shared with parishioners what would become a refrain in the funerals to come. "You will hear me say this at every single funeral celebration that we have. We are not in the house of God to celebrate her death. We are here to celebrate her life. We are here to celebrate the life that allows her to continue to be among us." He also implored his flock not to allow anger to turn into hate.

The service for Maite Rodriguez started at 7 p.m. in the Rushing-Estes Knowles chapel. The ten-year-old's hand-painted coffin featured sea animals. It rested at the front of a long rectangular space that held perhaps 200 people and felt like a living room lined with pews.

Maite's favorite color was green and she loved lime-green Converse shoes and jalapeños. She was "focused, competitive, smart, bright, beautiful, happy," her mother said. When she was a kindergartner, Maite had decided that she wanted to become a marine biologist, and she had held firmly to that goal. She had researched a program at Texas A&M University in Corpus Christi and told her mother she was set on studying there.

Two months after her death, a scholarship was established in her name, the Maite Yule-ana Rodriguez Scholarship, to be awarded to a Uvalde student.

The following day, June 1, Father Eddy returned to the altar at 10 a.m. He was joined by Archbishop García-Siller in celebrating a Mass of Christian Burial for teacher Irma Garcia, forty-eight, and her husband, Joe. The archbishop delivered the homily. The church overflowed for the widely loved couple. Irma had been an educator in the school district for twenty-three years, all of them at Robb. She had also won teacher of the year honors as recently as 2019. Joe had worked at the H-E-B grocery for more than twenty-five years, where he had interacted daily with hundreds of community members on a first-name basis. "They began their relationship in high school and it flourished into a love that was beautiful and kind," read the death notice in the *Leader-News*.

Cease Martinez of Houston, an artist who painted a mural for Irma and Joe, said he learned that they were practically inseparable, which was also true in death. That was his inspiration for depicting them in a niche box, often used for devotion or altars. He named it *Amor Eterno*, or eternal love.

The second Mass on June 1, for Jose Flores, took place at 2 p.m. Josecito, as he was known to family, was buried in a bespoke coffin. His step-grandfather, George Rodri-guez, said that the ten-year-old had recently begun playing baseball with the Blue Jays and was taken by the sport. "He was not an all-star but he was my all-star," the two-time city golf champion said. Jose never lacked for attention, support, or love. "You would just love him, and he will love you back 100 times." George said that the boy "was a pleasure, a treasure, a gift from God . . . *un lindo muchachito*," a beautiful boy.

Room 111 classmates Nevaeh Bravo and Eliahna Torres, who had both been born on January 12, 2012, at Uvalde Memorial Hospital, and Maranda Mathis from Room 112 were laid to rest on Thursday, June 2. Services for both Maranda and Eliahna were conducted in the Rushing-Estes-Knowles chapel, while Nevaeh's family chose Sacred Heart for a Mass.

Eliahna's family and friends filled the Rushing-Estes-Knowles chapel at 11 a.m. for the ten-year-old who loved playing softball and making people laugh. "In her short time living with us, Eliahna managed to have a huge impact in many lives. She was a loving and compassionate person who loved to be silly. She had the most beautiful smile that could light up a room," her mother, Sandra, wrote.

Her teacher, Arnulfo Reyes, called Eliahna "sassy and dramatic." Several days before the shooting, the child approached Reyes teary-eyed, saying that she was wor-ried that when the school year ended, she would never see him again. "I'll always be here," he soothed her.

Nevaeh's and Maranda's services both began at 2 p.m. Father Eddy celebrated the Mass of Christian burial for ten-year-old Nevaeh (heaven spelled backward). Family described her as a sweet and sensitive girl who loved butterflies and unicorns—and wearing mascara and lip gloss every chance she got. Nevaeh's father said his daughter also loved to eat—even salad. She also thrilled at visits to his ranch, where she rode horses and fed the animals.

Mourners filed into the Rushing-Estes-Knowles chapel to say good-bye to eleven-year-old Maranda. Family said she was a shy, sweet tomboy who loved nature and preferred to be outside. "She had a grand imagination and often expressed her love for unicorns and mermaids, especially if they were her favorite color—purple."

On Friday, June 3, the priest spent virtually the entire day mourning the lives of three departed children: Mass was celebrated for Jayce Luevanos, Jailah Silguero, and Jacklyn "Jackie" Cazares, who less than a month earlier had received her First Communion.

Services for cousins Jailah and Jayce were combined and began at 10 a.m. Again the church overflowed with the interconnected families, grieving two ten-year-olds—one who loved to dance and make TikTok videos and the other who liked to bring friends home to his grandparents' house, only a block from the school, to play in the yard with his dog, Fifi. Jayce brewed the morning coffee for his grandparents.

The church filled once again at 2 p.m. as mourners gathered for Jackie, a free spirit who was always willing to help people in need. Her favorite color was sage green and she loved to make videos for TikTok and interact with her friends on Snapchat. She also loved animals and wanted to become a veterinarian and to visit Paris. "She had a voice," her father said. "She didn't like bullies, she didn't like being picked on. All in all, full of love. She had a big heart."

And there was one other thing that her teacher pointed out. She and Jayce were an item. "The only time Jayce had a bad day was if Jackie was mad at him," Arnulfo Reyes said of the two. "And then I would go over and say 'What's going on, Jackie?'"

Jackie's father, Javier, later noted that during the funeral procession to the cemetery, they passed an out-of-town female police officer directing traffic. She stood at attention with a crisp salute as tears rolled down her cheeks. "My whole family was crushed. They all thought Jackie was their daughter, too," Javier said.

Saturday, June 4, brought two more funerals, one for Makenna Elrod at First Baptist Church and a second for Rojelio Torres at 10 a.m. in the Rushing-Estes-Knowles chapel.

Mourners for Makenna came dressed in their finest purple attire, a request from the family to honor the ten-year-old's favorite color. Her mother, April Elrod, said "She was a light to all who knew her. She loved her family and friends. She loved to play softball, dance and sing, participate in gymnastics, play with fidgets, and spend time with her family."

"Makenna made friends wherever she went. She had brothers, sisters, and cousins she loved to play with. Her smile lit up a room," her family wrote. And Makenna wrote notes that she left for her mother and others to find.

Makenna was buried in a purple dress stitched with butterflies. The casket bore her picture and a butterfly, and at the gravesite, the family released dozens of live butterflies. "The butterflies landed on all of us, landed on my shoulder, landed on her daddy's tie and landed on her big sister's shoes," her mother said.

Her "daddy," Chris Seiler, saddled his horse, which Makenna insisted on riding no matter what the temperature was outside, and trailered it to Hillcrest Memorial Cemetery. He put Makenna's "little boots" in the stirrups and led the horse to the gravesite accompanied by the Conway Twitty song "That's My Job." It was one of the ten-year-old's favorite—a tune she had often danced to with Seiler.

Rojelio Torres, another ten-year-old who always had a smile on his face, was interred in his favorite football shirt. "He was always eager to help and had many hobbies, including playing Pokémon, football, and video games. And he loved life and being outside." His teacher said he was self-confident and wanted to be the best he could be. When Arnulfo Reyes was asked if Rojelio had made a call to 911 on May 24, the teacher smiled. "If anyone was going to do it, it would have been Rojelio. He wanted to be successful." His Aunt Precious said the boy was the life of the party and always the first one on the dance floor. "He was a gifted child who was so giving and loved his friends and family."

On Sunday, June 5, First Baptist Church was the site of another service, this one for ten-year-old Alithia Ramirez. Her parents, Jessica Hernandez and Ryan Ramirez, had called on the pastor from their former church in Dilley to conduct the service. "She was a smart, talented, reliable, extremely loving young lady who dreamed of attending art school in Paris. She wanted to take care of everyone and was a role model to her siblings. She also loved to play soccer," the minister said. When her younger siblings Akeelah and Jonah had been too long on their screens, Alithia's mother, Jessica, would ask the older girl to distract them with her art. The children were soon drawn to the task, practicing happily with their talented big sister.

The following day, Monday, June 6, Father Eddy celebrated yet another Mass, this one for Eliahna Garcia, who died less than two weeks before her tenth birthday on June 4. Jennifer Lugo said her daughter prayed out loud every night, and her DJ father,

Steven Garcia, recalled how she loved to come to the studio with him and sing into the microphone. She was a joyful child who was already planning her quinceañera for her fifteenth birthday by creating dances. In a TikTok video, posted by her father, she said "Jesus he died for us so when we die we'll be up there for him."

Ellie's grandparents, Nelda and Rogelio Lugo, said that Ellie had wanted to be a teacher and loved the movie *Encanto*. That information made its way to Disney, and the family received a call. The Walt Disney design team in California wanted to create a special funeral dress for Eliahna. The finished product was stunning—purple with flowers and butterflies from the waist down. The wardrobe makers also included a handmade crown complete with veil as well as pieces of the dress to be kept as a keepsake.

To top it off, musician friends of Steve, including Carlos Rodriguez and Matthew Luna of Carlos Y Los Cachorros, performed "Te Vas Angel Mio" at the gravesite.

Ten-year-old Xavier Lopez was buried on Tuesday, June 7, following services in the Rushing-Estes-Knowles chapel. His parents, Felicha Martinez and Abel Lopez, said that on the day of the shooting Xavier was honored for making the honor roll for the first time. His mother had quipped that it may have been because classmate Annabell Rodriguez's smarts were rubbing off on him. The two fourth graders were an item, and both mothers laughed at the way they texted each other "I love you" before bed each evening. The kids' relationship was so special that it brought the parents together for weekends of barbecuing.

Annabell's service was held the following day in the same Rushing-Estes-Knowles chapel. She was born on November 29, 2011, in Uvalde to Monica Gallegos and Jessie Rodriguez. Her family said she was a sweet girl whose favorite color was blue, especially on butterflies. She enjoyed watching TikTok and spending time with her sisters and family. She loved the family dog, Patrona, and wanted to be a veterinarian. A scholarship in her name was created at Texas A&M University in Bryan-College Station.

Her mother said Annabell came home one day talking about a boy in her class who dressed well and "smelled nice." She and Xavier were buried next to each other at Hillcrest Cemetery.

Two days later, on Friday, June 10, Father Eddy celebrated Mass for forty-four-year-old Eva Mireles, who died next to her students. Irma Garcia had told the newspaper in an earlier interview that Mireles, with whom she had co-taught for five years, was "such an amazing partner." Eva loved hiking, biking, her CrossFit brothers and sisters, and life in general. Her sister Maggie Mireles said her older sister was the family favorite, a force to be reckoned with. "Whenever she arrived at a family gathering, she honked the horn and then dashed into the house screaming the children's names. We loved her and will never forget her. She was the center of our life."

Her only child, Adalynn, wrote "Thank you for being the best mom anyone could ask for. You are so known by many now, and I am so happy people know your name and that beautiful face of yours and they know what a hero looks like. I don't know how to do this life without you . . . but I will forever say your name so you are always remembered: Eva Mireles, fourth-grade teacher at Robb Elementary who selflessly jumped in front of her students to save their lives."

Mireles's and Garcia's names were engraved onto the National Memorial to Fallen Educators, a monument in Emporia, Kansas, that honors school workers who died "in the line of duty." The creation of the memorial had been spurred by the Sandy Hook shooting a decade earlier. Carol Strickland, the executive director of the National Teachers Hall of Fame, which oversees the memorial, said she had just turned in a list of about a dozen educators' names to be engraved onto the massive granite blocks for the rededication ceremony on June 17, 2022. On Wednesday morning, May 25, following the news of the Uvalde school shooting, she placed a call to add two more.

The service for Alexandria Aniya "Lexi" Rubio took place on Saturday, June 11, in the First Baptist Church, which was full to the choir loft. Her great-grandfather, Julian Moreno, who had retired after fifty years as the pastor of Iglesia Primera Bautista, led the celebration of her life. Lexi was a committed athlete who excelled at softball and basketball, which she practiced often with her father Felix. Her goal was to win a softball scholarship to St. Mary's University in San Antonio, where her mother, Kimberly, was a student, and then study law. Lexi's five siblings described her as fierce but with a beautiful contagious smile that more often than not turned into a hearty laugh. She was sarcastic but caring and giving. Following the service, the funeral procession to Hillcrest Cemetery was accompanied by dozens of patrol cars in a tribute to Lexi and her deputy sheriff father.

Two days later, on Monday, June 13, Tess Mata, another talented softball star who played on the same team with Lexi, was buried following Mass at Sacred Heart. Tess played second base, the same as her idol, José Altuve with the Astros. She was saving money for a return trip to Disney World. Her walls were purple and her grandparents, Raymundo and Rosemary Mata, drove her to school and picked her up each day. "Tessy, mom, dad, and I won't be the same without you, but we are comforted knowing you are waiting for us up in heaven and have a spot for us," her big sister Faith said. "We have one sassy guardian angel that I know is going to protect our family."

At the burial, a mariachi group sang *Amor Eterno*.

Tú eres la tristeza de mis ojos (You are the sadness in my eyes)

Que lloran en silencio por tu amor (That weep in silence for your love)

Me miro en el espejo y veo en mi rostro (I look in the mirror and see in my face)

El tiempo que he sufrido por tu adiós (The time I have suffered for your goodbye).

Father Eddy celebrated the last Mass for a Robb victim on Thursday, June 16. Eleven-year-old Layla Salazar loved dancing, singing, and the Dallas Cowboys. She and her father, Vincent "Vinnie" Salazar III, sang "Sweet Child O' Mine" by Guns and Roses each morning on the way to school. Layla was also a runner and a swimmer. She had won six first-place ribbons on field day and was extremely proud of her accomplishments. "If you ain't first, you're last," she declared, quoting a line from the movie *Talladega Nights: The Ballad of Ricky Bobby*. When her grandparents would pick her up from school, they would treat her with tacos. She requested a ride from them often. "Our hearts will forever be broken. Layla's love will create an opening in heaven where her love will pour through and shine down upon us to let us know she is happy."

The final funeral service for a Robb student, Uziyah Garcia, took place on June 25 at Immanuel Baptist Church in San Angelo, Texas, where the boy had been born ten years earlier. "Sweetest, biggest heart. He loved school, he loved friends. He loved basketball," his guardian and aunt, Nikki Cross, said. "He loved gaming with his brothers and his sisters, and every morning he made sure to tell me he loved me before he went to school. He loved hanging out with mom making TikTok and Snapchat videos, and we miss him every day."

There was a final funeral for a Robb casualty that was not held in Uvalde. Both Rushing-Estes-Knowles and Hillcrest declined to handle arrangements for the eighteen-year-old who had broken thousands of hearts. In fact, Justice of the Peace Lalo Diaz reported that it was almost a month before Salvador Ramos's body was claimed by his family and transported to the Crown Cremation Center on the western edge of downtown San Antonio for cremation. Castle Ridge Mortuary in Crystal City, 45 miles southeast of Uvalde, handled the funeral services.

Uvalde Leader-News

LOCALLY OWNED INDEPENDENT NEWSPAPER— INFORMING SOUTHWEST TEXAS SINCE 1879

ONE SECTION, 12 PAGES | THURSDAY, MAY 26, 2022 | VOL. 142 NO. 24 $1.00

MAY 24, 2022

The newspaper's front page for the Thursday issue after the Tuesday shooting. We felt that black captured the devastation better than any words or photographs. Courtesy *Uvalde Leader-News*.

Newspaper staff gather beneath the mural of Lexi Rubio, 100 paces north of the *Uvalde Leader-News* office. Pictured are (front, left to right) Skylar Scott, Kimberly Mata-Rubio, Norma Ybarra, and Olga Charles; (middle) Alesandra Gonzales, Meghann Garcia, Julye Keeble, Melissa Federspill, Joanna Garza, and Josh Haby; and (back) Sofi Zeman, Craig Garnett, James Volz, Neil Sturdevant, and Pete Luna. Author's photograph.

Newspaper staff display awards won during the South Texas Press Association convention held April 20, 2023, in Boerne, Texas. Pictured are (front, left to right) Neil Sturdevant, Pete Luna, and Craig Garnett; and (back) Julye Keeble, Meghann Garcia, Melissa Federspill, and Norma Ybarra. Author's photograph.

The author greets Kimberly Mata-Rubio during the November 7, 2023, Election Night party in front of the *Leader-News* office. Kimberly lost her race to become mayor of Uvalde. Pictured at right are Kimberly's husband, Felix, and son Julian. Photograph by Sam Owens, courtesy *San Antonio Express-News*.

CHAPTER 20

"Fire the Cowards"

Pete Arredondo knew that criticism was coming. He had given voice to that fear in the Robb hallway when he said "people are going to wonder why we're taking so long." Still, nothing could have prepared the school district police chief for the storm of recrimination that swept over him and his hometown with the weight of a thousand broken hearts.

Almost at once, Arredondo began to receive death threats, and, in an irony not lost on many, Department of Public Safety troopers were assigned to guard his home on Larkspur Drive in the small subdivision just south of the city. A neighbor said that Arredondo had recently built a boat barn behind his house and was able to slip into it by turning down the alley. She observed that at least two patrol cars were parked in front of the chief's house around the clock and that the media had become a constant presence and a frequent nuisance. Camera crews set up in the street and prowled the neighborhood in search of comments. The neighbor recalled a San Antonio television crew knocking on her family's door and loitering in the front yard after being turned away. Her husband turned on the sprinkler system.

On May 7, Arredondo had won election to a District 3 City Council seat in a landslide (he received 69 percent of the 182 votes cast), but because of growing unrest, a public swearing-in ceremony set for May 31 was canceled. When families began to demand that the city block the officer from taking office, McLaughlin responded that officials lacked the power to prevent it.

"As mayor, I have no authority to tell anybody they can't take their seat. There's nothing in our charter, there's nothing in the election laws, and there's nothing in the state that says he can't," McLaughlin said. "That will be Pete's call. The voters in his district elected him."

108

On May 31, out of respect for victims' families who had begun burying their children that day and in the hope of avoiding a spectacle, a private swearing-in ceremony was conducted for Arredondo in the afternoon. Newly elected council members Everardo "Lalo" Zamora and Ernest "Chip" King were administered the oath of office during a regular meeting.

A week later, on June 9, the city called an emergency meeting to renew an ongoing local disaster declaration. The noon gathering at city hall, which was held with little advance notice, turned into a press conference crowded with national media bent on quizzing the beleaguered school chief. Arredondo chose not to show up, which only served to fan the flames. When pressed by reporters as to why Arredondo skipped the meeting, McLaughlin replied that he had not spoken with the chief in a week and a half and would not presume to speak for him now.

"We want to be very clear, our priorities are for the families who lost children and for the children who survived. There was another funeral this morning. It was sad. . . . We want to give families the time that they need to grieve. And, I'm sorry, but it's getting very frustrating for us, at every funeral there's a reporter trying to stick a camera in the family's face," the mayor said.

That same afternoon, in a wide-ranging interview published by the *Texas Tribune*, Arredondo broke a self-imposed silence (he had declined numerous requests to speak with the *Leader-News*). In the interview, he denied that he had been the incident commander. He insisted that he had not issued any orders and that he and fellow officers had desperately wanted to confront the shooter but were stymied by a locked and fortified door.

"Not a single responding officer hesitated, even for a moment, to put themselves at risk to save the children," the chief said. "We responded to the information we had and had to adjust to whatever we faced. Our objective was to save as many lives as we could, and the extraction of the students from the classrooms by all that were involved saved over 500 of our Uvalde students and teachers before we gained access to the shooter and eliminated the threat."

According to the *Tribune*, their reporters spoke to seven different law enforcement experts about the chief's description of the response and all but one, who opined that breaching the locked door would have resulted in police casualties, asserted that there were serious lapses in judgment. Most pointedly, the experts said, by running into the school with no key and no radios and failing to take charge of the scene, the chief appeared to have contributed to a chaotic approach in which officers deployed inappropriate tactics, adopted a defensive posture, failed to coordinate their actions, and wasted precious time as students and teachers remained trapped in two classrooms with a gunman who continued to fire his rifle. Audio evidence from the hallway showed that after police arrived and drew fire at 11:36 a.m., the attacker fired a single shot at 11:44 a.m., and then fired another four rounds at 12:21 p.m., well after he was considered a barricaded suspect.

The *Tribune* article did nothing to lift the ignominy in which Arredondo found himself in his hometown. Demands for his dismissal from the city council and the school police force grew to near-vigilante proportions and when the *New York Times*, also on June 9, published a story based on leaked body camera and hallway video showing that officers knew early on that students were alive in the two classrooms, the chief attained pariah status.

Meanwhile, continued leaks from the press and the wall erected by the school district further antagonized the families of victims. The school district's communications director, Anne Marie Espinoza, added to the acrimony at a press conference on a very busy June 9 when she said, "Our district continues to collaborate in the ongoing investigation. Therefore, information on the investigation will not be included in today's press conference. I would like to share with you that the district cannot comment on personnel matters. I ask you to be mindful, this is our home, our district and our community. We are grieving."

Families wondered if that meant that the district had cornered the market on grief. If the message was aimed at the media, it should have been spelled out instead of couched in ambiguous language that would become standard fare. Tragically, the district had adopted a policy of no comment at a time when hundreds of school patrons—especially those directly impacted by the shooting—deserved to hear from the people elected to represent them and their children.

A painful example was a request to know who authorized an almost incomprehensible text message delivered to parents at 11:40 a.m. on May 24 that stated: "Robb Elementary is under Lockdown Status due to gunshots in the area. The students are safe in the building."

District officials declined to comment. District Superintendent Hal Harrell also refused to answer questions about whether he trusted the school police chief to handle responses. "That falls in line with personnel, and I am not going to comment on it," he said.

The only solid news gleaned from the meeting was that students would not be returning to Robb but would attend Guillermo Flores Elementary and that Department of Public Safety officers would be called on to patrol campuses until more school police officers could be hired.

Once again, families felt betrayed. How could the district employ Department of Public Safety officers who had stood idly by while children remained trapped in two classrooms with a murderer? In response, Harrell pledged that the schools would not employ any officer—from Department of Public Safety or any other agency—who had responded to the mass shooting. In the months to come, that commitment would prove to be the undoing of the district's top administrators, including the superintendent.

In the meantime, cries of "fire the cowards" punctuated virtually every meeting of the school, the city, and eventually the county. Angry families demanded that elected officials take action to clean house of any officer who had been present in the Robb hallway, a number that at any given time included at least nineteen officers from multiple agencies.

Some people mistakenly believed that the city could fire Arredondo from his school position. That misconception, which was fueled by the fact that school officials refused to comment on their patrons' demands, was eventually cleared up, but it did nothing to quell the calls for Arredondo to be removed from his council seat or for the firing of Lt. Mariano Pargas, who as acting chief of UPD on May 24 had commanded the city's twenty-eight-officer force.

In the weeks that followed, Pargas, who also served as the Uvalde County commissioner for Precinct 2, would become a lightning rod for criticism during meetings of the commissioners court. The same was true for Uvalde County sheriff Ruben Nolasco, who had escaped the fiercest scrutiny in the beginning but was soon singled out to turn in his badge with the others.

For weeks, city council members endured harsh criticism for the police response, and patrol units were eventually deployed to protect the mayor's residence. McLaughlin and city council members continued to listen—allowing speakers to deliver their messages—and continued to insist that they had little information to share.

McLaughlin told me that the day after the shooting he and County Judge Bill Mitchell visited the Department of Public Safety and the Texas Rangers in their command trailers in front of Robb to request a sharing of information. State police had assured the Uvalde officials that the information they were seeking would be shared.

"To this day, I have not even gotten a 'Hello, mayor, how are you doing,'" McLaughlin said nearly ten months later.

A school board meeting on June 20—the second since the tragedy—ushered in a new level of outrage. The agenda included one personnel matter, and it did not pertain to Arredondo. That reality gutted families who had watched the failed police response in real time and were acutely aware of whom state police had singled out for blame.

"Mr. Pete Arredondo is also my friend. It is true, we all got along with him," said Jesse Rizo, the partner of Jackie Cazares's aunt, at the board meeting. "At one point or another, we're going to have to decide if we hold him accountable. I pray that you make the right decision, not for me—for these people that come here bearing the pain, carrying the weight."

Rizo went on to praise Superintendent Harrell but also suggested that his resignation might become necessary. "You're the top person in this program. Everything unfortunately falls on you, sir," he said directly to Harrell.

The eight people who signed up to speak were allotted a maximum of three minutes apiece. However, the board had lifted the fifteen-minute maximum for the audience participation section of the meeting.

Javier Cazares said "I think our babies' lives are worth more than three minutes. Think about that next time." Cazares, who read the district's Preventative Security Measures document, which was posted online, questioned whether any of the protocols were enough or had even been followed.

"I could have a gun right now. Did anyone check? No," he said. "So where is the safety there? It's ridiculous."

Brett Cross, guardian of ten-year-old Uziyah Garcia who was killed at Robb, told trustees that allowing Arredondo to remain on duty was failing the community. "Having Pete still employed, knowing he is incapable of decision making that saves lives, is terrifying," Cross said. "I implore you, all of you, to do what is right, remove Pete from your employment, show us that you are Uvalde Strong."

The sixteen-year-old daughter of Irma Garcia also called for action. "I need you to know that the horrifying manner in which my mother was murdered and taken from us completely shattered our hearts but made my dad's stop," Lyliana Garcia told trustees. She went on to share an agonized cry from her sister. "She said 'My mom died protecting her students, but who was protecting my mom?' This will always haunt me and should haunt all of you."

In a press release issued after 5 p.m. on June 22, the school district announced that Arredondo had been placed on administrative leave from his $90,750-per-year position. Officials declined to say whether the chief was being paid while away and said that there would be no further comment. Harrell said that Lt. Mike Hernandez of the school police would assume the duties of chief.

June 21 proved to be a pivotal day in the aftermath of the tragedy. Speaking before a state senate committee in Austin, Department of Public Safety director Steve McCraw labeled the response to the Robb shooting an "abject failure," adding that police could have stopped the attacker within three minutes of arriving if on-scene commander Pete Arredondo had not decided to "place the lives of officers before the lives of children."

The director described Arredondo's conduct as being antithetical to decades of active-shooter training since the 1999 Columbine High School massacre. That protocol called for officers to confront the shooter as quickly as possible.

The timeline McCraw presented—which was supported by video from the Robb fourth grade hallway and body cameras and by transcripts of police communications— showed that within three minutes of the attacker entering the school's west door at 11:33 a.m., a sufficient number of armed officers wearing body armor had assembled to "isolate, distract and neutralize the subject."

McCraw's most damning testimony concerned the finding that the classroom doors were not locked. Arredondo claimed that officers had tried both doors, but video recorded no such evidence. In addition, the doors can only be locked from the outside using a key, and video footage showed the shooter emerging into the hallway on at least two occasions. There was also the fact that the lock on Room 111 was known to be malfunctioning, a problem that teacher Arnulfo Reyes said he had reported to school maintenance.

"And . . . the on-scene commander waited for a rifle, then he waited for a shield, then he waited for SWAT, and finally he waited for a key that was never needed," McCraw said. "Officers had weapons, the children had none; officers had body armor, the children had none; officers had training, the subject had none. One hour, 14 minutes and 8 seconds. That's how long the children waited and the teachers waited in Room 111 to be rescued."

Back in Uvalde, the mayor seethed in response to McCraw's latest narrative and to the fact that the evidence the director used to make his points was inaccessible to city officials. The city still had possession of its officers' body camera data and a record of 911 calls, but almost everything else had been scooped up by the Texas Rangers and the FBI. And District Attorney Mitchell had ordered that that evidence be sealed. In fact, early on, the fifty-six-year-old prosecutor had threatened legal action against any entity that released evidence before she completed her criminal investigation.

That threat combined with anger over McCraw's ever-changing narrative and his assertions that the city was not cooperating with the investigation compelled Uvalde officials to request a meeting. Eight days after the shooting, McLaughlin, City Attorney Paul Tarski, County Attorney John Dodson, and County Judge Bill Mitchell sat at a table in city council chambers with Capt. Victor Escalon of the State Police, Gov. Abbott's chief of staff Luis Saenz, District Attorney Mitchell, Col. McCraw, and half a dozen other Department of Public Safety troopers.

"We told them that if they were going to say we were not cooperating, we were going to release what we knew about what happened," the mayor said. "We didn't ask them to change a narrative or to support a narrative. We were tired of the bullshit stories changing every day . . . and we didn't say this is our narrative."

McLaughlin recalled the district attorney "raised her head" and told him that the city was going to do what she told them to do, and he responded "Let me tell you what. I'm not going to do anything you tell me. You didn't elect me. The citizens of Uvalde did. You're not going to tell me shit what to do with the city. Now your side of the ball game, you got all the play, but you're not gonna tell us."

The mayor added that at that point, Tarski said to the district attorney in a raised voice "Hush!" and told her to leave because she was not invited. "So needless to say, he and I better not have to appear before her."

In yet another contentious city council meeting held the evening of June 21 in the civic center, former council member and practicing attorney Rogelio M. Munoz, the son of Rogelio F. Munoz, appeared out of concern that the city was attempting to block open records requests from media organizations seeking facts about the shooting.

Munoz cautioned officials not to adopt an "us versus them mentality" but to realize that their constituents had elected them to be a voice of city government. "The children that died were your constituents. You represent them. And they and their families deserve answers. You as a body should be angry and speak . . . and should demand within the city administration that they provide more answers."

The 1998 graduate of Uvalde High School whose late lawyer father had long fought for the civil rights of the Hispanic community said that facts had been hidden behind a law enforcement investigation. "And today in Austin, the head of the DPS said everything. So why is it that state senators in Austin can be given the full accounting of what happened but people . . . or the family members can't be told what happened?"

McLaughlin answered that he "had raised hell with the governor, the district attorney, the DPS" and that he was equally frustrated. "I'm just like you, I'm fed up."

Munoz underscored his point, saying that "the community needs you to be advocates. These families need you to be advocates. . . . You weren't elected to protect an institution or department. You were elected to serve your constituents in the people."

The mayor insisted that McCraw had an agenda, which was to withhold a full report on what had happened, including the fact that the Department of Public Safety had the officers and the expertise to take command at Robb. "So as I told you earlier . . . the gloves are off. We, as we know it, will share. We are not going to hold back anymore," McLaughlin said.

CHAPTER 21

Advocating for Angels

T hree days before the June 11 funeral service for their daughter, Kimberly and Felix signed up for a new life: fighting for gun laws that might have saved Lexi, her classmates, and her teachers. There would be no time to rehearse the part. On June 1, US representative Joaquin Castro contacted the newspaper to request that we relay an invitation to Kimberly to testify before the US House Committee on Oversight and Reform. The decision to participate was easy. The couple had already decided that they would speak for Lexi at every opportunity.

The Rubios did not undertake the arduous trip to Washington but rather participated via Zoom. With Felix at her side, Kimberly told members of Congress about dropping Lexi and her brother Julian at Robb at 7 a.m. and then returning for separate awards ceremonies. After Lexi's event ended around 11 a.m., they had promised her ice cream at the end of the school day.

"I can still see her, walking with us toward the exit. In the reel that keeps scrolling across my memories, she turns her head and smiles back at us to acknowledge my promise. And then we left. I left my daughter at that school, and that decision will haunt me for the rest of my life," Kimberly testified, barely containing her emotions.

She went on to insist that her fourth child was not just a number, describing Lexi as intelligent, compassionate, and athletic. "She was quiet. Shy, unless she had a point to make. When she knew she was right, as she so often was, she stood her ground. She was firm, direct, voice unwavering."

Kimberly told the committee that she and her husband stood for Lexi and as her voice, demanded action, including a ban on assault rifles and high-capacity magazines. "We understand that for some reason, to some people, to people with money, to people who fund political campaigns, that guns are more important than children, so at this moment we ask for progress. We seek to raise the age to purchase these weapons from 18 to 21 years of age. We seek red flag laws, stronger background checks. We also want to repeal gun manufacturers' liability immunity."

The grieving mother shared an image of who Lexi would have become—a little girl who wanted to attend St. Mary's University in San Antonio on a softball scholarship to major in math and go on to attend law school.

"I'm a reporter, a student, a mom, a runner. I've read to my children since they were in the womb. My husband is a law enforcement officer, an Iraq War veteran. He loves fishing and our babies. Somewhere out there, a mom is hearing our testimony and thinking to herself, 'I can't even imagine their pain,' not knowing that our reality will one day be hers, unless we act now."

Miah Cerillo, who had survived the slaughter in Room 112, and her father, Miguel, along with the girl's pediatrician, Dr. Roy Guerrero, also testified to the House committee. Miah spoke via a prerecorded message in which she answered questions Guerrero posed. The doctor and Miguel Cerillo both traveled to Washington to appear in person.

The eleven-year-old described her teacher Irma Garcia going to lock the classroom door and making eye contact with the attacker. "She went back in the room and she told us, 'Go hide,' and then we went to go hide behind my teacher's desk and behind the backpacks, and then he shot through the window [of the door]."

Miah said the gunman entered from the interconnected classroom, said "good night," and shot Garcia in the head. "He shot some of my classmates and the whiteboard," she said.

The child recounted how she smeared her friend's blood all over herself, "stayed quiet," and retrieved her dead teacher's phone to call 911. When asked if she felt safe at school after the massacre, Miah shook her head. "I don't want it to happen again," she said.

Guerrero, a 1996 graduate of Uvalde High School, told lawmakers about racing to the hospital where he found Miah covered in blood and with a shoulder that was bleeding from a shrapnel injury. He also saw two of the children who had been killed. Their "bodies had been so pulverized by the bullets fired at them, decapitated, whose flesh had been so ripped apart that the only clue as to their identities were the bloodspattered cartoon clothes still clinging to them."

"I chose to be a pediatrician. I chose to take care of children. Keeping them safe from preventable diseases, I can do. Keeping them safe from bacteria and brittle bones, I can do," Guerrero said. "But making sure our children are safe from guns, that's the job of our politicians and leaders. In this case, you are the doctors and our country is the patient. We are lying on the operating table, riddled with bullets like the children of Robb Elementary and so many other schools. We are bleeding out and you are not there. You are sitting in your office filling out the paperwork so you can get paid."

A message to the community from actor and Uvalde native Matthew McConaughey on June 9 appeared on the front page of the *Leader-News*. He described the five days he and his wife, Camila, had spent in Uvalde getting to know the families of victims. "You brought us into your homes and hearts where you shared tears, hugs, hopes and dreams. . . . Now Camila and I are headed to Washington to give voice to your stories, to make sure you are remembered, and to share your desires and inspirations for change that[,] as many of you told us, 'can make your losses matter.'"

The actor was as good as his word. In fact, by the time his story was being read in our newspaper on Thursday, McConaughey had already delivered an impassioned plea in a White House press briefing that followed a visit with President Joe Biden two days earlier.

"We start by making the loss of these lives matter," he told reporters. "We start with laws that save innocent lives and don't infringe on our Second Amendment rights."

He insisted that the regulations he and the families sought were not a step back. "They're a step forward—for a civil society, and, and the Second Amendment."

The star shared mementos of the lost children their families had given him—a self-portrait Alithia Ramirez had drawn and the green Converse sneakers Maite Rodriguez had worn. McConaughey noted that Maite had wanted to be a marine biologist when she grew up. She had drawn a heart on the toe of her shoes. It was meant to signify her love of nature. McConaughey went on to say that those shoes "turned out to be the only evidence that could identify her after the shooting. How about that," he said, slamming his fist on the podium.

McConaughey told reporters that Uvalde was his birthplace—where he used his first Daisy BB gun, his first .410 shotgun—and where he learned responsible gun ownership. The actor insisted that the country could pass laws that made it harder for malicious actors to get their hands on weapons and at the same time respect and uphold the Second Amendment. "Responsible gun owners are fed up with the Second Amendment being abused and hijacked by some deranged individuals," McConaughey said.

He called for investment in mental health care, safer schools, and federal legislation to address red flag laws, background checks, waiting periods, and raising the minimum age for owning an assault-style rifle from eighteen to twenty-one. "These regulations are not a step back. They're a step forward for civil society and the Second Amendment."

"There is not a Democrat or Republican value in one single act of these shooters," McConaughey said. "But people in power have failed to act. So we're asking you and I'm asking you . . . can both sides rise above? Can both sides see beyond the political problem at hand and admit that we have a life preservation problem on our hands? We got a chance right now to reach for and to grasp a higher ground above our political affiliations."

———————

After two deadly mass shootings in May 2022—massacres at the Tops supermarket in Buffalo, New York, and the school shooting in Uvalde—the Democratic-majority House (on a near-party-line vote) passed a package of gun safety bills, including a safe storage bill and bills to increase the minimum age to buy semiautomatic rifles to twenty-one, ban large-capacity magazines, and establish universal background checks. Sadly, the bills were not taken up by the more divided Senate, which was evenly split between the parties.

On May 24, 2022, Sen. Krysten Sinema met with Senate Minority Leader Mitch McConnell and Senate Minority Whip John Thune for advice about which Republican senators might be willing to negotiate a gun safety bill. They directed her to Senators John Cornyn and Thom Tillis. Thirty minutes later, Sen. Chris Murphy texted Sinema to join the negotiations with himself, Cornyn and Tillis the next day. Murphy had been one of the Senate's most prominent gun control advocates since the Sandy Hook shooting in his state in 2012.

The fact that Democrats appeared to be willing to avoid more controversial gun issues and to include some Republican-backed measures such as school safety and mental health appealed to McConnell. He and Senate Majority Leader Chuck Schumer signaled support and both senate leaders pursued a hands-off strategy of trusting senators to reach a deal that would be agreeable to their respective parties.

It was far from a straight line and there were many threatened ruptures, but on June 12, a group of ten Democrats and ten Republicans came to an agreement on a framework outlining the provisions of the bill. On June 21, almost one month to the day after the horror at Robb, Congress passed the Bipartisan Safer Communities Act.

Although the new law was a long way from what most advocates of responsible gun ownership had sought, especially the families of victims in Uvalde, the measure was "something"—the first comprehensive gun legislation in the last thirty years.

"I appreciated the progress. And I felt it needed to be done after Uvalde, but it just wasn't enough. Never would be enough," Kimberly said months later. "You know, even here at the state level, I do my best, but my focus will always be federal level, because I know it's Texas. I can't leave it alone."

———————

On a blistering July 10, with temperatures pushing into triple digits by early afternoon, approximately 500 people, including most of our newspaper staff, gathered in front of the now-deserted Robb Elementary for an Unheard Voices March and Rally. Victims' families, members of the community, and local and national advocacy groups had organized the event as a show of solidarity and mounting outrage at the lack of transparency regarding the police and school district response to the tragedy.

Before the rally began, teenage sisters Sofia and Aracely Torres helped host a sign-painting party at El Jardin de los Heroes Park on the city's West Side. Using donated materials, the young women guided the creation of dozens of hand-lettered messages with themes like "What if it was your kid?" "Protect our kids, not coward cops," "Fear has no place in schools," and "No more silence, end gun violence." Most dominant, of course, were the enlarged images of those who had perished.

Protesters included families and friends who had lost loved ones as well as community members intent on showing their support. Members of the Brown Berets, a decades-old Chicano social justice group, handed out bottled water. They also prompted loud call-and-response chants—"No justice, no peace" and "Gun reform, now"—throughout the course of the one-mile walk to the downtown plaza. A few marchers dropped out after becoming dizzy from the heat. Others carried umbrellas or wore broad-brimmed hats and water-soaked bandanas.

Upon reaching the shade of the plaza's towering pecans, participants funneled to the north side of the square, where a podium and a PA system had been erected. Kimberly was among the family members who addressed the crowd.

"What I want, no one can give me. I want my daughter back," she told the audience through tears. "If I can't have her, then those who failed her will never know peace. We want answers. We seek justice, and we demand change. We will never rest. Remember their names."

Abbot's refusal to consider gun reform and the fact that the Texas Legislature had passed laws that had made guns more readily available even after mass shootings drew the ire of many of the speakers.

"A war weapon is more important to our current governor than the lives of his people," twenty-one-year-old Faith Mata, the sister of slain student Tess Marie Mata, told demonstrators, who responded with an often-repeated chant: "Vote him out!"

Other family members who stood in the front of the mic included Felicha Marti-nez, the mother of Xavier Lopez; Jazmin Cazares, the sister of Jackie; Angel Garza, the stepfather of Amerie Jo, and his mother, Berlinda Arreola; and Alysandra Garcia, the daughter of Irma Garcia.

Alysandra said that her life and the lives of her three siblings had been turned upside down since the death of Irma in her classroom and her father, Joe, of a heart attack two days later.

Arreola, as had many of the marchers through chants and signs, focused her wrath on law enforcement. "I challenge all of you cowards who were in that class . . . in that hallway to step down. Turn in your badge and resign. You do not deserve to wear a badge. You did not protect and serve."

Caitlyne Gonzales, a ten-year-old who had survived the massacre, also walked the mile to the plaza and spoke in memory of her best friend, Jackie Cazares, and others. On "that day," as Caitlyne referred to May 24, she had huddled behind her teacher Mer-cedes Salas's desk in Room 106 with fifteen of her classmates. The class was directly across the hall from the horror in Rooms 111 and 112 and at least one bullet had torn through the wall of her classroom, leaving behind the smell of gunpowder. Caitlyne said that when the gunfire first erupted, she heard a scream that she immediately recog-nized as Jackie's.

"A school is a place where a teacher and child should feel safe, but it isn't," Caitlyne told the crowd, her voice often quavering. "I should feel safe. My friends should feel safe, but we don't. . . . I can't imagine the pain my friends and teachers felt in their last moments. Jackie and the rest of the classmates and teachers died because law enforce-ment did not protect us like they should have. I am so mad. So many lives could have been saved. I'm here today to be their voice, since we can longer hear their voice."

Democratic candidate for governor Beto O'Rourke waited patiently toward the back of the makeshift stage for his turn to speak. During the wait, people approached him for photographs and shared prayers. Kimberly had also engaged in conversation with O'Rourke, and when Pete Luna noticed a reporter sticking a camera in her face, he moved to defend her.

Kimberly waved Pete off, showing him that she was wearing a microphone and that Andy Fredericks with ABC News had permission to film her. In fact, ABC had recently announced a yearlong project called "Uvalde365" to chronicle the communi-ty's response to and recovery from the tragedy.

During a brief four-minute speech, O'Rourke, perhaps somewhat chastened after his ambush of Abbott at the press conference in May struck a philosophical tone. He recalled the mass shooting that had crushed his hometown of El Paso only days before the start of school in August 2019. But he said that in darkness, "there comes a strength, there comes a community . . . and there comes something that is more powerful than we knew that we had in us before these tragedies, and you heard that today."

He also remembered the power of Kimberly's June 8 testimony before the US House Committee on Oversight and Reform and reiterated her message that unless we effect change, the grief that she and other families of Robb victims have experienced "will be the future for far too many of us."

Afterward, I thanked the candidate for his remarks and for advocating for the slain children and teachers. He replied that Kimberly had the opportunity to make a difference, that "her message was important."

Two months later, the Rubio, Cross, Cazares, and Garza (represented by Amerie Jo's step-grandmother Berlinda Arreola) families began to talk about forming an advocacy group. They had appeared together for dozens of meetings with elected officials, rallies, and marches in Uvalde, Austin, and Washington, so it made sense to become more organized. The result of their collaboration was an organization called Lives Robbed. Brett Cross assumed the president's post and Kimberly was happy to serve as vice president, largely because she didn't think it would be too demanding.

Later, when the Crosses dropped out, Kimberly found herself as head of the group. "I didn't see that one coming," she laughed. But she felt strongly that the organization clearly helped focus their activism, making it far more impactful.

When the Mata family joined the group in October, Lives Robbed became more than advocacy. It was now four women—Kimberly, Gloria Cazares, Berlinda, and Veronica Mata—who drew strength from each other. "I love it now, it's just all women. I feel like Lexi would love that," Kimberly said.

When I asked about an interview that Kimberly, Gloria, Veronica and Ana Rodriguez (the mother of Maite) had done for ABC's *Nightline*, Kimberly sighed. "We thought it was awful. We were not at all prepared." But that's not the way it came across. The women agreed that their friendship had helped them through some of their darkest moments.

"There are a lot of times that we feel alone. You know, even if there are 100 people in the room you still feel alone. But I don't feel that way when I'm with them," Cazares said in the interview.

Veronica, who lost Tess, said it was difficult for her to go for extended periods without talking with the group. "I think because I feel that connection with them because of the girls, and I feel like if I don't talk to them, I'm missing a part of Tess."

Growing up, Kimberly had been especially close to her mother. They had slept in the same bed when her father Ruben was away for work. She laughed as she remembered Ruben coming home to find his place in the bed occupied by Kimberly. After May 24, it became more difficult to be around family because "they want to fix things that can't be fixed," Kimberly said. Being with the women of Lives Robbed allowed her to share feelings that other friends and family, with the exception of her husband and children, might not understand.

Rodriguez described a similar feeling with the close-knit group of women who had lost children—and more specifically daughters. "There's some sort of connection. It's not comfort or anything like that. It was that I wasn't alone. I wasn't feeling these feelings alone. I knew that Kimberly . . . that Gloria and Veronica . . . felt the exact same way," Ana said.

If any of the women "had a moment . . . if I see one of them break down, I know exactly what she's feeling, because I go through the same thing." Ana said that in those moments, none of them try to fix the other. Rather, "we just kind of sit there and in a sense absorb what she's feeling."

In the months that followed, Lives Robbed would undertake scores of trips, most of them to Austin or Washington. But now there was more flexibility. If any woman could not participate, she rested easy in the fact that the others would speak for all of them.

CHAPTER 22

A Monumental Project

Fifty-seven-year-old Abel Ortiz could not remember a time when art had not brought him peace. As a boy growing up in the small Mexican town of Zaragoza, he sketched images of Snoopy and Mexican wrestlers. A Hindu superhero named Kaliman who possessed mental powers also became a favorite subject. It was that artwork that saved Ortiz when his family emigrated to West Texas in 1973 and the seven-year-old found himself in a classroom in the tiny town of Ozona with no English skills and no friends.

The first day in Mrs. Wilson's class was a disaster. The boy screamed and cried and tried to scale a wall to escape. The tall red-headed teacher with "kind blue eyes, wearing an orange paisley dress and a ten-gallon hairdo" directed her students to coax the new kid back. He calmed down when classmates offered to teach him how to swing. Back in the classroom, Mrs. Wilson kept a firm grip on Ortiz's wrist until she sat him down next to her desk and provided pencils and crayons.

In the weeks and months that followed, the boy came to class and worked on his drawings. Another Hispanic student spoke broken Spanish, but his halting translation was not enough to enable the young Ortiz to participate in basic subjects. "I came in every day and just drew. And I felt like, you know, it was therapeutic. And calming me down for the rest of the year. Yes, I failed the first grade. But at least I felt a sense of belonging."

Five decades, two master's degrees, and a marriage later, Ortiz found himself deeply wounded by the horror at Robb. He was friends with Steve Garcia and his wife Jennifer Lugo, who lost their daughter Ellie, and as the longtime art instructor at Southwest Texas Junior College, he had taught Kimberly. Many other members of families who had lost someone in the May 24 shooting had participated in his wife Evelyn's Zumba classes.

Ortiz searched for the appropriate response. He wondered if he should host a barbe-cue or a car wash. And then it hit him: "No; it's art. Art is my power. I know that art heals, and I know this community is going to be in pain forever now. Especially the families."

The genesis was a single painful sentence Felix had uttered the day after the shoot-ing. "He was hugging Kimberly during an interview, and he said 'These deaths should not be in vain,'" Ortiz told me a year after the tragedy.

He recalled telling his wife that he was going to do a mural project to "make sure that Felix's words resonated." Initially, it was to be one painting on the side of his Art Lab building located on North Getty Street. That plan quickly expanded into the twenty-one murals that the artist now envisioned across the city. Only on that vast scale could he address the "pain that was monumental."

The first steps involved reaching out to building owners to secure space. In the first week, rejection dogged Ortiz. Four owners had turned him down outright, a response he attributed in part to his shortcomings in selling the vision. One of the buildings was particularly coveted because it had what he called "the perfect wall."

Ortiz felt he needed to give the community and the people who controlled the walls a sample of his vision: 20-foot-by-35-foot renderings of each child, two teachers, and a husband. He offered to paint Ellie Garcia on his building, but Jennifer preferred a different wall because the view of the Art Lab's alley was restricted. She decided to reach out personally to the owners of the "perfect wall." The building housed Security Finance, and Jennifer knew the manager.

Once again the owner, who lived in Wisconsin, said no, but by the next day they had experienced a change of heart. The green light resulted in Ellie's mural and eventu-ally two others, for Nevaeh Bravo and Rojelio Torres, going up on the Security Finance building. Nevaeh's mural ended up being moved twice because of wall texture issues, and Rojelio's family did not care for the first mural painted for their son. Ortiz sided with the family, because the original artist's efforts had produced an expressionist-like image that was not readily recognizable as Rojelio.

Ortiz soon secured fourteen walls to serve as canvases, which was seven short. But he had a plan. The sister of his good friend John Aviles was Sister Dolores Aviles, who oper-ated the St. Henry De Osso Family Project. The nonprofit's home was a long, cement-walled building hardly a block from downtown. John Aviles felt certain his sister would embrace the mural project—some of the victims had been in her program—but she was ensconced in a retreat with her Teresian Sisters and could not be reached for a week.

When Ortiz finally made contact, Sister Dolores "jumped on it right away, 100 percent . . . she gave me all the walls and in that sort of saved the project." Today

Sister Dolores's building is home to nine towering images of vivacious children and one loving teacher.

With most of the wall inventory secured, the artist turned his attention to the actual mechanics of creating the bespoke renderings. In his fervor to complete the vision, Ortiz imagined doing the work himself. It was an impossibility, and he smiled as he described the dilemma.

"At first I was really ambitious. I can do twenty-one—in eight years probably," he laughed. "Well, at least I can do one and if I had to, I could do two if we didn't have enough artists, because I didn't know how many people were going to respond."

Ortiz got his answer straightaway. His wife, Evelyn, posted video on social media of the artist listing the wall possibilities and people began to respond. One of the texts came from Dr. George Meza, a psychologist and collector of art in Los Angeles who managed a Facebook page, Collectors of Chicano/Latino Art and Allies. Ortiz belonged to the group, and Meza was checking in to make sure the Uvaldeans' two children were okay and to ask how to provide assistance. Once Ortiz explained the plan—not one mural but twenty-one—Meza's response was "Brilliant, what can we do to help?"

The Chicano artist group tackled the need for money by organizing an online art auction that attracted national attention. Within days, the group had collected $42,000 in sales from artwork that had been donated by concerned people across the nation. The stars continued to align for the murals when Monica Maldonado with the non-profit MAS Cultura in Austin visited Uvalde. She was already assisting Uvalde native Kimi Flores, who had painted murals depicting a dove and a coyote.

The following Monday, six days after the tragedy, Ortiz met Maldonado at his gallery and they walked together to inspect the walls that had been secured, potential other sites, and the spaces that had remained elusive. Maldonado was already fundraising for Flores's work and offered to use their GoFundMe account for the new murals. In short order, the effort raised $12,000. Maldonado, who knew artists and muralists across the state, was designated as project manager.

Muralists are the rock climbers of the art world. Their work is far more physical than standing in front of a canvas. The tasks of raising and lowering ladders, lifting heavy cans of paint, and constantly moving back and forth to maintain the proper perspective require strength and stamina. And then there is the brutal Southwest Texas sun that beats down on artists at the height of summer.

Even so, within two weeks of the shooting there were so many muralists ready to work—some with long résumés—and canvas artists who wanted to learn and give back that Ortiz found himself assigning assistants to muralists who had already been chosen.

"This is why we had a waiting list. So that fear that maybe I'll have to do twenty-one murals because I don't get enough artists just completely dissolved right there."

Another obstacle that Ortiz had feared—opposition from the City of Uvalde's Historic Preservation Board—failed to materialize. He had approached Diane Treviño about using her wall in the alley of 115 West Main. It so happened that Treviño sat on the board, and once she gave her permission, there appeared to be no resistance. The artist said that clearing that hurdle had been "the biggest relief of stress for me" in the entire process of retaining walls.

Obtaining lifts to reach the thirty-five-foot-tall murals presented another problem. Much of the equipment from local firms like Baker Rentals and Reno's Rentals had been drawn away by Operation Lone Star. Law enforcement used the lifts to place sentries in observation towers along the southern border. According to Ortiz, when lifts did become available locally it was so expensive to rent them that it would have exhausted their funds. Once again a timely solution arrived when Moses Valdez, who owns United Rentals in Carrizo Springs, offered to donate lifts at no charge, including transporting them to and from Uvalde.

Ortiz said the assistance, especially coming from out of town, "restored his faith in humanity." He posted on social media that "Moses can part the sea" and thanked United Rentals, because they "were a godsend."

The last piece of business, following the burial of Layla Salazar at Hillcrest Cemetery on June 16 (the final victim to be laid to rest was Uziyah Garcia on June 25 in San Angelo), was to present families with a consent and background form. Ortiz was prepared to proceed if only twelve to fourteen said yes to the project. When all twenty-one agreed, he "was very, very happy." He was in Spain on a planned vacation, keeping up on the progress in Uvalde through Monica Maldonado. By the time Ortiz returned, the first three murals had been completed.

For the artists to be effective, they had to forge a relationship with the family members. That was evident to Ortiz as he began work on the mural for Ellie. He had known the Garcias for years—since Jennifer had participated in one of his wife's quinceañera choreography sessions as a fourteen-year-old—but as he painted, the relationship grew more special. Jennifer added things to the painting like flowers and Takis tortilla chips and made suggestions that reflected Ellie's personality.

When other parents saw the Takis and other specific treats, they suddenly remembered their own children's fondness for snacks. Ortiz asked artists to return for updates, and of course they were more than willing. In fact, some artists were so anxious to return that they offered to serve as assistants to painters who had murals in progress.

Ruben Esquivel had already painted Jayce Luevanos on the St. Henry De Osso building when he returned to create the mural for Lexi on the north wall of the Kessler Courtyard Properties building next door to the *Leader-News*. I caught up with him and his co-worker Carmen Rangel after the project had been sketched and painting had begun. Virtually all of Lexi's painting was done with spray paint, which is faster but in some ways more difficult.

"It's a lot of pressure," Ruben said. "The first day there were like forty people watching. And of course nothing went right." Rangel said that she had previously worked on projects involving some degree of tragedy but "not on this scale . . . this is more planned out, with family involved and documentation."

They need not have fretted over the outcome, because Kimberly loved Lexi's image. "It's perfect. He nailed it. The nose is amazing. We thought it was going to be her smile, but the little nose is perfect. And I love the five butterflies. Those are her siblings."

Lexi's mural has become a touchstone for Kimberly. It is where she finishes each three-mile run, a practice that has become an integral part of her attempt at healing. Other families of victims have been equally pleased. The murals call to them, and they visit them to drink coffee, take group photos, eat dinner, gather with birthday balloons, or post video to Facebook of themselves driving by, as Steve Garcia recently did.

"It really makes me happy to see that the murals are doing their job," Ortiz said, referring to the mural walk on May 24, 2023, when families joined together to mark the end of the first year with a visit to each painting before attending a candlelight vigil on the city's river walk.

According to Ortiz, that was the original idea: a memorial art walk. With twenty-one murals spread across downtown, people could reflect as they moved from one painting to the next, and they could have an "experience" as they remembered the children. "We might forget anything we write or study in a book, but when we have an experience . . . people don't forget that," Ortiz said.

Of course, there have been plenty of naysayers, people who felt the murals were gaudy or were roadblocks to the city "moving on." Some critics have even suggested painting over the murals. Ortiz found an analogy for that kind of thinking in the reaction of Parisians to the Eiffel Tower after it was introduced during the 1889 World's Fair.

"The Parisians hated it. They signed a petition to bring it down as soon as the World's Fair was over. Can you picture Paris without the Eiffel Tower? It's the same people that hated the impressionists. It's the same period, they made fun of them. And they printed jokes in the newspaper—cartoons and stuff like that."

The truth is no single endeavor has lifted the families of victims and the community like the Healing Uvalde mural project. The loving faces of nineteen children and their two teachers scattered across eight buildings in the heart of Uvalde have become symbols of joy wrapped in tragedy. The paintings continue to attract residents and visitors like no tourism campaign the city could ever have imagined.

Future plans call for lighting and landscaping and the addition of QR codes next to each painting that would allow visitors to access a biography of the victims and even listen to their voices. The possibilities are many, and the effort to protect and promote the unique expressions of life—contributed selflessly by a host of talented artists as gestures of giving back—are befitting of a community treasure.

Ortiz said that he will stand as caretaker for as long as he is able. An exciting first step was to ensure that the murals received two coats of a special sealer donated by MuralColors. The first coat protects the color and the second coat allows for graffiti to be washed off. The treatment is expected to extend the life of the artwork for up to thirty years. That does not guarantee that the images will not degrade earlier, as the texture of the walls beneath the paintings is the paramount factor for longevity. But like the city's iconic Grand Opera House, which was built in 1891 and requires expensive upkeep, the paintings of victims are as permanent as we will allow them to be.

"The murals are there to remind us of the children and celebrate their lives. It's how you respond to the tragedy that's going to define you," Ortiz said.

CHAPTER 23

Failure Becomes Official

The seventy-seven-page Texas House Investigative Committee report landed on families and the community in the form of a fresh tragedy. Gone were any questions about whether law enforcement had responded honorably or if the Uvalde school district had taken adequate measures to ensure the safety of its students and teachers. The report made clear in blunt language that revered institutions had failed in their most fundamental mission—to serve and protect the community.

In a press conference on the afternoon of Sunday, July 17, at the Ssgt. Willie de Leon Civic Center, state representative Dustin Burrows described "multiple system failures," including law enforcement's failure to follow active shooter protocol by eliminating the threat immediately and the school district's complacent approach to security.

"At Robb Elementary law enforcement responders failed to adhere to their active shooter training, and they failed to prioritize saving the lives of innocent victims over their own safety," the report read. In addition to Burrows, who chaired the committee, other members were state representative Joe Moody (D-El Paso), who served as vice chair, and former state supreme court justice Eva Guzman as a public member.

The report found that the hour-plus delay in breaching the classrooms may have resulted in additional deaths. "It is likely that most of the deceased victims perished immediately during the attacker's initial barrage of gunfire. However, given the information known about victims who survived through the time of the breach and who later died on the way to the hospital, it is plausible that some victims could have survived if they had not had to wait 73 additional minutes for rescue."

Criticism of the school district also cut deep. "Robb Elementary was unprepared for an armed intruder on the campus," the report read. The committee singled out the school's inadequate five-foot perimeter fencing and doors that either malfunctioned or were routinely left unlocked for convenience—which was against school policy but "appeared to be tacitly condoned by school police and administrators."

The committee had conducted its first meeting on June 9 in Austin, an extensive session with McCraw. The group then met on five different days in council chambers at Uvalde City Hall to gather testimony. Members interviewed a total of thirty-five witnesses, including law enforcement, school employees, and the attacker's family, in closed sessions. They also reviewed thirty-nine interviews other investigators had conducted.

The house report concluded that a major error in the response of law enforcement was the "failure of any officers to assume and exercise incident command." The study stated that since Uvalde police officers arrived first in response to a vehicle crash and shots fired, it made sense for one of them to assume the role of incident commander. "However, after chief Arredondo arrived and the attack shifted to school property, he became the logical choice." That was especially true because when Arredondo had crafted the school district's active shooter plan in 2019, he had named the person occupying his position—school district police chief—as incident commander.

Throughout the house investigation, television crews hovered outside city hall, hoping to snag people coming and going from the interviews. Few obliged the camera operators, as most stood little to gain by exposing themselves to public scrutiny.

On Sunday, before the afternoon press conference, the committee had met privately with families to deliver the report and answer questions. The parents had been notified on Tuesday, July 12, that they would receive the results of the investigation, including hallway video, the following Sunday, before it was made public. However, later that same Tuesday, the *Austin American-Statesman* and its television partner KVUE preempted those plans by releasing two versions of the hallway video—a four-minute segment called "critical moments" and the full leaked version of one hour and twenty-two minutes.

Grieving families felt blindsided by the harrowing images of the black-clad teenage shooter strolling casually into the school, followed by explosive gunfire as he triggered more than 100 rounds before police arrived. Days before, media outlets such as the *Texas Tribune* had reviewed the leaked video and had reported the scope of the delay. But it was the actual images of law enforcement's bungling response that smacked families in the face. They responded with smoldering rage at police agencies and at the *Statesman* for releasing the leaked evidence.

Angel Garza, whose stepdaughter Amerie Jo Garza had been killed, was quoted as saying "Who the hell do these people think they are?" The bereft father lashed out at officials, perhaps in an effort to smoke out the leaker. "You want to go ahead and air their final moments to the entire world. What makes you think that's OK? The least you can do is have some freaking decency with us."

Kimberly and Felix, along with other Uvalde families, were attending a rally in Washington sponsored by March Fourth, a group that advocates a federal ban on assault weapons, when the video went viral. Kimberly later told me that families had not wanted the evidence published until they had been able to view it on Sunday.

"We understand that the media—it wants to hold people accountable because the government hasn't been transparent with us," Kimberly told me after her return from Washington.

In a post Kimberly wrote "The world sees a person shooting into an obscured door. I see, hear him murdering my 10-year-old daughter, and her classmates. How much pain is one person expected to endure?"

The video showed Felix, dressed in his sheriff's deputy uniform, looking on as shots exploded at the moment the BORTAC team finally breached the classroom. Clearly emotional, Lexi's dad wiped away tears as a fellow officer restrained him. When medics rushed forward in hopes of triaging victims, Felix turned away in anguish.

"I didn't see my baby walk out or be carried out," Felix said later.

Javier Cazares, who had been among the families meeting in Washington with members of Congress, said during a press briefing on the evening of Tuesday, July 12, that they had not seen the video despite repeated requests. "They weren't supposed to do it without our consent,"

"We've been asking the DA for this video for a while and she refused to let us see it," Nikki Cross said during the same briefing. "So once again, the world got to see it before us."

During a city council meeting at the civic center the same day the video appeared, Mayor McLaughlin referred to the leaked evidence as a "chicken" move. "This was wrong to do it this way. The video needed to be released, but the families should have gotten to see it first."

Council member Chip King put a finer point on the mayor's description, saying that McLaughlin had said "chicken, but it was chicken shit. They did that for ratings, and they did that for money and that's the only reason they put that out there."

Adam Martinez, whose third grade son had been at Robb, shot back, "What about the cops, are they chicken shit?"

King replied that the city planned to take care of that issue.

"You said they did a good job. Do you still think they did a good job?"

McLaughlin replied that he had not yet seen the video. "But I can tell you that one of the officers that you called—that got grazed in the deal—in that video he goes back down that hall three times trying to get in that room."

Martinez suggested that the council poll others present to see what they thought, but McLaughlin insisted that he knew the answer. Still, the investigation of the city police force needed to be carried out.

"He's a chicken shit, he got hit, grazed, by Sheetrock. Y'all are attacking the media, y'all should be attacking the cops who did nothing."

In a final piece of seemingly routine business, the council accepted the resignation of Pete Arredondo from the seat he had won on May 7. At the urging of family members, council members had refused to grant him a leave of absence, and he had now missed the number of meetings (three) that were grounds for dismissal. He tendered his resignation at the beginning of July.

––––––––––

Fueled by the Texas House Investigative Committee report and the hallway video, the meeting of trustees of the Uvalde Consolidated Independent School District on July 19 flared into an angry confrontation between families and the administration. Two trustees chose to skip the meeting. J. J. Suarez, who held an oversight position with the Southwest Texas Junior College Law Enforcement Academy and had responded to the Robb shooting, was reported to be attending a Major League Baseball event. No excuse was provided for trustee Anabel White's absence. When trustees were asked to call Suarez to join the meeting by phone, they responded with the same maddening silence they had maintained since the day of the attack. "I cannot understand what could be more important than to be here tonight to face the fire," Jesse Rizo told trustees seated on the stage.

More than twenty people had signed up to speak during the meeting in the John H. Harrell Auditorium that turned into a three-hour grilling of school personnel. "If things are not done the way they need to be done, we're prepared to walk out, we are prepared to leave our children home, and not start school," Brett Cross told the board.

Mixed with the angry accusations were renewed demands for the immediate termination of Arredondo, whose face—now more than ever—dominated the "most-wanted poster" for police officers. The net of culpability cast over school administration had also widened, ensnaring officials who ranged from Robb principal Mandy Gutierrez to District Superintendent Hal Harrell.

"We held Pete accountable because he was the chief. Y'all held Mariano [Pargas] accountable because he was the [acting] chief of police and now we are holding you accountable and asking you step down," Berlinda Arreola told the school board.

Another speaker, Rachel Martinez, whose four children attended district schools, said, "The failures from your employees caused such heartbreaking loss. . . . Why do you continue to employ these officers?" Martinez said that adding new officers to the existing staff would be a mistake: "The current staff is incompetent and liable for the already massive failures. You need to clean house . . . start from zero."

In an editorial that appeared in the *Leader-News* on July 24, 2022, I called for the same action: "So how do we restore these ailing institutions to something approximating health? The school district took a halting first step on June 22 by placing Arredondo on administrative leave. His termination was the sole agenda item for yesterday's special school board meeting. Assuming the chief is gone, the district should not simply add more officers to a force born of a failed culture. Administration needs to start over or disband the department altogether."

CHAPTER 24

Goodbye, Chief(s)

After three months to the day of being pilloried for his botched handling of the Robb massacre, Pete Arredondo's judgment day was at hand. On August 24, school district trustees convened a special meeting that Arredondo and his attorney, George E. Hyde, had requested. The two men, citing safety concerns, chose at the last minute to ghost their own event, which was probably prudent.

The months of pent-up anger regarding the police response would have exploded at the sight of the man who, because of his own handiwork in drafting the school district's active shooter policy in 2019, was the de facto incident commander. Arredondo could have offered nothing to placate the crowd of about one hundred except "I'm sorry, I should have done more." The threat of lawsuits prevented that admission, even if it had come from the heart.

Instead, 28 minutes before the meeting was scheduled to start in the high school auditorium, Hyde issued a seventeen-page public statement that asserted, among many other things, that the school district had not properly provided his client with complaints about his performance. The document also maintained that Salvador Ramos was the sole responsible party.

Trustees opened the 5:30 p.m. meeting without addressing the lawyer's statement. Instead, the board moved immediately into closed session. It now felt as though we were part of an unedited courtroom drama, waiting for the jury to return with a verdict. The Texas House committee had put on record their damning evidence, as had McCraw. Arredondo had supplied his defense through an interview with the *Texas Tribune*. Now it was in the hands of school trustees. As time ticked by, the crowd grew increasingly impatient, commanding the PA system designed for public comment to implore officials to return and take action.

"School board members, if you can hear me, it's Nikki Cross, Uziyah's mom. We're reaching a little over an hour now. You brought us here on this date, hijacking this date from us. Please stop wasting our time and get out here."

Felicha Martinez, choked with emotion, said she missed her son and best friend Xavier Lopez. "Three months and we have forever to live. I don't know how we are going to be able to do that. My baby was a wild kid. He was happy, he was a dancer . . . he could dance anybody through the night. . . . He left behind a one-year-old niece who talks to his picture every day. Because of them doing us wrong, she will never get to grow to meet the awesome *tío* that he would have been. If the board can hear me, please change everything for our kids. . . . Protect our kids. No more lies."

State senator Roland Gutierrez of San Antonio stood at the microphone to proclaim, "It's not just the cafeteria school cop. It's not just Pete Arredondo. . . . You had the federal government that waited, the state government. There are some DPS troopers here. I like many of them, I think they are fine people. But they failed that day. The sheriff's office failed on that day, the police failed on that day. It's hard for me to say, as a person that has voted for things in their interest. I do back the blue. I get it. But you have to do things the way they should be done. They had a duty and an obligation."

At the suggestion of Nikki Cross, family members followed her to the microphone to memorialize their children, while a phalanx of camera operators representing a dozen media outlets zoomed in on the emotion.

"Uziyah was the sweetest little boy I've ever known. Sweetest, biggest heart. He loved school, he loved friends, he loved basketball. He loved gaming with his bothers and his sisters, and every morning he made sure to tell me had loved me before he went to school," Cross said before recognizing Uziyah's friends. "Jayce [Luevanos] . . . he loved spending the weekends with him, almost every weekend he asked to go spend the night. Xavier Lopez . . . I love you, he loved going to your house. Loved hanging out. The only surviving friend from there is Aiden. Precious little boy, he comes to check on me all the time. I love him. Jackie [Cazares], I figured out in Uzi's phone, was his queen. . . . They were all such amazing kids."

Amerie Jo Garza's grandmother, Dora Mendoza, who was described as the ten-year-old's best friend, said she "was a very happy little girl, wanted to be an artist, teacher. Had good grades. We hurt because we are not there to help her out. We need justice for our kids. Twenty-one lives lost, and Mr. Pete Arredondo is asking for justice. . . . Just think about all the lives lost, please, and we will forever not have Amerie here with us."

When the trustees finally reconvened after one hour and thirty minutes, board secretary Laura Perez made a motion that "good cause exists to terminate the non-certified contract of Pete Arredondo, effective immediately." Her motion received a second, and the board voted unanimously in favor. They rose immediately and walked off the stage as families called for them to return.

It seemed almost anticlimactic. Finally the families rose and began to file out of the building. They carried away an important victory—the first and only since the shooting—along with the oversized pictures of their deceased children, who had observed the proceedings from chairs in the front rows of the auditorium.

Arredondo was not yet finished. He took another bite out of the school district's credibility a little over five months later. On January 31, a letter arrived at the central office announcing that the Texas Commission on Law Enforcement was elevating the former chief's termination status from general to honorable. A State Office of Administrative Hearings law judge had ruled in favor of Arredondo because the Uvalde district had failed to respond to a notice of a formal F-5 appeal to the commission that Arrendondo had filed the month after his termination.

It seemed impossible that the school district could commit such an unpardonable blunder. Even staunch supporters of the district fumbled for an explanation. Possibilities ranged from administrators taking their eye off the ball to an office-wide stroke.

Interim superintendent Gary Patterson, who began working on November 1, provided a simpler answer. The messages from the Texas Commission on Law Enforcement had come at a time when the district was transitioning from the departure of integral staff, including Hall Harrell, interim district police chief Mike Hernandez, and Student Services Director Ken Mueller. Quite simply, the communications regarding Arredondo's appeal had fallen into a digital void.

More specifically, Patterson wrote in an opinion piece that appeared in the *Leader-News* on February 26, 2023, "All correspondence from TCOLE [Texas Commission on Law Enforcement] was sent to the person of contact during that time, the Interim Police Chief. Our database confirms that all the correspondence from TCOLE, other than the January 31st email, was opened but not forwarded to any other email address in the [school district's] Directory."

On February 24 and 27, more than a month after Arredondo had won his upgrade, the school district filed a motion for a rehearing to submit evidence and uphold the original discharge status of "general." By the time of the tragedy's one-year mark, that hearing had not been conducted.

Lt. Mariano Pargas of the Uvalde Police Department was next in line of ranking officers who failed to assume command at Robb to fall victim to national reporting. On November 14, CNN journalist Shimon Prokupecz reported on a call Pargas had placed to dispatch requesting clarification of a radio message he had picked up outside Robb school that said that there were victims in the classroom.

Ten-year-old Khloie Torres, using her slain teacher's phone, had dialed 911 at 12:12 p.m. to tell the operator that there were "victims in the classroom."

"Victims?" the sixty-five-year-old Pargas had repeated when he heard the recorded message. Four minutes later, at 12:16, the veteran police officer had telephoned dispatch directly to ask about the call. "The call you got from . . . from one of the students, what did they say?"

"Okay, Khloie [Torres] going to be in Room 112, Mariano, 112."

Pargas asked how many were still alive, and the dispatcher replied "Eight to nine are still alive. She's not too sure . . . she's not sure how many are actually DOA or possibly injured."

The acting chief had disconnected and walked back into the Robb hallway. He mentioned the victims to a Border Patrol officer, but at 12:18 p.m., Pargas said nothing about the children when a Texas Ranger talked to him about organizing the flow of information. According to a CNN video analysis, Pargas left the building and never attempted to respond to the children's calls for help.

In an interview two days later, Mayor McLaughlin told me "Mariano will be gone by this week, whether he chooses to retire or whether he's fired." The mayor later expressed his ongoing frustration with the piecemeal release of evidence by news agencies in the six months since the attack: "We have not been briefed by anybody since the day this happened. Nobody. And it's frustrating. If we'd had those videos that [Shimon Prokupecz] showed on Pargas, then we would have done something two months ago."

"I think a lot of bad decisions were made. And I think that they lacked leadership that day. I honestly believe in my heart, that if those officers had been told to do something, they would have done it, but they were told to stand down," McLaughlin said.

The mayor said he told Prokupecz that his work "was appreciated" but that it should not be necessary for a "reporter from New York City releasing something, and he can get access to every fucking thing and we can't. I mean that shows incompetence in my opinion . . . in the district attorney, the DPS, and everybody."

Pargas chose to retire from the force on November 17, three days after the story Prokupecz aired broke. However, he continued to serve on the Uvalde County Commissioners Court, a decision for which he was sharply criticized. Families of victims appeared frequently during meetings to call for his resignation and that of Sheriff Ruben Nolasco.

Two days before families observed the one-year mark since the shooting, Javier Cazares, who had run in the November 2022 election as a write-in candidate for Pargas's Precinct 2 commissioner's seat, stood before the commissioners court to once again ask Pargas to vacate his post.

Cazares and others also objected to the fact that Pargas, like Arredondo, had petitioned the state to upgrade his Texas Commission on Law Enforcement status from the "general" designation the city had reported to "honorable." The city plans to oppose the upgrade during a hearing in the summer of 2024.

"It was the worst day of my life. Unfortunately, Mr. Pargas is not here. I would tell him that he failed that day—him along with a lot of others," Cazares told the court. "Nothing about you or your inaction on May 24 are honorable. You, sir, are a bacteria in stagnant water that needs to be flushed away." Cazares continued, "Honorable are the survivors of Room 112. Even when faced with an AR-15, death, carnage, and chaos, their fragile little hearts outdid you and your men."

The grieving father, who had been allowed to review autopsies sealed to the public, told commissioners that his daughter, Jackie, did not die in the first fusillade of more than 100 rounds but about half an hour into the attack.

"I can only imagine what she was thinking. I'm sure she cried for her daddy, hoping, praying to be saved. She was so scared, she wet her little pants. Her death has broken me as a man, husband, and father."

CHAPTER 25

Back to School

During the dramatic run-up to the start of school, it felt as though parents and their students had boarded a giant transport ship that was sailing toward Niagara Falls. Everyone knew what lay ahead and yet there was no confidence in a unified command to avert the disaster. It was a haunting reminder of May 24.

To buy more time to complete security measures, the district had pushed the start of the fall 2022 school year forward a full two weeks. Classes were scheduled to begin on September 6. Even then, there were so many unanswered questions and concerns that the district convened a town hall meeting on August 29.

The event attracted only about a dozen community members, but their concerns carried significant weight, especially since many of the security projects remained unfinished. The district had announced plans for new fencing, more cameras, new doors, and single-entry-point vestibules. District officials blamed labor issues and supply-chain issues for the delays. Plans to hire additional police officers, including the engagement of an outside firm to evaluate staffing levels, were also announced, as was an investigation into district policing. The harsh reality was that few officers looking for work cared to set foot in a community where cops were so widely disdained.

During the town hall meeting, trustee Laura Perez, who had worked as a nurse at Uvalde Memorial Hospital for the previous eighteen years, embraced the idea of an investigation but rejected claims that the board was not interested in accountability. "It is important. I have a lot of questions. I've asked a lot of questions, and I was told, not by the district . . . that I was not privileged to that information because I was a board member," she said. "I was at the hospital. I know what I saw. It's been very personal for me. I was there. I know the injuries. I know the deceased. I watched my friend walk down the hallway to identify her child. It's very personal. To say that I don't and we don't care, it's not true. I just want make sure change comes correctly."

Perez's response was among the paltry few that had been offered from trustees over the preceding three months. What came across as a lack of empathy (or interest) had become such an obvious disconnect that I asked a close friend and former Uvalde school board member what was going on. How could people elected to represent their community sit in stone-faced silence while anguished patrons pleaded for answers about the murder of their children? It was antithetical to the whole concept of representative government. And it was certainly nothing like the independent spirit of participation members of the city council and commissioners court routinely demonstrated, people who were also elected by the community.

His answer was that school trustees are indoctrinated to believe that educating children is such a complicated business that the surest way to succeed is by being a team player who adheres to the administration playbook. Even to the point that board members are essentially scripted before public meetings about how to respond and what items are better left unaddressed. Of course, my friend had not always been a "team player," and his independence had not been appreciated by district administration.

By August of 2023, the school district's attorneys had supplanted the established playbook with one of their own. Perhaps their guidance would end up saving taxpayer dollars in the face of multiple lawsuits, but there was another cost that could not be quantified: public trust. At that point, school district administration had squandered a sizable portion of it—at least for those who felt that justice was not being served.

That point was front of mind during the town hall when activist Jesse Rizo questioned how trustee J. J. Suarez—a licensed peace officer and instructor in the Southwest Texas Junior College Law Enforcement Academy who had responded to Robb—was able to vote on whether to terminate school police chief Arredondo. A second question sought answers about how Suarez had traveled to the crime scene and who had advised him that officers were dealing with a barricaded suspect.

"The fact that you sit up there on the board and you, yourself, were in that [Robb] hallway. For whatever reason, with the training you had, you left Arredondo to just basically create a disaster and yet you, sir, have to sit up there and judge Arredondo."

Suarez offered to discuss school board business only, adding that anyone with questions could contact him by phone, adding that he had reached out to many families, including Rizo's family.

Dozens of children, especially those who had survived the attack on the fourth grade wing, told parents flat out they were not going back to school. Of the four girls who survived Room 112, none started classes in the fall. Mayah Zamora, who was shot seven times and spent two months in University Hospital in San Antonio, was still recovering, and Khloie Torres, Kendall Olivarez, and Miah Cerillo simply were not emotionally prepared. All three girls struggled to sleep or even to leave their homes.

Four of the six surviving boys, Jaydien Canizales, Noah Orona, Jordan Olivarez, and Samuel Salinas, began classes, two of them at Sacred Heart. The remaining boys, Gilberto Mata and A. J. Martinez, chose to stay home.

Other children from the fourth grade wing as well as those from higher and lower grades also elected to postpone classes. On the first day of school, 3,724 students were enrolled, about 100 shy of the 3,821 recorded for the previous year. The district also reported that of the 136 students enrolled in its virtual academy, only 59 students had attended.

Two fourth grade teachers who were wounded at Robb were physically unable to return to teaching. Arnulfo Reyes and Elsa Avila were still healing, although both educators said they missed interacting with their students.

Reyes owns a gift shop and a nursery called Arnie's Nursery & Gifts at 640 North Grove Street in Uvalde. It had been closed for awhile, but if he chose not to return to teaching and his health permitted, the shop would keep him occupied.

Veronica Mata and April Elrod had both lost daughters in Room 112, and yet both teachers returned to their classrooms for the new year. Veronica was not ready, but the couple's only other child, Faith, was resisting a return to Texas State University for her senior year, saying that she did not want to leave her parents alone in the house. Veronica and Jerry Mata felt that if Faith opted to stay away, she might never complete a degree, and that "would be a disaster."

Taking the cue from her parents, Faith returned to Texas State and graduated the following May. "It was the toughest year of her life. I don't know how she did it," Veronica said.

Veronica was determined that her twelfth year of teaching would be different. She would not remain at work in her kindergarten class until 8 p.m., as she had often done in the past. Going forward, she would make sure her students got what they needed, but family would always come first. There was also the fact that she and her husband now spent chunks of time traveling to advocate for more sensible gun laws.

For April, it was a matter of continuing her passion as an educator. "I mean, this is my nineteenth year teaching. I love what I do. I can't imagine doing anything else," she told me. She added that the school had been "taking really good care of all of us and making sure that we have what we need."

Both Veronica and April had been supplied with aides, which gave them more flexibility. Even so, April was not able to join other families traveling for advocacy. She had three children still at home, ages eight, fourteen, and sixteen, and only so many sick days. "My kids and I have gotten every single illness that has come through this year. . . . Oh, my gosh, my doctor says it's probably because of stress that our immune system is down. So I have two days left for the year to get me through that, you know, and it's February. So, you know, I can't afford to take off and go," she said.

Still, she supported everything the families were doing. "You know, we don't want to take guns away from people, we just want the age to be raised from eighteen to twenty-one. I just feel like for kids to be more responsible and mature when they own this type of gun that can cause this kind of devastation."

The two teachers felt fortunate to have each other. "As I'm walking my kids to recess, she's walking hers to lunch," April said. "So we pass each other every day in the hallway and give each other a hug and a little bit of encouragement. And, you know, nobody knows except for the ones that are having to go through this. So I mean the twenty-one are a family . . . we really are because we pull on each other's strength . . . and we can help each other through the rough days."

Other veteran teachers like Nicole Ogburn and Mercedes Salas did not have the luxury of not working, even though they clearly suffered from trauma. "I didn't have that choice not to go back to work because I have to pay my bills," Ogburn said. She and Patricia Albarado made a pact over the summer, telling each other "if you go back, I'll go back."

An educator friend who had moved away but recently returned to teach in Uvalde observed that the two women had not had a real break from the tragedy. All summer long you "were never out of the spotlight . . . Uvalde was never out of the spotlight," she told them. "Now that school started, and I'm seeing you and I'm hearing you, and I'm watching you . . . you're not the same people you were. You're suffering. But yet nobody's supporting you."

In an interview with NPR on September 2, Nicole Ogburn had acknowledged that she had concerns about starting school again, this time on a newly repurposed campus named Uvalde Elementary School. She worried about her own mental health (she was receiving therapy in San Antonio) and that of her students. Instead of picking out decorations for her new classroom, which would have been a priority in previous years, she bought a door jam and a curtain that could be pulled down over the door window in the event of an intruder.

As she thought about physical security measures, the special education teacher was also trying to anticipate what it would be like when students returned to the classroom for the first time since the shooting. "I think I'm scared for how some of these kids are gonna react when they get here, and if I'm gonna be able to handle that part of it," she said.

Ogburn told me that she had granted previous interviews and that she had granted one before school started because she felt like "people needed to know what I experienced. It's not what everybody else . . . it's what I experienced that day. Other teachers (who were in the west wing) were scared to do it. And I was like, I need to say how I feel."

She almost did not return to the classroom. But she thought about her own children and about Uvalde students. "I thought, I gotta go back and show them first of all, we can't live in fear. I mean, you just never know when something's gonna happen," she said. "So I thought, I have to try not to live in that fear. I have to go forward and show these kids, 'Okay, Ms. Ogburn can go back to school, then so can I.'"

Still, it had been difficult and there were days when the anxiety was overpowering and the teacher asked to stay home. Ogburn said that on those occasions, her new principal had been more than understanding. "'You take care of yourself. Don't worry about what's here. We'll take care of that,' the principal told her. "Luckily I have days built up," Ogburn said. "Because before I never, I rarely took off ever. . . . But there's some teachers right now they don't even have anything left. And so they don't have those days just to be like 'I need a day to decompress.'"

School bus driver Silvia Uriegas also returned to driving with the new school year, but with a different bus and a new route. Each morning in the 2023–24 school year, beginning at 6:47 a.m. she gathered eighteen to twenty elementary students from Farrar Street and returned with about forty kids in the afternoon. That was the first route. The second trip involved picking up and delivering junior high and high school students. The last passengers arrived at their homes by around 5:15 p.m. It made for a long day.

The week before school began, Uriegas had begun to worry what it would feel like—whether the trauma from May 24 would return. She also thought about the passengers who would not be there, like ten-year-old budding artist Alithia Ramirez, who had written her name on the back of one of the seats in bus no. 19 (it was still there) and whose little sister, Akeelah, would now ride alone.

"But yeah, I mean, it's a sad situation. We all know a lot of the kids. It was interesting, because I keep going back to that image of [the officers] carrying the kids, but they said nothing was going on. That's all I thought about . . . that nothing was going on."

The PTSD from the shooting is a constant companion. Uriegas described the sound of the nail guns at new construction near her home sending her into a near-panic. "Yeah, that was like, you know, like, it's surreal. I was sitting in my living room, like, 'What is that'? And then I realize, okay, no, it's all good. It is screaming or yelling kids. Like, they get too excited. It's like, okay, it takes me, takes me back to that day."

Mercedes Salas said that the first thing she did before returning to class on September 6 was to test the new eight-foot fence. She was pleased to discover that neither she nor other teachers were able to climb it.

CHAPTER 26

A Widening Divide

Fed up with school administration's refusal to remove the four remaining officers who had responded to Robb, thirty-two-year-old Brett Cross adopted a new tactic. On the morning of September 27, he and a dozen supporters planted themselves at the front of the Uvalde Consolidated Independent School District administration building on North Getty Street and refused to budge.

At that moment, the central office ceased to function. Employees circled the block in their vehicles, like worker bees trying to return to a plugged hive, looking for a way around the chaotic scene. When Cross was ordered away from the front door, he migrated to the back entrance, leaving a handful of protesters in his stead.

For most of the first day, the thirty or so men and women charged with supporting the small army of teachers, aides, and auxiliary staff that educated the district's 4,100 students were afraid to enter the building. A handful diverted to a nearby facility normally used for school events.

In an interview that afternoon, Cross said, "It's been 18 weeks [since the shooting]. I've been to every one of the [school board] meetings, I've begged, I've pleaded, I've cried—everything—and they don't care. So I'm not asking any more. I'm demanding."

The wiry and amply tattooed wind turbine technician, accustomed to working dangerously high above the earth, had no reservations with confrontation. In fact, he said his role in the negotiating process was to assert force on school administrators while others in the Lives Robbed group pursued diplomacy.

"I've done the meetings. I've done the behind closed doors . . . but the way I see it is anybody who has ever made change, you have to have both. You have to have the private meetings, the civilized discussions . . . and you have to have the loud in your face so that they will listen to one without the other."

146

According to Cross, district superintendent Hall Harrell told him in a conversation in front of the office that the district could not suspend the school police until an investigation of their actions was complete. Cross suggested that the superintendent call the investigator right then on his cell phone, which he did. Cross then asked the investigator himself if suspension would impede the review. "No, sir, it won't," the man replied. With that confirmed, Cross again asked Harrell to suspend the officers, but the superintendent offered to send them home for the day instead, saying that he needed to speak with district's lawyers before taking any permanent action.

Cross, who came across as more measured in private conversation than in public, told me that he didn't have anything against police in general (his nephew Uziyah, who died in the shooting, wanted to be a cop), but the officers who responded to Robb "sat on their asses for 77 minutes . . . and the school cops are the ones that when we go to school board meetings, they are the ones wanding us down [checking with a metal detector]. Like I have to look into the eyes of the people that sat there in that hallway and listened to our kids scream and bleed out."

The first day ended without resolution, and Cross established a rudimentary camp in the back parking lot. Supporters erected a sunshade and folding chairs. They also delivered ice chests with soft drinks, cases of bottled water, and food items. The first night, Cross dragged a cot into the alcove at the back door and slept under the glare of a security light—albeit fitfully. One of the biggest drawbacks was the absence of restroom facilities. As the days dragged on, the number of people holding vigil fluctuated from the committed protestor alone during the overnight hours to dozens mingling in earnest camaraderie by day.

Almost at once district officials posted signs directing the media to stay away from the camp. Many of us ignored the prohibition, paying routine visits. It was, after all, a major news event. In the forty years I had been reporting on the city, no such protest had ever occurred. But neither had there been a mass shooting.

If not for a major revelation on Wednesday, October 5, Cross might have languished for weeks in his grim camp. On that day CNN journalist Shimon Prokupecz broke the news that a former Department of Public Safety trooper named Crimson Elizondo had been hired as a school district police officer. The report was a direct affront to families, as Harrell had pledged that no officer who responded to the shooting would join the school force.

Not only had Elizondo responded, she had arrived within minutes of the shooter and was the subject of a pending Department of Public Safety investigation for her actions. That information had been conveyed to acting school district chief Mike

Hernandez on July 28. As a final glaring insult, the young trooper was captured on body camera video outside Robb on May 24 answering fellow officers who asked if she had a child inside the school: "If my son had been there, I would not have been outside. I promise you that."

The incendiary news fueled a firestorm among families. Protesters jammed the front entrance and lined the street in front of the district's central office holding up signs that demanded the termination of Elizondo and the rest of the force. The next day the administration fled to the high school, where they could regroup.

The district fired Elizondo within twenty-four hours of the CNN story, and the following day it suspended its police force. Acting chief Hernandez and student services director Ken Mueller, who was implicated in the hiring of Elizondo, tumbled next. Both were placed on administrative leave, but Mueller elected to retire rather than linger. The final shoe to drop belonged to Harrell. On Friday, October 7, the school district announced in a press release Harrell's plans to submit his retirement to the board the following Monday.

The same press release outlined plans for the Texas Police Chiefs Association to continue a management and organizational review of the police force. "The results of this review will guide the rebuilding of the department and hiring of new chief of police. We expect a report later this month." The communication also informed patrons that the district had requested that the Texas Department of Public Safety provide additional troopers for campus and extracurricular activities. Thirty-three members of the state police would fulfill that mission.

Over the long weekend, Harrell's retirement announcement galvanized Uvaldeans who had been longtime supporters and admirers of the superintendent. The sixty-year-old had spent more than thirty years with the district, rising from classroom teacher to superintendent, a career path that emulated that of his father. For six decades, the name Harrell had been synonymous with dedicated service to Uvalde Consolidated Independent School District and the students it served. That had to count for something.

The response was a rally that was organized to coincide with the October 10 school board meeting. Beginning around 5:30 p.m., hundreds of supporters lined both sides of Bohme Street outside the Benson Educational Complex, where the meeting was scheduled to be held. When Harrell arrived, he was greeted as a hero. The crowd chanted his name, sang songs, and offered hugs and prayers. The juxtaposition of the superintendent's line of supporters and the families of victims who had to navigate the street between them on the way to the meeting was jarring. Especially in view of signs with messages like "Thank you Dr. Harrell. We stand with you and we are sick of the blame game, the bias . . . media . . . fear . . . politics . . . lawsuits."

Inside, where the families were dressed almost exclusively in black T-shirts memorializing their loved ones, the atmosphere grew even more inflamed. "How dare you decide now, when a job is at stake, to come together, but you stayed home [as] we, the families, have been demanding transparency and accountability?" Kimberly Mata-Rubio said. "How dare you attack those of us who lost our children in the worst possible way?"

Kimberly reminded trustees that she had not sought Harrell's retirement, a position she had made clear in correspondence with the board in July. Her comments came during the open forum portion of the meeting that included seven speakers.

Many Harrell supporters and families remained outside, as the capacity of the boardroom was limited to ninety people. At different points, tense words were exchanged and troopers stepped in to keep the peace.

Over the weekend, after Harrell announced that he was leaving, his wife, Donna, posted a note on Facebook in which he said the decision to retire was his alone. Our newspaper's social media post announcing Harrell's decision elicited more than 350 comments between Friday afternoon and Wednesday morning. Most expressed gratitude and admiration for the longtime educator.

"Nineteen children and two teachers died and we couldn't get that out there," Brett Cross said of the glaring disparity in support. "I will say this: if it had been seventeen white kids, all of these people out there would have been in here," he continued, referencing the Hispanic ethnicity shared by all but two of the twenty-one people who died in the May 24 attack.

Another family member, Berlinda Arreola, offered back-handed support for the superintendent when she said, "I hope and pray we find a superintendent qualified enough to fill your shoes. Twenty-one brutally murdered teachers and students wasn't enough to outrage our Uvalde Strong community, but your retirement is."

That week I asked Kimberly about the divide in the community. She felt that it had been "building for a while, because there are those who want to forget already and move on, because they can move on." She said some had also objected to Brett Cross's protest—to the public spectacle of it and its interference with school activities—even though it was not directed at Harrell but at the police force.

"I respect him for his decision to retire. He feels like he is not the right person to bring the school back to what it was or better. I am sure he will help lead the search for a new superintendent," she said.

Still, she thought that if the people who had come to support Harrell on October 10 had been with the families from the beginning, they could have helped advise the superintendent. "If they are Hal's friends, they should have been speaking out to help guide him and instead they waited for him to fall, and now they are there."

Months later Kimberly told me that Harrell's leaving had been a setback for the families' push for information. She knew that the superintendent was in a bad place because of the line he was forced to walk between genuine concern for those who had lost children and the lawyers' directives that were tantamount to a gag order. "Hal genuinely cared about the children and the district. And I felt that we could have worked with him," Kimberly said. "More so than the man who replaced him."

For Javier Cazares, the rally in support of Harrell confirmed that the community was more willing to stand up for one man than the dozens of grieving family members who had "attended meeting after meeting" without any show of support. "I think a lot of people are still afraid to speak [for us] because of the backlash of their bosses, or co-workers or families or political views or whatever," Cazares said.

CHAPTER 27

Día de Los Muertos

Those who have watched the movie *Coco* have gained a fanciful insight into a celebration that is deeply ingrained in modern Mexican culture and has been borrowed into the Latino families in Southwest Texas. Typically held on November 1 and 2, it is not quite Halloween and not quite All Saints' Day but something in between. Día de los Muertos is a holiday for visiting the graves of the departed with food and mementos of the things they most enjoyed. Many families construct an *ofrenda*, or altar, to place the coveted objects on. The idea is to lure the beloved's soul into the embrace of the living family.

According to tradition, at midnight on October 31, the souls of deceased children come down from heaven and reunite with their families on November 1. The souls of deceased adults come to visit on November 2.

Five months after Robb, any hope of reunification was badly wanted, and families responded with an outpouring of decorations, food, and love for dear ones buried in Hillcrest Cemetery. In the growing twilight of an autumn afternoon, individual gravesites beckoned with the soft glow of candlelit *ofrendas* and the more colorful lights that ringed the graves themselves.

No *ofrenda* was complete without the candles and marigolds, or *flores de muerto* (flowers of death), to provide a beacon and an enticing scent for visiting spirits. And of course, each altar included photographs of the departed, in addition to their favorite foods and drinks. In that sense, each grave reflected the individual tastes of the person buried there as interpreted by parents, siblings, extended family members, and friends.

Music plays an enormous part in all Latino culture, and this holiday was no exception. The plaintive sound of mariachi trumpets wafted across the normally silent cemetery, adding to the drama of the evening and moving many to dance, including adults and young children.

The Rubios had visited Lexi's gravesite almost daily since her death. Not two weeks earlier, on October 20, her 11th birthday, they had gathered for a private celebration with Lexi's favorite red velvet cake with cream cheese filling, party balloons, and gifts.

Día de los Muertos was not a holiday the family had celebrated previously, so they turned to the internet for instructions on how to construct an *ofrenda*. The first step was to procure an appropriate table and cover it with a serape with its own distinct striped pattern. Next came Lexi's *ofrenda*. It featured her favorite meal from McDonald's: a cheeseburger, plain and dry, topped with French fries and nuggets [aka a Lexi burger]. Accompanying that were Toffifay bites, Taki chips, and a Starbucks sweetened tall peach green tea lemonade. For Kimberly, visiting the other families to see what things their children liked and listening to the mariachi music proved soothing.

Not far away, in the same area of what was considered the new cemetery, the Mata family celebrated the memory of Tess. Her father told a reporter that he was happy visitors paused to take photographs of Tess's altar, but he was still overcome with emotion.

"I'm happy that they are not forgetting about her," Jerry said. "You just don't think you are going to be doing this for your daughter in the fourth grade. She was not supposed to die. But the goal today is to remember the good times."

Ana Rodriguez found the celebration at the cemetery to be helpful even though Maite's ashes rested in the place she had loved more than any other, her home.

The nursing instructor at Southwest Texas Junior College found comfort that came from being with other families whose pain was as unbearable as her own. Like Kimberly, she particularly relished visiting the children's graves to learn what their favorite treats in life had been. "I think to myself, they are going through the exact same pain I'm going through and they're still here . . . they're still here. So I battle with my own demons. That's why for me, it's helpful," Ana said.

For Ana, the death of Maite represented more than the loss of a beloved daughter. The little girl had been becoming a smaller version of her mother. They had bonded in a way that was different from Ana's bond with her two boys. Mother and daughter were both into photography and scary movies, which they watched together on "movie nights." Maite also possessed a remarkable ability to read and respond to her mother's sometimes troubled heart. That was probably because they had spent so much time together, Ana surmised.

They shared the same bed, but Maite always slept facing the wall. If Ana was experiencing hard times, she would hug her sleeping daughter. "I would put my ear to her back and hear her heartbeat. She didn't know she was helping me . . . but it helped so much to hug her."

Ana remembered another especially difficult day, which happened to be her birthday. "I went to bed after dinner and Maite said, 'Mom, will you come dance with me?' I just had a feeling she knew I was having a hard day. I'm glad that I forced myself to get out of bed and go dance with her."

The mariachi group strolled from gravesite to gravesite, asking families to choose a song for their departed child. When asked what song Maite would like to hear, Ana chose "Remember Me" from the movie *Coco*, a film her daughter had adored.

This is where the fantasy of Coco departed from the reality of nineteen children murdered in a classroom. The families had the "want to," the fervent desire to summon their babies back into the living world for however brief a moment. If that meant suspending the harsh reality of what had happened for half an hour or even 10 seconds, no effort was too great.

Uvalde's downtown plaza pulsed with its own celebration. A central *ofrenda* provided a place for remembrances of all twenty-one victims, and the semi-permanent crosses that encircled the plaza's central fountain took on decorations befitting the holiday.

As is customary, an attempt at light-heartedness pervaded the celebration. Women wore faces painted in the image of La Calavera Catrina (or elegant skull) and wore elaborate, ghostly costumes. Booths also beckoned, offering holiday-themed goods as well as food and drinks. Visitors, including members of the media, mingled with locals, always mindful of the fountain's twenty-one crosses.

When I entered the plaza after walking the half-block from the newspaper office, a Hispanic couple I had known for thirty years hailed me. The moment the pleasantries ended, the woman launched into a criticism of families of victims, including our former assistant editor. "You need to put a lid on her," the wife told me bluntly. "If not, she's going to cost you a lot of readers."

I reminded the woman, who with her husband belonged to an upwardly mobile demographic, that Kimberly was not currently working for our newspaper and that I had zero influence—and wanted none—on what she chose to say or do. I also suggested that if any of us had lost a child at Robb, we would not have a problem with Kimberly or any other family seeking justice.

The woman persisted, explaining that her family was caught in the middle of the Robb tragedy. Some of her relatives served in law enforcement and others had children at the school. In essence, she was living the nightmare that had cleaved the community into painful slices of humanity.

Before I took my leave to explore the celebration, the woman launched one last bid for action. "You get her to stop, and I'll find you 100 new subscribers," she tempted. Not surprisingly, none of that came to pass.

In fact, the following evening Kimberly and Felix joined about 200 people, including a dozen other family members from Uvalde, in delivering the Day of the Dead to the front door of the governor's mansion in Austin 160 miles away. The family's fathers carried a large *ofrenda* decorated with photographs of lost children and teachers to the front of the residence and demanded more responsible gun laws, especially raising the age to purchase a semiautomatic rifle from eighteen to twenty-one.

"We are here today celebrating our children's lives but also trying to reach out to parents on a personal, on a mom-and-dad level. Just, if you care about your children, protect them, go out to vote for candidates who support sensible gun legislation," Kimberly announced to the crowd watching the marchers.

Monica Muñoz Martinez, a 2002 Uvalde High School graduate and associate professor of history at the University of Texas at Austin, joined the march in Austin, which was led by the Mexican American Legislative Caucus. Similar marches and vigils, called *Marcha de los Niños*, took place in five other Texas cities to remember loved ones and advocate for stricter gun laws. Prior to the Austin walk, the group staged a rally on the capitol steps, where participants held candles in honor of the victims.

When the marchers reached the Governor's Mansion, a security guard appeared and warned participants to be sure to remove all of their display items. Martinez said, "It was a solemn event."

Growing up in Uvalde, Martinez recalled trips to the cemetery where generations of her father's family were interred. They would clean the site and leave flowers and reminders in the form of food or other objects. It was also an opportunity to learn family history.

There were also trips to Mexico to visit the graves of her mother's family in Piedras Negras and Nava. The holiday in Mexico was a starkly different affair, where the entire community attended with a more specific purpose. In most towns and cities, the upkeep of graves was the responsibility of the families. If a plot became overgrown, another person might take it over, Martinez said.

The Yale-trained historian has written extensively on Mexican culture, including *Injustice Never Leaves You: Anti-Mexican Violence in Texas*. She called the trips to Mexico "an annual pilgrimage" to do the requisite cleaning but also to have fun. In the process, she learned the stories of her ancestors and the sacrifices they had made while acquiring "generational wisdom."

"So we grew up celebrating Día de los Muertos and had these very different experiences: in Uvalde, private, and in Mexico, very public," she said.

Martinez was not surprised that most young Uvalde families did not have a long-standing tradition with Día de los Muertos, which is most closely associated with the Catholic Church. She has a photograph of Sacred Heart deacon Hector Garcia (who died in 2023 at the age of eighty-two) at Hillcrest Cemetery with a spray bottle of holy water. On Día de lost Muertos, dressed in full vestments, he walked the cemetery and blessed every headstone.

Martinez noted that the warmth the victim's families drew from visiting each other that evening was also important. Día de los Muertos is a time when it is not so much a celebration but a chance "to process the grief that you are still carrying . . . an opportunity to mourn collectively or to feel comfort up front . . . grief and loss collectively as a family or as a community," she said.

In various locations around the state and across the nation, Hispanics used the holiday to pay tribute to the victims of Robb. Students from Sidney Lanier High School in San Antonio assembled a display that featured nineteen small desks. Each one uniquely honored a student who died on May 24—what they liked, what they were into, their favorite colors and superheroes.

And in Chicago, the thirty-sixth annual Day of the Dead exhibition at the National Museum of Mexican Art in Pilsen, Chicago, paid tribute to the Uvalde victims by including an *ofrenda* installation created by students from Bernhard Moos Elementary School in Chicago. Monarch butterflies represented the souls of students who died, and two skeletal angels above symbolized the teachers who had died trying to protect them. Mock yearbooks featured brief descriptions of things each child loved.

In the corner, next to two desks and a chalkboard, was a pecan tree, which represented Robb Elementary School. On the board appeared a poem by the Nahuatl poet Mardonio Carballo highlighting the relationship between every living being and those who have nurtured and cared for them.

And at the University of Texas in Austin, a similar *ofrenda* was created that remained in place until the one-year mark of the tragedy.

CHAPTER 28

Vote Him Out

The 2022 midterm elections on November 8 offered the first real opportunity for victims' families to effect change at the ballot box. They were convinced—largely through suffering and blind faith—that Texans would join them in limiting access to the weapon of war that had mutilated their children. Families were not asking to ban assault-style rifles altogether, only for a commonsense measure to raise the age to purchase one from eighteen to twenty-one, the same threshold for acquiring a pistol, a pack of smokes, or a six-pack of Bud Light. The tight-knit Lives Robbed organization planned to help make it happen.

The first order of business was to elect a new governor. Abbott stood as proud defender of Texans' rights to own—and openly carry—virtually any weapon capable of killing. The National Rifle Association loved him for it—he consistently earned an A rating from them—as did his vast base, which included most of rural Texas and big swaths of conservative metropolitan areas. The sixty-four-year-old also owned a mountain of cash. These plus the fact that Texas had not elected a Democrat to statewide office in the previous thirty years meant that defeating Abbott would be more difficult than banning barbecue, and yet Democrats saw vulnerabilities.

A polar vortex on Valentine's Day in 2021 paralyzed the state's power grid, stranding millions in a weeklong ice age. Temperatures plunged to single digits the night of February 14, as 6 inches of snow blanketed the county. The resulting power failure shut down the city's water pumps. Four days later a second 5-inch snow blanketed the city as temperatures hovered in the teens. Still without power or water, Uvaldeans slept in front of their fireplace—if they were lucky enough to have one and the fuel to burn in it. Others heated their homes with propane fish fryers or simply bundled up like Nanook of the North until electricity was finally restored. The big chill, which caused hundreds of deaths and billions of dollars in structural damage statewide, frosted the hearts of many voters.

Things on the southern border with Mexico were not going swimmingly either. The governor had pumped billions into Operation Lone Star. Two thousand National Guard troops patrolled the southern boundary and hundreds of Department of Public Safety troopers prowled the borderland highways and still immigrants piled into the state in record numbers.

The Supreme Court decision scuttling *Roe v. Wade* also blew an ill wind into the state, especially for many female voters. The governor had helped pass legislation that made abortion almost impossible after ten weeks, way before most women—and especially their partners—had any idea that a pregnancy existed.

The Uvalde Lives Robbed alliance—along with a substantial number of Democrats statewide—felt that the tragedy on May 24, 2022, represented a crucial underpinning of the Democratic Party's platform, which included more responsible laws for gun owners.

With the imagined stars lining up against the governor, all that was needed was someone to execute the miracle, a candidate who could inspire Democrats to vote in a state where barely half bestirred themselves to go to the polls in presidential election years and fewer than that in between. What was needed was a politician who could reel in independent voters weary of the state's abysmal track record on health care and education funding and a state awash in firearms.

That kind of magic was in short supply, but there was one man who had name recognition and whose energy measured in megawatts. In 2016, Beto O'Rourke clawed his way to within 2 percentage points of knocking off Texas senator Ted Cruz, a man reviled by Democrats as the second most unctuous man on the planet. The race was close, despite O'Rourke's insistence on treading the high road against a man with whom rolling in the mud was mandatory.

Beto had also expended a large measure of his Texas senate campaign political capital in a failed attempt to secure the 2020 Democratic nomination for president. Less than eight months after launching his campaign on March 14, 2019, the Texan called it quits. Sinking poll numbers in the crowded twenty-candidate field and inadequate funding were cited as reasons for the decision to halt the campaign.

Two years later, Beto once again slipped on rose-colored glasses and saw blue in the latest call to lead long-suffering Texas Democrats out of the wilderness. The El Paso native held off three challengers in the March 2022 primary in the governor's race, and over the next few months—after being schooled by the Cruz race—attempted to saddle Abbott with the failed power grid, miserable health care, insufficient school funding, and a fruit salad of other failures. And then on May 24, a rampage killing in Uvalde appeared to hand Beto a blood-soaked gift. The deaths of nineteen children and two teachers at the hands of an eighteen-year-old with an assault-style rifle would surely motivate a sufficient number of voters to sweep the two-term Republican from office.

It was not an unreasonable expectation, and Beto wasted little time. The day after the shooting, he interrupted the Abbott press conference at the Uvalde High School auditorium with a simple message: the blood of Robb victims was on the governor's hands for his serial refusal to support commonsense gun laws. Some objected to the timing of the confrontation and to the fact that Beto's supporters appeared to have been planted in the audience. For others, including members of Lives Robbed, the event revealed a candidate who was willing to fight for gun reform at any cost.

That sentiment was reinforced on July 10, when Beto spoke on the downtown plaza at the end of the Unheard Voices March and Rally. He shared three things he considered to be vital after listening to the families of the children and teachers who had been murdered. First and foremost was the desire to never forget the victims' names. Second was the burning need for justice and accountability. And third, the message he heard with compelling conviction was that the grieving families wanted their devastation never to be visited on another person in the state or nation. "We need to make sure, as difficult as this can be, to find consensus and to move forward . . . to make legislation that will save lives, that we end gun violence or sharply reduce it in our communities and this country," the candidate said.

He added that the state and the nation could defend the Second Amendment "while doing a far better job of protecting the lives of those in our classrooms, those who lead the classrooms as teachers in front of them and the people who are in our stores and our movie theaters—in our homes."

O'Rourke called out Democratic state representative Tracy O. King of Uvalde, thanking him for being in the audience. "We may not agree on everything, but I bet you we can agree on things like a background check, like a red flag law, like safe storage. Let us start where we have an agreement and move forward. Because we need action today. The next mass shooting is right now with each and every single one of us."

––––––––––––

By late September, Abbott and O'Rourke had amassed more than $50 million each, well on their way to a record-setting $160 million combined. O'Rourke outraised his opponent by about $6 million and spent all but $200,000 of the $81.6 million total. The governor kept about $7 million of his $78.5 million campaign chest.

Much of the money went toward television advertising, and Uvalde families happily agreed to appear in commercials promoting Beto's platform. One ad began with parents looking straight into the camera, holding photos of their children and sharing what they had hoped to do when they grew up: Lexi Rubio wanted to be a lawyer, Jackie Cazares hoped to become a veterinarian, and Layla Salazar wanted to be a track star.

Another ad focused solely on Maite Rodriguez. Ana Rodriguez narrated the video. "She wore green Converse with a heart drawn on the right toe. Those shoes ended up being one way to identify her body in that classroom. I never want another family to go through this. Greg Abbott has done nothing to stop the next shooting. No laws passed. Nothing to keep kids safe in school. So I'm voting Beto for Maite," the mother said in the video.

On September 30, nearly three dozen family members boarded a bus for the five-hour trip to Edinburg in the Rio Grande Valley. The occasion was the first and only debate between Abbott and O'Rourke. During a pre-debate press conference, the Uvalde contingent excoriated Abbott for refusing to call a special session to change gun laws—specifically to raise the legal age for purchasing assault-style weapons from eighteen to twenty-one.

"I'm speaking directly to moms when I say our babies' lives are on that ballot. It happened to me, it can happen to you, and this pain, it'll bring you to your knees begging for an end," Kimberly said. "I implore you to ask yourself, do you want to send your child off to school and have them return? Do you want to hug them every night? Do you want the opportunity to watch them grow? Then vote accordingly. Vote for Beto, because a vote for Abbott is a grave mistake. He has repeatedly refused to enact stricter gun laws and has instead expanded gun rights. Had Abbott prioritized the lives of his most vulnerable constituents over guns, then I wouldn't be here today. I would be at home with Lexi."

Felix, who completed two tours in Iraq, said, "I held a weapon of war. It doesn't belong at home, and especially not in the hands of an eighteen-year-old kid. I went to war and I made it home. My daughter went to school and was murdered in her classroom."

During the one-hour debate, Abbott stuck to the practiced line that the raise-the-age law was a nonstarter "purely from a legal position." He maintained that other states that had passed such laws—for example, Florida—would have to deal with legal battles. Of course, a year after the Robb shooting and five years after the attack at Parkland High School, legislation signed by Rick Scott, who was Florida governor at the time, that increased the age to purchase all weapons to twenty-one was still law. That measure, which the Republican governor had championed, went into effect within weeks of the shooting that killed seventeen.

Abbott also refused to budge on red flag laws or background checks, asserting that they would deny "lawful Texas gun owners their constitutional right to due process." Red flag laws allow judges to temporarily seize weapons from people who are deemed dangerous. That measure and the higher age limit alone would have saved lives in Uvalde.

O'Rourke hammered Abbott for signing a law that allows Texans to carry handguns without a license or training if they are otherwise legally able to carry a gun and for sending a video message to the 2022 annual convention of the National Rifle Association in Houston a few days after the Uvalde shooting.

"I want every parent out there to know that the lives of your children are more important to me than the NRA or any special interests or any other political consideration," he said. "I will prioritize them ahead of everything else."

The lanky Democrat who had been compared with the Kennedys did not escape his own political past. The toughest questions probed his position on guns, particularly a statement he had made during his 2020 run for president. At the time Beto had famously said that he would take assault-style rifles from gun owners. Asked to clarify his position on the confiscation of such firearms, O'Rourke had said, "The only place that an AR-15 or an AK-47 makes sense is on a battlefield."

A month before the November midterm election, I met Christina Delgado from Santa Fe at Brett Cross's makeshift camp behind the Uvalde Consolidated Independent School District central office. Delgado's friends had lost children in the mass shooting at the Sante Fe High School in 2018 that had killed eight students and two teachers, and her daughter, who had been in lockdown at the Santa Fe junior high while the high school was under attack, had been traumatized by the deaths of her friends. Delgado said that her goal was to help Uvalde avoid the same treatment that had plagued Santa Fe. She called Abbott's response to the Robb shooting on May 25 "the exact same bullshit" that had been fed to her friends at home.

"We had representatives that were continually coming in, meeting with families and taking photographs, posting on Facebook, talking to them about legislation, putting legislation on paper, taking the photographs, posting it, sharing it . . . then watering it down to where it either died in committee or watering it down so much that it really isn't effective. It was just to suffice the need at the moment to quiet everything down," Delgado lamented. She urged Uvalde families to stay focused on the "principles" and not to get bogged down in Republican versus Democrat.

"It's not about non gun owners. It is about the fact that these babies went to school and did not come home, they went to school and they were hunted. And these babies went to school and had no way to fend for themselves. At the very least, our kids fought. These kids did not have that opportunity and never should have been put in that situation to begin with."

Throughout the campaign, Abbott continued to resist requests to call a special session. Not only families but also the governing bodies of every institution in Uvalde asked him to do so. The Uvalde City Council, the Uvalde County Commissioners Court, and Uvalde school district trustees voted unanimously for resolutions in support of a special session, as did governing bodies across Southwest Texas. The governor ignored everyone.

By the time early voting began on October 24, the race was thought to have tightened, as in some polling Beto had drawn to within 5 percentage points of the incumbent. Supporters remained enthusiastic, especially since their candidate had now raised more money than any office seeker in state history. Money was pouring in, especially from small donors, but it was flying out just as fast, as television commercials for both men continued to flood the state.

On the evening of November 8, a large crowd gathered outside the *Leader-News* office for our traditional Election Night party. The practice of posting returns on chalkboards (we had since upgraded to whiteboards) for the community to view dated to 1932, when native son John Nance "Cactus Jack" Garner ran as vice president on the Democratic ticket for president with Franklin D. Roosevelt. That year, the Democrats carried Uvalde County and the nation, and they repeated their success in 1936.

The Election Night party enjoyed renewed enthusiasm in 1973, when Dolph Briscoe Jr., also a Democrat from Uvalde, was elected governor. His campaign had been powered by a wide assortment of Uvaldeans who had crisscrossed the state on behalf of the affable and fabulously wealthy Uvaldean.

Members of Lives Robbed had posted up at Lunkers Grill & Bar a couple of blocks from the *Leader-News* offices to watch returns. Early in the evening, Kimberly Mata-Rubio dropped by the newspaper to check in. Instead of helping with our coverage, as she had done for almost a decade, the journalist was followed by reporters and cameras representing other media organizations. We tended to be protective of our inner sanctum, but on that night I allowed people inside, a decision the staff did not wholly agree with.

While the ballots were still being counted, Kimberly explained to a camera crew in our conference room that she never considered men and women elected to public office as "saviors, but [as] officials who had a job to do." She had previously supported gun reform because it saved lives and wondered why people needed access to weapons designed for war.

"I did my part and voted responsibly. And I still ended up the mother of a mass shooting victim. That doesn't seem very fair. And then I just realized that I didn't do enough. It isn't enough just to vote. You have to be at the forefront. You have to encourage people to vote, you have to educate," she said.

When Fox News, the first major media outlet to issue a declaration, named Abbott the winner at around 8:15 p.m., the mood darkened. Not only had the governor triumphed, he had thrashed Beto by 22 percentage points in Uvalde County. By contrast, Cruz had beaten O'Rourke in the county in 2018 by only 10 percent. To add more insult, the governor had surpassed both of ex-president Donald Trump's margins in 2016 and 2022. He also performed better than he had against underfunded challenger Lupe Valdez in 2018.

Families were stunned. They had poured their hearts into support for Beto and other like-minded candidates and nothing had changed. Not only had Democrats statewide been unmoved, but friends and neighbors who pledged to be "Uvalde Strong" had sat on their hands.

Javier Cazares was one of three write-in candidates who had sought to replace Uvalde County Commissioner Mariano Pargas, the acting UPD police chief at Robb. Javier responded to Pargas's reelection by saying, "Uvalde is Uvalde. I figured, you know, we saw the results in our locals who don't like change. I am a little disappointed things didn't go in the way I thought they were going to go." He added "We're in it for the long haul. . . . I mean, this totally changed my views on a lot of things. We're not going anywhere."

Brett Cross reacted with stinging criticism. "Uvalde Strong—You come to us saying how you hurt for us but turn a blind eye to the corruption and deceit. Uvalde Strong—You vote for a man who said 'It could have been worse.' A man who hasn't lifted a finger to help us in Uvalde—a man who wants to take away your right, your wife's, mother's, aunt's, daughter's and nieces' rights to their own bodies."

Democratic candidate John Lira, who had challenged incumbent US representative Tony Gonzales for the congressional district that sprawled from San Antonio to El Paso, joined the families at the watch party. He said that while Abbott's victory was "crushing," he was proud of the families for becoming politically engaged after experiencing a tragedy.

"It just means that the fight goes on," said Lira, who also lost on November 8. "This community, these families, they fought their ass off for change, for a new vision, for somebody that will listen to them and be responsive to them and what happened to this community."

The sense of betrayal the midterm elections inflicted compounded the earlier hurt and the families' bitter disappointment was entirely understandable. And yet they (and countless others) had probably expected too much from voters. It was not that all of those in Uvalde County who cast ballots for Abbott lacked empathy. The problem was that the fear of being replaced by immigrants, of abortion on demand, and of a crumbling Second Amendment was greater than the threat of an eighteen-year-old with a weapon of war killing more children.

CHAPTER 29

Survivors

E leven-year-old girls, especially close friends sharing feelings, don't search for words as much as words find them. The sounds that tumble from their lips coalesce into sentences a nanosecond ahead of their brains' ability to complete the narrative. That is why they finish each others' sentences or pounce on the last syllable as a springboard to a new, entirely unrelated topic—princesses of non sequitur.

These are the conversations Khloie Torres, Kendall Olivarez, Miah Cerillo, Leann Garcia, and Rakenzie Muñoz immersed themselves in when they carved out valuable time together. The friends dished about the usual stuff: the latest craziness on TikTok, games they were playing, their sports ambitions, classmates, teachers, and boys—if they were at all interesting. And one other topic, a more haunting and dominating subject: how to cope as a survivor of a mass shooting.

Khloie, Miah, and Kendall had watched a haunted eighteen-year-old turn two classrooms full of joyful souls into an abattoir of torn, bleeding, terrified victims. One hundred and fifty seconds. That's how long it took the killer to destroy so much that was beautiful. He used the remaining seventy-four and one-half minutes of his time as a sentient being to torment, torture, and continue to kill.

Rakenzie had been spared the trauma of being wounded or watching others die, but she was there that day—cowering with her teacher Mercedes Salas directly across from the killing—hearing the sounds and sharing the smell of fear and gore.

Khloie's dad, Ruben Torres, above all others, understood what the surviving girls and boys had endured. He called it "their firefight," a reality the veteran had lived as a .50-caliber machine gunner on a Humvee during tours in both Afghanistan and Iraq. "They were in the shit . . . in the shit, but the biggest difference is they didn't have anything to protect themselves with."

Almost nine years in the Marine Corps—especially eight months in Al Ramadi, Iraq, in 2005—had changed Torres. Frequent firefights with insurgents and the never-ending threat of improvised exploding devices (IEDs) ensured that he never stopped surveilling—scanning motorists, shopkeepers, and even public officials as potential attackers. Every vehicle that drove parallel to their convoy was a potential target. If a driver came too close, the marines followed strict rules of engagement. The interloper first received a warning shot from an M-16 or a "popped" flare to get his attention. If those measures failed, the Americans opened fire with their .50-caliber machine guns and even more powerful weapons.

Ruben acknowledged that when he returned stateside it was not easy for his kids to live with his hypervigilance. "Every time they went with me it was a fucking mission," he said of his family, which in addition to his daughter included his wife, Jamie, and two teenage sons. "It's a mindset and you just don't get rid of it."

There was a certain way to leave the house and enter the family vehicle. You memorized cars in the neighborhood, which families they belonged to, and what did not fit in. And in malls, restaurants, and other public places, Ruben scanned for anything that did not feel right. He talked with his children about previous mass shootings and survival techniques that included isolating the source of the gunshots and then—if you were mobile—moving away from the shooter or remaining still, as though you were dead.

At the end of the day, Ruben's experience as a combat soldier saved lives in Room 112. It was Khloie who called 911 four times to beg officers to intervene. And while her efforts failed to elicit an immediate response, one could argue that without those calls, officers might have waited even longer to rescue the wounded. But for sure it was Khloie's cool head in the classroom, whispering for her classmates to be quiet while the killer lingered in the adjoining room and suggesting that students like Miah smear blood on herself to appear dead, that helped preserve life. A former marine deserves credit for having implanted that blueprint for survival.

And yet no one walked—or was carried—away from Classroom 112 unscathed. Virtually all of the ten surviving children sustained some form of physical wound—from gunshots to shrapnel and even hearing damage. Most recovered quickly and moved on to an even more challenging emotional healing.

Khloie's father told me that tough as she had been in the classroom, she suffered in the present. I had made repeated attempts to connect with Ruben—to learn how his daughter maintained such poise in the face of death—and he was always extremely courteous. We made several appointments, only for them to be broken at the last minute.

I offered to come to his house (which might be upsetting for Khloie) or for him to visit the newspaper. Without fail, his explanation for why he could not come—or did not show up—was that "my baby didn't sleep last night" and she could not be left alone. Sudden loud noises, young men with long hair, and especially young men with a "Goth look" set her on edge. Certain music impacted Khloie the same way.

Finally, on a blustery, rain-spattered afternoon at the end of January 2023, I called Ruben's cell and waited yet again. When a burly man on a 2007 Suzuki 750 wearing a heavy knit parka and an impressive chin beard rolled to a stop in front of the office—well past closing time—the interview was on. An hour and a half later, it was clear why Khloie's survival had been more than chance. It was also obvious that even exceptionally brave ten-year-olds—boys or girls—could not outrun the trauma of what they had seen.

Before he left, Ruben confided that the only time he cried after the shooting was months later when the district attorney invited families to the courthouse to review evidence. When the prosecutor played recordings of two of Khloie's 911 calls, the first one lasting 18 minutes and the second one 28 minutes, Ruben said "it was fucking insane." The combat veteran simply could not fathom how police could hear his daughter's pleas and do nothing.

Miguel Cerillo reacted with the same bitterness after hearing his daughter Miah's attempts to summon help. The eleven-year-old was talking with the 911 dispatcher at 12:21 p.m. when a burst of gunfire erupted. "He's shooting," Miah said matter of factly. Miah told her parents that she heard someone say "this is the Uvalde police department, if you need help call out." Miah said that after a classmate responded, the killer appeared suddenly from Room 111 and shot the student, whom she could not see.

When Miah finally watched video from the hallway outside her classroom, she flushed with anger. "What kind of piece of shit is that?" she blurted at the cluster of officers gathered there. When she used more profanity to describe police, Miguel said he told her to "watch your language." She replied "No, dad, you don't understand," and began to cry.

When Miah could not sleep, her mother, Abigale Veloz, or Miguel would lie down in the room with her and her siblings. There were other symptoms of PTSD, including unpredictable responses to sudden noises like an object falling when the family was shopping in H-E-B. "She just ran straight out. She had no hesitation," her father said.

Although Miguel was born in Houston, he spent chunks of time as a young boy and teenager with family in the Mexican border town of Matamoros. It was there that he found an appreciation for what he called "the woods." He had discovered that same tranquility in Uvalde—until the shooting upended everything.

Father and daughter had been close, but now Miah seemed distant, preferring the company of her mother. Miguel attributed the separation to the fact that the attacker had been a young male. His daughter now mistrusted men, especially those with long hair. She also refused to return to school.

"The other day she's kind of ready, but she's not ready yet. So I mean we still struggle with her. . . . It's gonna be a long process, gonna be a long road ahead," Miguel said.

Virginia Vela's son Jordan lived that same reality. He went days without symptoms and then relapsed at the image of a stranger outside the family's home, a car passing the house too slowly, or the crashing of thunder. At the same time, it was Jordan who months later bravely led students from an elementary school gym after someone attempted to prank those on the inside by beating on the doors. The children were terrified, but Jordan guided them to the exit, even circling back to help a student who was struggling to keep up. The boy's actions were not surprising, since it had been he who pulled his cousin Kendall from beneath Irma Garcia and dragged her toward the curtain-draped table for hiding.

Vela remembered that in the days immediately after the shooting, family had gathered at the Olivarez's home. A school photograph rested on the table and relatives were commenting on students who were missing. "No, they are not missing," Jordan corrected them. "They're dead."

"He was telling us, and sure enough, that's how I knew that he didn't close his eyes. He didn't. He saw everything, because every kid that he mentioned from his classroom, they were gone," Vela said.

Just before Thanksgiving, Jordan's recovery suffered a shocking setback when his thirteen-year-old cousin Ethan Anthony Rios was killed with another seven-year-old boy in a car crash in Temple. Vela dreaded telling her son the news because the cousin had become the one person with whom Jordan felt comfortable talking to about Robb.

The boys had connected most evenings via online games. They wore headsets while they played and talked. On the evening of the accident, Vela tried to head Jordan off from his routine contact with Ethan, but she was too late. Another cousin, Robert, had already told Jordan about the accident.

"We walked into his room, and he was sitting with the headset in his phone and holding it in his hand, just staring at the TV. I just looked at him. . . . Is he having a flashback? Or did he just find out? Because that's how he has flashbacks." Vela said Jordan looked at her husband and said "You know, Robert said something. He texted me something, but I don't think I understand."

The family had been invited by Minnesota Vikings player Kris Boyd to attend a game in Minneapolis, but they wrestled with whether to go so soon after Ethan's death. Finally, feeling that Jordan badly needed an escape, they chose to travel to Minnesota—a trip that Boyd funded. "It was amazing," Vela said. "My son was like walking away from me [in the stadium]. He was a kid again."

Jaydien Canizales should not have been in Room 112. His regular teacher in Room 108, Chastity Martinez, was out on May 24 for a wisdom tooth extraction, and four of her students had been assigned different classrooms to lighten the load on the substitute.

Jaydien's mother, Azeneth Rodriguez, told me in an interview two weeks before Christmas 2022 that she had not intended for her son to attend Robb. She had hoped to enroll him at Sacred Heart, but when it came time for school to start, she did not have the money for tuition.

Small for his age, Jaydien smiled often, although his smile surely masked a deeper anxiety. His Christmas wish was for a larger home, where he did not have to sleep in the room with his two-year-old brother, whom Azeneth said was definitely immersed in the "terrible twos."

"I'm pretty sure there's times when he wants to cry. I'm pretty sure there's times where he wants to be by himself. He doesn't want to be bothered but how can that happen? There is no money for a bigger house."

There was good news, however. Jaydien was headed to Sacred Heart in January, thanks to a scholarship. The Catholic school was especially appealing because another survivor, Noah Orona, would also be attending.

Azeneth wondered how long it would take for her son to recover mentally. "I mean, you read about people with PTSD—battles and stuff. You know, it subsides. I'm not sure it ever goes away. But maybe with a child it's better. A better chance."

In many ways Leann Garcia had served as a bellwether for the horror on May 24 that was soon to be revealed. Blood had streamed down the eleven-year-old's face as she ran from her classroom. Parents, pushing against the police line, had cried out at the girl's appearance, seeing for the first time that children—maybe their children—had suffered serious injuries.

I visited the apartment where Leann lives on Pearl Harbor Day, after her mother, Angelica Rodriguez, agreed to an interview. Inside the small living room, which was dominated by an artificial Christmas tree, I perched on an ottoman while Angelica leaned back on the sofa. She recounted the moment she heard that there was an active shooter at her children's school. The plural word "children" took me by surprise, because all I knew was Leann, who was widely known as a survivor. What was not common knowledge was that her ten-year-old brother Ivan had been only steps away.

And while Leann's nose wound had not been serious, it did require surgery. Doctors in San Antonio performed an orthoscopic procedure to retrieve shrapnel from her sinus cavity. She was released to her parents two days later. However, she reported pain in her teeth and her cheek. Subsequent examinations revealed tiny metal fragments embedded in the gums above her front teeth as well as a piece of metal in her cheek. The metal shard was extracted from her face, but a dentist said that removing the fragments from her gums would be more invasive than just leaving them to eventually work their way out.

By the time I met Leann, the tall, sassy girl wanted a new house for Christmas. She showed me her nose, which revealed an almost imperceptible scar. Her large brown eyes fairly glowed as she added a visit from Bad Bunny to her Christmas wish list. "Baaaaad Bunny," she said, drawing out the name of the Puerto Rican rapper, singer, and songwriter.

Her brother Ivan seconded the request for a new house, especially in light of an incident in the parking lot of their apartment complex. Someone had fired seven bullets into the driver's-side door of a parked vehicle that happened to belong to a Garcia family cousin. That event had rattled the entire family and Jaydien Canizales, whose house was less than a block away.

Angelica said she thought Leann was doing "pretty good," which the girl seemed to be at first blush. It was Ivan, however, whom the mother worried about more. The boy's classroom had been steps away from Rooms 111 and 112, which had exploded in gunfire and the screams of victims.

Another survivor struggled with a severe physical wound and even more grievous emotional distress. His left forearm had been ripped apart and rebuilt with a titanium rod and screws courtesy of the skilled surgeons at Brooke Army Medical Center. More than ten months after Arnulfo "Arnie" Reyes was dragged from his classroom, he could not shake a sense of loss and abandonment.

Seated in the same comfortable recliner I had found him in six weeks after the shooting (his father had delivered it when the teacher returned from the hospital), Reyes described days when he was suddenly overwhelmed with emotion while performing simple chores. "I see a color. I'm like 'Oh, Jackie [Casarez] would have loved that.' It's purple or whatever. Stuff like that. And I'll just have to sit down, cry about it. Let it all out."

In addition to his arm and hand not working, other frustrations intruded on Reyes's life. His worker's compensation insurance no longer funded the full course of physical and occupational therapy his doctor had prescribed. Initially he attended several sessions a week, and now the routine had been cut in half.

"The doctor says I should go three times a week, and she knows what she is talking about. And [the insurance company] has their own doctor or something like that. I don't think that has been very beneficial."

Asked how he would grade the school district's support for him as a wounded teacher, Reyes said "An F—absolutely," because he had not received any encouragement from the district's central office. In our original interview, Reyes said that he had heard nothing from administration during his hospitalization at Brooke Army Medical Center. In the intervening months, contact had been nonexistent except for two brief calls—one in December and a second in January—from interim superintendent Gary Patterson.

Reyes said that he was receiving 30 percent of the salary he had earned before the attack on his classroom, but the "district makes it sound like they are doing me a favor. . . . It makes me wonder what they are doing for Ms. [Irma] Garcia's family. I mean, their parents died."

CHAPTER 30

Happy Birthday

On a brilliantly clear January afternoon, families gathered in Hillcrest Memorial Cemetery to celebrate the shared birthdays of Nevaeh Bravo and Eliahna Torres. Born on January 12, 2012, the girls died an arm's length apart in Classroom 111. On January 12, 2023, they would have turned eleven and would have been feted with cake topped with brightly burning candles and perhaps a piñata filled with goodies. Loud squeals followed by a mad dash would have ensued when the piñata spilled its rich contents across the patio floor.

The girls' mothers, Maggie Garcia and Sandra Torres, did not realize their daughters shared the same birthday until it came time to bury them. The women had labored the same day in the town's only maternity ward, and yet their paths might never have intersected. Theirs was one of many connections that surfaced after the tragedy. Parents who had cheered kids on the same softball team and yet never formally met, like Kimberly Mata-Rubio and Veronica Mata, became inseparable. Former high school classmates reconnected in shared grief after the deaths of their children.

On this day, the mothers refused to let death stand in the way of a celebration. Party food was prepared or ordered, balloons were filled, and guests were invited. Siblings, grandparents, nieces, nephews, uncles, aunts, and cousins attended. And yet no one knew exactly how to act. The adults stood a little stiffly, speaking in lowered voices. Children reverted more easily to normal—cracking jokes and smiling. But how can anyone truly party in a cemetery, where the diminutive celebrant lies two yards beneath the hard winter ground?

Ever since the shooting, graveside parties had been a recurring event. They represented a family devotional that will continue as long as mothers and fathers, siblings, and friends hold on to the memory. The size of the celebration may diminish with time, but the poignancy of the day will live as long as family hearts continue to beat—and a child leaves behind plenty of strong hearts.

Eliahna's mother said that finding her daughter's gravesite had been a stroke of good fortune. Initially the family believed that the only available plots were located in a newer, more distant section of the cemetery. Sandra was not happy with that possibility. Eliahna was among the first to be buried, and her mother could not abide the thought of her burying her little girl without knowing if her best friends Jackie and Tess would be nearby. Plus, she said, Eliahna had been afraid of the dark.

Finally Sandra contacted the city's local registrar, Jennifer Potter, and asked if there was any way Eliahna could rest near Sandra's grandmother. When Potter said there was in fact one space left, it was an enormous relief. "She loved taking care of the elderly," Sandra said, pointing out the adjacent graves of her grandmother, Solia Samora Castillo, and an aunt, Guadalupe Samora Castillo, both of whom died in 2019. "She helped my mom take care of them."

The ten-year-old also played softball for the Lady Bombshells, or, as Sandra jokingly called them, the "Bad News Bears." The team's last game of the season had been scheduled for May 24 and at its conclusion players would have learned if they had made the All-Stars. The night before, Sandra had told Eliahna that she would pick her up after school and they would grab something to eat before getting ready for the game.

Sandra's job required her to leave the house each morning at 5, but she sometimes woke Eliahna early so the child's grandmother would not face the task of awaking, supervising dressing, and delivering her granddaughter to school on time. Sandra said that that morning, Eliahna "looked so peaceful while she slept . . . so I reached in for the kiss, and I left because [it was] just like another ordinary day. I know this isn't supposed to happen in Uvalde . . . and I go to work and get my last phone call, my last 'I love you.'"

Asked what the family had done the previous year for Eliahna's birthday, Sandra explained that her daughter had been in quarantine at her grandmother's house after being exposed to COVID-19. She said the family had taken a treat and dropped it off outside the home and then told Eliahna they were going to eat Chinese food in San Antonio.

"She was crying and crying because that was her favorite—especially crab legs and crawfish." Sandra smiled, remembering how they had teased her.

Pastor Jaime Cabralez with Jesus Christ Revealed Ministries on South High Street joined the birthday crowd that numbered at least fifty. For the fifty-one-year-old minister, who had found God at twenty-three while serving a three-year sentence for felony drug possession, the loss was personal. Eliahna was his brother's granddaughter, and two of Cabralez's own nine-year-old granddaughters had cowered in fear at Robb during the massacre. His daughter worked in the school's cafeteria. Seven months earlier, Cabralez had presided over services for Eliahna.

Now he offered a deeply emotional prayer, calling on the celebrants to raise their hands in affirmation of the holy spirit. He was followed by Tejano singers who performed soulful pieces, including "Amor Eterno."

I was standing next to Jesse Rizo, Jackie Cazares's step-uncle. The sun was beginning to slide down the western sky, and the wind seemed to have subsided out of respect. The tender words in Spanish conveyed the depth of the unimaginable sadness, Jesse told me.

Tú eres la tristeza de mis ojos (You are the sadness in my eyes)
Que lloran en silencio por tu amor (That weep in silence for your love)
Me miro en el espejo y veo en mi rostro (I look in the mirror and see in my face)
El tiempo que he sufrido por tu adiós (The time I have suffered for your goodbye).

Not sixty paces away, the party for Nevaeh Bravo was going strong, with her siblings and numerous family members gathered near the gravesite. Party food filled nearby tables and a raft of balloons danced overhead. Maggie Garcia explained that Nevaeh got along with everybody but was an extremely sensitive child who always cried on her birthday. Her mother said she entered the world that way, "crying and yelling."

On May 24, Maggie had not attended the awards ceremonies at Robb even though she "always, always goes. . . . I never missed and that day I wanted to go but something was telling me not to go." She said it might have been Nevaeh saying that she was not receiving an award.

Maggie selected her daughter's gravesite because of a grouping of mesquite trees on either side of the plot. It seemed less lonely there. Her husband had preferred the new area of the cemetery, certain portions of which allow for landscaping.

Over the last year, families of victims had beaten a steady path to their children's gravesites, regardless of time of day, weather, or special occasion. And they had added many fixtures, especially benches with backs, lights, and wind chimes, which in some cases were not allowed. The city had thus far looked the other way, but a year after the tragedy there was discussion about whether to enforce the cemetery rules.

There was also talk about erecting a fence and closing the cemetery after sunset. City registrar Jennifer Potter said that the problem had nothing to do with visiting families but with people engaging in illicit behavior. "We've found a lot of inappropriate things out there . . . and so that leads us to believe that there is a lot of stuff going on after dark."

Earlier in the year, Kimberly Mata-Rubio had requested during a city council meeting that families be allowed to install upright headstones instead of the flat markers. City officials hesitated at first because upright stones would interfere with the sprinkler system and with mowing. Approval was finally granted but with height restrictions to allow for uniform watering.

Remembering the days after the shooting, Potter said she had attempted to keep the cemetery as a quiet and reverent place for families. Reporters and camera crews had pestered her for interviews and access to the cemetery, but she had held firm. "It was my job to make their lives at that point a little bit easier. So like I said, I did my best to accommodate what they asked for. And I tried to console them, help them through this really difficult time. I hope I did present that to them . . . that I was here to help take care of them and grieve with them," she said.

CHAPTER 31

Banking on Grief

Mass shooting documentarian Charlie Minn found himself in the eye of an emotional hurricane as the details of his film about Uvalde took shape in January 2023. Minn had appeared in the city within thirty days of the tragedy, promising to produce a film that would honor the lives of the victims. That commitment paved the way for a series of interviews in August 2022. Seventeen of the twenty-one families who had lost loved ones in the attack had agreed to participate, as had six of the survivors from Room 112.

By the time the film, titled *Robb-ed*, was scheduled to be released at the Forum 6 Theatres in Uvalde on February 3, 2023, far ahead of the original one-year mark, Minn's motives had become suspect. A trailer for the film appeared to focus more on raw grief than on honoring the victims, as Minn had promised to do. Dozens of Facebook posts said that *Robb-ed* had been produced to make money (Minn had promised that 25 percent of ticket sales and a portion of future streaming revenue would go to the families) instead of accomplishing a more noble purpose. Some participants called on the community to boycott Minn's production.

"Charlie Minn took advantage of how vulnerable we were at the time," wrote Gloria Cazares, Jackie's mother. "He said our children/moms were going to be honored. He lied to us."

Family members felt such betrayal that they issued a cease-and-desist letter, instructing the filmmaker to delete their interviews from his footage. "After further consideration, we are terminating any written and verbal agreements with Charlie Minn, Angelica Silva or anyone associated with the production of ROBB-ED: 77 Minutes of Police Incompetence," the letter read in part.

Theater owner Jacob Hensen had scheduled the film for a screening well before the controversy erupted. Caught between a commitment to Minn and the desire to serve the best interests of the community, Hensen scheduled a private screening for family members in order to gauge their response before committing to a public showing.

My first contact with Minn came within thirty days of the attack. In a phone call from the Broadway 830 pizza restaurant around the corner he said he wanted to stop by the newspaper to discuss an interview as part of a broader project.

His pitch was that Uvalde, like El Paso, was another example of Hispanics being targeted in a mass shooting. I disagreed with the premise. The Uvalde school district is almost 90 percent Hispanic, the same demographic of the attacker and his victims. Minn's other angle, that Robb represented yet another tragic example of a failed police response to a mass shooting, was more difficult to dismiss.

The caller's specialty was documenting mass murder, and his résumé reflected broad experience. A former staffer on the TV series *America's Most Wanted: America Fights Back*, Minn's work included *915: Hunting Hispanics*, about the Walmart shooting in El Paso in 2019; *The Kids of Santa Fe*, based on the rampage shooting at Santa Fe High School in 2018; *Parkland: Inside Building 112*; and, in a bit of irony, *77 Minutes: San Diego McDonald's Massacre*.

The fifty-something Minn, who spoke in a clipped, confident manner, explained that his goal was to give a voice to innocent people who had been murdered. He also wanted to borrow from our reporting on the tragedy to use it in his documentary.

I told him our staff had no interest in being interviewed or sharing information. Minn was unfazed, which was not surprising given the fact that his stock in trade was asking difficult questions of traumatized people. He promised to keep me apprised of his progress and suggested that I review samples of his films.

My curiosity piqued, I purchased *Inside Building 12* on Amazon and watched about half of it. I also viewed parts of the El Paso film and then forgot about Minn until he called again at the beginning of August 2022 to say that he was back in town to begin filming. He and his crew had set up what passed for a studio inside Room 116 at the Days Inn, and he invited me to watch the process.

It was after 5 p.m. on a stifling Wednesday afternoon. The motel room door stood ajar, spilling cool air into the outdoors as people milled around. I inquired after Minn, who arrived shortly thereafter. We exchanged greetings and he invited me inside. A pretty woman whom I recognized as April Elrod, the mother of ten-year-old Makenna, was directed to a chair. Her ex-husband, Chris Seiler, took a seat a few feet away.

Minn instructed the grieving former couple to look squarely into two separate cameras trained on each of their faces. The director sat facing his subjects, his head bowed over a sheet of paper. "The natural instinct is to look at the person asking the questions," Minn said. "I am going to be looking down the whole time, so you won't be tempted to look at me. Stay focused on the camera."

Over the next 45 minutes, during which the interviewees exhibited an astounding measure of grace, Minn posed a series of questions and requests for information that he later said were standard for most of the interviews. He began by saying he was sorry for their loss, adding that there should be a word in the English language for a parent who has lost a child.

April and Chris's response to the initial question about how they were coping was that they leaned on their faith in God. "Makenna had a big faith, and she loved the Lord big before all of this happened. We've always gone to the Baptist church here, but Makenna would wake me up early and push for me to take her to Sunday school," April said.

April described the tender notes her daughter left for her to discover while teaching first grade. "I love you, mom. Have a great day. You're the best teacher ever. You rock," were among the messages. The family also found a white folder upon which the 10-year-old had written "'This is Makenna's. Keep out or else!' Inside was a letter to each one of her siblings and to me. It's brought us a lot of peace," April said.

A particularly poignant moment was April describing her last moments with Makenna on the six-mile drive from the family's property to Uvalde. "I remember holding her hand the whole way to the grocery store. We talked about everything we were going to do that summer, because it was three days before school was going to be out." They stopped at H-E-B to buy bubbles because it was "bubbles day" in Room 112. Makenna and her younger brother Holden were also treated to four doughnuts apiece.

When they reached Robb, the kids got out, weighed down by the bubbles and doughnuts in their backpacks. "I saw her help her little brother carry his doughnuts, and she stopped at every single person that she met along the way to say hello and good morning." April returned for Holden's awards ceremony but said there was not one for Makenna that day. "So in the morning was the last time I saw her, but she was happy and excited. And showing love all the way to her classroom."

When asked about the failed police response, a recurring theme with all of the interviews, April and Chris demurred. They wondered about the actions of police but also felt that the ongoing investigation would ultimately assess blame where it was needed.

Minn made it clear that the 77-minute delay had helped fuel his quest to document the tragedy. "I think the videotape [of the Robb hallway where officers waited] is just damning. It's just damning," the documentarian said.

Both April and Chris wept frequently during the interview. It was still all so fresh. In fact, Minn told me during an interview afterward in the motel lobby that he had received criticism for asking families to discuss their losses so soon. His response was that parents wanted their children to have a voice and his work provided that opportunity.

"I don't think I ever shot a film where all of the families broke down," Minn said of the emotions exhibited during two days of filming in Uvalde. "It's grueling, and I can only imagine what these families are going through. They lost their kid, which is probably the cruelest situation one can face."

———————

About twenty family members attended the private screening Hensen hosted and came away with an unfavorable opinion of the film, which was almost two hours long.

"After talking to and reading feedback from the family members impacted by the tragedy last year, I have decided we will not play 'Robb-ed' at our theatre. The only reason we were going to play the movie is because we were presented with information that all the families that participated in the film wanted the feature shown, that is no longer the case, therefore we have pulled the movie from our schedule," Hensen wrote on the theater's Facebook page.

Minn said he wished that families had advised him of their objections sooner than one week before the film was to be released. "Had they done this half a year ago, adjustments could have been made to remove them from the movie," he said.

The documentarian, who split his time between New York and El Paso, added that he had done nothing illegal and that after producing forty films over the course of fourteen years, "I know the rules."

"Nobody is being forced to watch a movie. My films are not for everybody. I am not everybody's cup of tea. If people don't want to go see the movie, then that's their right, no problem," he said.

The filmmaker acknowledged receiving similar pushback from families who had participated in his documentary about the Parkland, Florida, high school shooting in 2018. The chief complaint was that the scenes were too graphic.

By the summer of 2023, the title of the documentary had been changed to *77 Minutes: Surviving the Uvalde Mass Shooting*. Minn had supplied me with a link to watch the original film before it was scheduled to be released. *Robb-ed* was not my cup of tea, but I could see the attraction for some families of victims who wanted to share the intimacy of their loss to ensure that their children's names were not forgotten.

CHAPTER 32

Twenty-One for Twenty-One

Beginning with the opening of the Texas Legislature's 88th session on January 10, 2023, Robb victim families rode a virtual conveyor belt between Uvalde and Austin. Once a week, generally on Monday or early Tuesday, they departed for the 320-mile round trip in the hope of persuading lawmakers to pass commonsense gun laws.

Uvaldeans generally traveled in their individual vehicles unless a husband or male partner could not attend, and then the women carpooled. When they arrived in Austin, the group would make its way to the state capitol office of Sen. Roland Gutierrez to check on the agenda for the day.

The senator's small office had become the visitors' briefing room and sanctuary. "We would just walk in—nobody would say anything. We would just walk back to his personal office space," Kimberly recalled. It was also a safe place when families were tired "or it just became too much."

The Robb tragedy had been deeply troubling for the fifty-two-year-old practicing attorney. Gutierrez was born in San Antonio to a Mexican immigrant father and a mother from South Texas who died while he was a baby. His father had remarried a Mexican immigrant woman, creating a family he described as a "Mexican Brady Bunch." Still, his father's job as an insurance salesman provided the family with more luxury than most who lived on the city's West Side.

Gutierrez went to private schools and eventually attended St. Mary's University School of Law in San Antonio. He began practicing as a criminal defense attorney but soon gravitated to immigration law. The state senator now maintains a small practice that focuses on deportation and asylum cases.

When he heard about the shooting on May 24, Gutierrez hurried to Uvalde and eventually ended up at the civic center. He remained for much of the night, watching and recoiling in horror at the screams of family members after learning that their children had not survived.

The senator could not bring himself to approach any of the families that first night. "They were just in such great pain. And I didn't think I'd be able—no state senator or president of the United States or anybody was going to help them in their grief. It felt a little bit disingenuous to just say 'Hey, what can I do for you?'"

On the Friday after the shooting, Gutierrez was in his car near Robb Elementary, listening to a radio broadcast of Abbott's press conference at the Uvalde High School. The lawmaker said he became furious and drove to the auditorium, where he confronted the governor and demanded that he call a special session to address the shooting.

"This thing wasn't just about failure," he said of Abbott and McCraw's narrative following the attack. "It was absolutely about lies, and messaging obfuscation and blaming and pointing fingers at everybody else but the Department of Public Safety."

It was not until several days later that Gutierrez found the courage to speak to the family of a victim. He first approached Kimberly Mata-Rubio at the prayer service for Lexi in the Rushing-Estes-Knowles chapel. It was a brief conversation, but one that bound the two in a joint mission. Over the following weeks and months, Gutierrez would seek justice for those whose children and parents had been murdered or injured.

By November, the senator had mapped out a campaign to change the way Texans looked at guns. Months of watching grieving families being rebuffed by Uvalde institutions, including the city and the school district, and being lied to by the Department of Public Safety and the governor had emboldened him to challenge the Republican-led legislature.

The first order of business was the announcement of a bill that would create a $300 million Robb family compensation fund. Several family members, including Kimberly and Felix, joined Gutierrez on Uvalde's Downtown Plaza for the formal announcement. A draft of the proposed legislation blamed local and state police for failing to confront the shooter before "victims bled out and perished." The proposal included $7.7 million for the immediate family or members of the household of victims. Another $2.1 million would be made available to those who had been physically injured.

Once the session began, the senator filed that bill and many more—a total of twenty-one. representing the twenty-one lives lost in the attack. Over the course of the 140-day session, like clockwork on almost every Tuesday, Gutierrez announced the next measures in a press conference. Without fail, he was flanked by Uvalde families and those of other mass shooting victims from across the state.

The highest priority was placed on a measure that would raise the age to own an assault-style weapon from eighteen to twenty-one. One bill called for making fragmenting bullets illegal, another proposed allowing anyone injured in the shooting to sue the state of Texas and any of its agencies, and a hugely significant proposal in light of the Robb massacre proposed eliminating qualified immunity for peace officers, subjecting them to damages for their failures.

For the duration of the session, Gutierrez implored and cajoled fellow senators to give his bills a hearing. Behind the scenes, family members worked in tandem, knocking on the doors of legislators to tell their tragic stories in person to men and women they had never seen—and who often were not interested in the message.

Over and over again, the refrain from the humble working-class families was "we should not be here." They lived in a community where it was not necessary—or in some cases even desirable—to speak out. Their focus had been caring for family and reporting to work each day without complaint. Now their dead children had thrust them into a most uncomfortable place. They had no choice but to speak truth to power. And somehow they mustered the courage to do just that. Gutierrez helped them fulfill that role.

Despite his unflagging determination and despite encouragement from like-minded lawmakers, none of Gutierrez's bills—even ones unrelated to the shooting—were granted a committee hearing. Without that first procedural step, no bill could become law. It was not a surprising outcome. Lt. Gov. Dan Patrick managed the state senate with an iron hand, and gun control measures were a nonstarter, even in the aftermath of Robb.

At one point, Gutierrez antagonized Patrick during a debate on a bill meant to keep kids from seeing sexually explicit drag shows. After state senator Bryan Hughes, a Mineola Republican who authored the bill, said the legislation was meant to protect children, Gutierrez said "We haven't done a whole lot of protecting the children when it comes to guns and ammunition."

The comment drew applause from Texans sitting in the senate gallery, but Patrick warned that if Gutierrez did not keep his comments focused on the legislation up for debate, he would stop recognizing the senator to speak.

Gutierrez put up a relentless fight. Toward the end of May, he spoke in desperation to Patrick and his fellow senators, describing in horrific detail what first responders found inside the two Robb classrooms. So gruesome was the scene that veteran officers were captured on body camera video vomiting in the hallway. "You have never seen so much blood," the senator said of the video he and a select few had been allowed to review.

Finally Gutierrez apologized to colleagues for his unbridled passion to effect change. "I sure am sorry to all of you, the way that I have behaved this session," he said on the senate floor. "I am angry as hell. And I see these kids when I go to bed at night. I see them in the morning when I wake up. Their parents are all my friends.

"I get what you guys have to deal with back home, and I get that you have to go and run for office," he said. "And you just gotta tell those people to go to hell and you're here to protect kids. That's all that matters."

Kimberly felt that Gutierrez was "as stressed as the rest of us" from fighting against long odds for gun reform. "I could see what that did to him. Personally, I don't know what that brings home to your family. I mean, every time he talked, it was with such emotion."

Martinez Fischer, the head of the house Democratic Caucus and a close friend of Gutierrez, said his friend had faced repercussions during the session. "He's given up his career, he's given up his reputation."

Meanwhile, state representative Tracy O. King of Uvalde had launched his own raise-the-age effort with the filing of House Bill 2744. King's bill called for increasing the legal age for purchasing an assault-style rifle from eighteen to twenty-one, but the measure was more tightly focused. The language specified "semi-automatic rifles with a detachable magazine in a caliber larger than .22."

It also included exceptions for peace officers, members of the military, and anyone who had been honorably discharged from the armed forces. There was an additional provision that allowed temporary loans of weapons to Texans under the age of eighteen for participating in sporting events at shooting ranges and on hunting trips.

In introducing his bill on April 18 to fellow members of the House Select Committee on Community Safety, the sixty-two-year-old lawmaker, facing his colleagues from the witness chair, confessed that he could not have supported his own bill in the previous session of the legislature, but that May 24 had altered his views.

"It changed everybody in Uvalde's life and it shattered the lives of 21 families and their family . . . and the truth is that had House Bill 2744 been the law in the state of Texas one year ago, 21 constituents of mine, plus the husband [Joe Garcia]—and probably two heroic teachers, 19 innocent children would still be alive today," King told the committee.

He went on to say that he had previously believed that if someone wanted to commit a heinous crime, they would figure out a way. They would steal a gun from their parents or neighbors or find an alternative weapon. That had been the method in countless shootings across the United States, King said. "But for some reason . . . this one wanted it bought legally."

Prior to turning eighteen on May 16th, 2022, the shooter had asked family members and friends to help him purchase weapons. They had all refused, and the teenager had waited.

King also told committee members that the majority of people he had spoken to about his legislation, including members of the National Rifle Association, farmers and ranchers, and other diverse constituents, had been receptive and candid. "They've got as many guns as I do—almost. And they say, you know this isn't that much, Tracy, this isn't that much to ask."

Family members, including the Rubios, had waited for more than nine hours to address the committee, which had been diverted to the house floor shortly after the session had convened. When it was finally their turn, Kimberly asked if members had watched the coverage of Robb and wondered what they could have done to prevent the tragedy.

"Do you look at the images of children running for their life and think 'What if we had enacted stricter gun laws?' Do you consider the children still inside? Those like our daughter who would never emerge? Did you imagine what it would feel like to bury your child?"

Kimberly advised lawmakers to sit with that image, because only then would Texas officials take the requisite action, including voting for HB 2744.

Christina Zamora, the mother of ten-year-old Mayah, who was shot six times and spent two months in University Hospital in San Antonio, testified that placing weapons "with the power to injure and kill so many in the hands of a young man is a huge responsibility." She said it was too much for teenagers whose minds are not fully developed and who still need guidance on the big and complicated issues of life.

"I am the mother of a son in his early 20s, and he is a wonderful young man but there is no shame in saying that he still needs—or turns to his parents for some issues, and we are happy to provide that support," Zamora said, adding that not all young men have people in their lives they can turn to.

"For everyone's sake, raising the age from 18 to 21 for the purchase of these types of assault weapons is common sense. What happened to my daughter's beautiful little body and her friends and teachers should never, ever have happened in the first place," Zamora ended.

Javier Cazares told the committee that the families were not there to take anyone's guns and that he was a gun owner, "a believer in the Second Amendment and a concealed carrier."

"I don't want you to see what I saw. I saw my 9-year-old daughter draped in a white sheet cold and alone in an operating room. I don't want any of y'all to see that. We need to change laws. Please have an open mind and please pass this law," Cazares said tearfully.

NRA lobbyist Tara Mica spoke against the bill, saying she did not "parachute in from Washington" but lives in Texas. "We're not mass shooters. We defend the Constitution. Realistically, a raise-the-age bill is likely to be litigated and found unconstitutional."

Michelle Mostert also signed up to oppose the measure, saying that she did not believe that legislation fixing the age at twenty-one for people to buy semiautomatic weapons would have prevented the shooting at Uvalde.

"You know, there's law-abiding people that are 18, 19, 20 years old, that aren't going to be able to use [semiautomatic weapons] for competition or, or shooting hogs or whatever, but . . . my point is it is not gonna stop it. I mean, we have the death penalty to stop murder. We have all these laws, but it doesn't stop it. It's just too bad. You know, criminals are criminals because they don't follow the law."

State representative Joe Moody pounced, saying that if laws do not matter and if people do not follow the law, why not abolish the penal code altogether? The representative, who is also a practicing attorney, said we have laws for two reasons: They create a "speed bump deterrent," and in the event the bad person still does the bad thing, they have punitive value.

Moody had experienced mass shooting on a personal level in the Walmart attack in El Paso. He had seen the destruction caused by high-velocity bullets impacting human flesh. He told Mostert that people who have bad intentions live in the same world as the rest of us, and the Robb attacker was no different. He had been thwarted multiple times from buying a gun before his eighteenth birthday and would have continued to be stymied had the legal limit been twenty-one.

Mostert injected that "he would have found a way."

"There's not many people up here that have looked at this [Robb] case more than me. Mr. [Dustin] Burrows is one, Mr. King is another," Moody said. He and Burrows had been part of the house committee that had investigated the Robb shooting. He insisted there was no chance that the Robb shooter would have been able to acquire a weapon illegally because he would have run into a law that was working and could not have figured out a way to circumvent it.

"So understand that they—criminals—don't operate in a world that's separate than you and me. They operate in the same world and have the same barriers. So we have speed bumps and deterrence. Guess what? Those work."

Moody also referenced the horrific message that Uvalde justice of the peace Lalo Diaz had observed on the whiteboard in Room 111. On one side of the board was a list of "puppy-love couples." The other side was blank except for the letters "LOL" that had been drawn with the blood of the victims.

"That's what he thought of. That's what he thought about what he had done. His message to us wasn't anger, hatred—just something flippant. He celebrated that he could do what he did. That's his critique of us because we let this happen," Moody said.

Despite the lengthy and moving testimony from victims' families, committee chair Ryan Guillen of Rio Grande City refused to call for a vote. As a result, King's bill died in committee. That changed on Saturday, May 6, when a man armed with yet another AR-15-style rifle shot dead eight people—including three children—at a shopping mall in Allen, just north of Dallas.

The fresh mass killing added a greater sense of urgency for gun-law advocates, who converged on the Texas capitol the following Monday. Their chants of "raise the age, raise the age" echoed off the rotunda walls prior to a press conference, where they implored lawmakers to vote on King's bill.

Kimberly told elected officials and reporters that she had awakened Monday after seeing Lexi in a dream the previous night. She recounted how in the dream she was parked at Morales Junior High in Uvalde waiting to pick up her son David. As she talked on the phone, Felix announced he was going to take the kids to practice on the outdoor basketball court.

"I watched him walk away and noted something was different, but I couldn't put my finger on it. I continued my conversation, then proceeded to walk toward the courts. That's when I saw her, my Lexi. I dropped everything I was carrying and rushed toward her. I held her so tight it should have hurt. She was damp with sweat, and I inhaled the scent of her hair like it was oxygen I'd been deprived of."

Kimberly told the committee she was awakened by tears. "I share this with you to say I'm so sorry I'm not strong today and maybe that's what y'all need to see," she sobbed. "At the end of every day, I'm just a mom who wants my daughter back and a mom who doesn't want another mom to know my pain."

To everyone's surprise, Guillen called the Select Committee on Community Safety together to cast their ballots. Members, including two Republicans, voted 8–5 to advance HB 2744 to the full chamber. Celebration broke out in the room as families simultaneously cried and laughed. They hugged each other and King, thanking him for helping them to achieve a much-needed victory.

The euphoria was short lived. The next day, with the 10 p.m. deadline fast approaching to include HB 2744 on the House Committee on Calendars, it stalled. Dustin Burrows, who had voted against the measure in the Select Committee on Community

Safety, also served as chair of the House Committee on Calendars. He simply refused to move the measure to a vote before the full house. The gallant fight to enact legislation that King had described as "not that much to ask" was officially dead.

Kimberly voiced the feelings of most families, saying that she was "angry, disappointed and disgusted by Texas politicians" but added that "Uvalde families did not fail. Texas politicians did. We were up against a brick wall but the dent we left is notable."

King's reaction to the outcome was measured. He knew going in that the chances were almost zero, but he felt compelled by the terrible loss that had befallen his community. "There is always another session," he said. Two months later, the long-serving representative announced plans to retire.

For Gutierrez, the almost five months of nonstop fighting was almost impossible to put aside. In an interview on June 26, he told me that while he had been shut out, "we made a lot of noise." The noise had been generated largely by people whose children had been the victims of mass murder—in Uvalde, Santa Fe, El Paso, and Sutherland Springs.

"These people, what they went through was extraordinary. And government completely failed. I mean, people need to understand that whether you're Democrat or Republican, it doesn't matter. . . . Government has failed us in rural Texas. And it continues to fail us. And yet rural Texas keeps voting for the people that are in power for the last thirty years. It is just astonishing to me."

Gutierrez, who would soon announce his candidacy for the US Senate seat held by Republican Ted Cruz, said, "Government is supposed to do those big things, supposed to get you out of a mess when you're in a mess. It's supposed to provide health care and education, all those things . . . but it has failed us."

The fiery senator added that Uvalde was more than a horrific tragedy, that what happened there was larger than the issue with guns. He called it "a complete and total meltdown of the safety blanket that we call government." Lawmakers that are in power in Texas are not being honest with the people, he said.

CHAPTER 33

More Bitter than Sweet

On April 21, 2023, the *Leader-News* won the Community Service Award at the annual convention of the South Texas Press Association in Boerne, Texas. The paper also claimed eight first-place honors—ranging from breaking news to editorial writing—on the way to securing the Sweepstakes Award (most points earned in each newspaper division) in the semi-weekly division. The paper amassed 1,200 points, believed to have been a record for the association, which was launched in 1927. (The first president was the founder of our newspaper, Harry Hornby Sr.) In addition, Pete Luna and Melissa Federspill won photographer and journalist of the year, respectively.

The accolades were far more bitter than sweet. Robb stood at the center of the vast majority of the material we had submitted for judging. We knew that better than anyone, and yet our peers were gracious enough to insist that our work had been exemplary. South Texas Press Association officers had also requested that we share with members what it had been like to cover a mass shooting—what we got right and what went wrong—and how it had impacted us and our readers.

Most of the staff signed up for the convention, despite the daunting assignment. In fact, during my forty years with the *Leader-News*, I could not remember a time when seven staff members and in some cases their spouses or significant others attended. It felt like our family had joined an extended family for its annual reunion.

Melissa wept when she won the Journalist of the Year Award. Her coverage had been exceptionally incisive and at the same time sensitive. But the almost impossible assignment of covering the Uvalde school district had taken a steep toll. There had been far too many days when contentious meetings and roadblocks to information had led to tears.

The Community Service Award proved most difficult to accept, as the plaque incorporated a facsimile of our front page from the Sunday after the attack, a page filled with the images of nineteen beautiful children and their two teachers. It was a perpetual reminder of our city's loss, as well as the supreme effort that the staff put into getting the coverage right.

Before the convention, we had sought permission for ABC News videographer Andrew Fredericks and producer Megan Hundahl Streete to shoot film during the event. Streete, who had lived in the community previously (she was a third-generation Uvaldean), had approached us the previous July seeking collaboration on a project called Uvalde 365. The investigative unit of ABC News, headed by Cindy Gali, planned to remain in the city for an entire year to document the community's response to and recovery from the tragedy.

Andy and Megan had spent so much time with us that they felt more like members of our staff than the members of the television network. In fact, when the head of ABC News Kim Godwin and Gali visited the newspaper the same day Kimberly returned to work, it was Andy who had greeted his bosses and led them on a tour. Andy and Kim Godwin had never met, and she thought Andy worked for us.

Andy had recorded the award ceremony and continued to film when it came time to recount the events of the last year. We took seats on a raised platform facing about one hundred people in the audience, and each of us—general manager Pete Luna, managing editor Meghann Garcia, staff writers Julye Keeble and Melissa Federspill, classified manager Norma Ybarra, and graphic designer Neil Sturdevant—relived May 24. Our peers posed thoughtful and sometimes probing questions, some of which elicited emotions that could not be contained. At one point Pete, who is emotionally bulletproof, had to gather himself before continuing. Others drew deep breaths in order to be able to speak. It was devastating, exhausting and yet somehow cathartic to share our experiences with like-minded and sympathetic people who might one day find themselves covering a similar tragedy.

Looking around the room was also a sad reminder of how much our industry had shrunk. The membership of South Texas Press Association stood at about thirty-two, half of what the total had been ten years earlier. Some of the absences were the result of deaths, which was only natural, since I had been attending meetings for four decades. More alarming was the fact that many publications had ceased to exist altogether or had transitioned to ghost papers—whose coverage comes only when nearby publications choose to dip in for the more sensational events.

In our region of Southwest Texas alone, we had witnessed the demise of at least four iconic newspapers. The *Del Rio News-Herald*, a daily that had served Val Verde County 70 miles away on the border with Mexico, had folded in November 2020. The publication traced its roots to 1884 and had served under its most recent masthead since 1929.

Given that Del Rio was home to Laughlin Air Force Base and served a community of almost 35,000 and another 100,000 just across the border in Ciudad Acuña, the shuttering came as a jolt. If a paper in a market twice as large as our own that was operated by a well-funded corporation like Southern Newspapers Inc. could not survive, what did the future hold for the rest of us?

The paper in Real County just north of us, the *Leakey Star*, had also closed, as had the *Texas Mohair Weekly* (founded in 1936) in Edwards County, which bordered Uvalde County to the northwest. A couple of counties away, the *Ozona Stockman* had temporarily ceased publication in June 2023. It dated from 1913.

There was another reason to escape Uvalde and its inherent stresses. The same week as the South Texas Press Association convention, the staff had completed a fifty-six-page magazine titled "We Remember" and had sent it to the printer in Louisiana. Scheduled to be inserted in the *Leader-News* on May 21, the product featured two-page spreads on each of the nineteen children and their two teachers. Meghann had poured hundreds of hours into designing and assembling the tribute.

The focal point of the left-hand page of each spread was a photograph of each victim's mural, including a message from the muralist. The right-hand pages were reserved for the families to fill as they saw fit. Most chose their favorite photographs and of course reminiscences of their loved ones.

Meghann had felt it necessary to begin with an outline to give families something to build on. She feared that it would be nearly impossible to gather enough input to design from scratch. To begin with, communicating with all of the parents was next to impossible. To help facilitate the work, we called on Kimberly Mata-Rubio and Jesse Rizo to spread the word.

Even with that help, it proved challenging to assemble enough information for each of the victims. Many photographs and messages were grabbed from social media and other creative sleuthing. Slowly the publication took shape, and in the final week before publication, as families visited the newspaper to proof their pages or check it from emails, they expressed sincere gratitude.

We also found ourselves talking with a handful of family members who had declined earlier interview requests. One in particular, Jose Luevanos and his wife, Christina, explained that they had wanted to talk about their son Jayce but had suffered a bad experience with the press in the early days of the tragedy.

Sitting in the newspaper's conference room, as the couple examined Jayce's pages in "We Remember," I wrestled with the fact that Jose was familiar to me. He worked at Ace Hardware, a place I frequented, and yet we had never actually met. In fact, he had continued to work even after the tragedy. In hindsight, I felt that he appeared melancholy—and yet that could have been my mind playing tricks. But I never saw him joking with the customers or fellow workers. To think that he soldiered on after his son had been murdered struck me as remarkable.

The magazine appeared as planned on Sunday, May 21, and we shifted immediately to coverage of the official one-year mark the following Wednesday.

Kimberly had been traveling nonstop as part of her ongoing advocacy. She said that she was exhausted and had decided not to respond to requests for interviews as the first year approached. But she said that when other families of victims began getting calls, "there was no way that I was going to leave Lexi out of the conversation."

She went back to her text messages and email and said yes to every one she had chosen not to answer. One of them was from a Swiss news magazine that had also asked the newspaper for an interview. Another publication from South Korea had also called and emailed us to schedule a talk. Their project had to do with news deserts in their native country. In hindsight, we probably should have agreed to an interview.

Kimberly confirmed that the families had planned a private walk on May 24, 2023, that would follow the path of the twenty-one murals and end with a candlelight vigil at the Memorial Park Amphitheater. The mural event was kept as quiet as possible to avoid the interference of the media and the curious. To help make that happen, city officials closed a series of streets around the downtown, forcing drivers to give the area a wide birth. Even so, plenty of cameras found their way into the procession.

The day had dawned clear and warm, but somehow it seemed considerably cooler than the previous May 24. Later that morning, Robb survivor Arnulfo Reyes gathered supporters on the downtown plaza, where they unfurled orange flags to demonstrate against gun violence. Vehicles passing the plaza honked and passengers shouted their approval of the wounded teacher's demonstration.

Reyes's rally included a period of silence for 77 minutes, and the Uvalde Ministerial Alliance conducted a prayer service at the Uvalde County Fairplex.

By 7 p.m., hundreds of people, including visitors and members of the media, had pushed into the amphitheater and spilled into the adjoining grassy areas of the park's river walk. It was a somber and simultaneously uplifting event. Attendees smiled easily but spoke softly, as though confirming their solidarity with the purpose of honoring the lives that had been lost.

Music for the vigil was provided by an assortment of people, including Amber and Johnny Arreola and freelance photographer Tamir Kalifa, who contributed to the *New York Times*. He performed "Blackbird" by the Beatles, as well as a song he had written to honor shooting victim Jackie Cazares titled "Jackie's Rock." The music had been inspired by a trip to Paris, where Kalifa left one of Jackie's decorated rocks in a place by the Seine River. A visit to Paris was one of the girl's dreams.

ABC News anchor John Quiñones, who had been part of the network's presence in the city during the previous year, addressed the audience, as did Junior Newtown Action Alliance members Geneva Wharf and Molly Zatlukal.

Christela Mendoza, a cousin of shooting victims Jackie Cazares and Annabell Rodriguez, served as master of ceremonies for the event. She shared a poem by Jill Haley, and then butterflies were released. The colorful insects had been distributed in envelopes among audience members.

As you release this butterfly in honor of me,
Know that I am with you and will always be.
Hold a hand, say a prayer,
Close your eyes and see me there.
Although you may feel a bit torn apart,
Please know that I am forever in your heart.
Now fly away butterfly as high as you can go,
I'm right there with you, more than you know.

As the poem ended, attendees tore open their envelopes and gently shook the colorful insects free. They fluttered among the audience, lighting on arms and shoulders, and then soared higher before disappearing into the fading light.

Arnulfo Reyes and young survivors from Room 112 initiated the lighting of candles, passing the flames to those nearest to them in an ever-widening circle. Soon hundreds of candles held by audience members flickered in the growing twilight. The result was striking, and it felt right to be sitting on the bank of the river walk among people who cared deeply for those who had been traumatized a year earlier.

CHAPTER 34

"Where Is the Empathy?"

If there was one takeaway from a May 20, 2023, program hosted by the *Texas Tribune* to examine the community's state of mind a year later, it was that local officials must be feeling pretty good. Or perhaps they felt really bad, guilty—or not much at all.

The question arose after a member of the audience noted that other than Southwest Texas Junior College president Hector Gonzales, whose institution provided its Tate Auditorium for the event, no other city official had bothered to attend. Not a single person representing the school district, city, or county. Of course, they could have been watching on livestream in the comfort of their homes.

"Where is the empathy?" asked Jaclyn Gonzales, a Uvalde native and licensed professional counselor who served on a panel titled "Resilience." She noted that over the previous year, institutions that should have acted to minimize the trauma inflicted on children and teachers had instead pushed for a return to normalcy, hoping to turn the page as quickly as possible.

She added that trauma work, which impacts about 80 percent of the population, is not just the incident itself but the response after the traumatic event. Specifically, Gonzales said it was a mistake for the Uvalde Consolidated Independent School District to expect children to return to summer classes two weeks after a mass shooting.

"It wasn't a very supportive response. It wasn't very understanding to their emotions. And I felt it was a disrespect to them." There were a lot of ways, obviously, that the system failed, but none of it was done maliciously, she said. "I think that people weren't thinking."

Gonzales told the audience that when you are operating in a broken system—both before and after the attack—you don't make great decisions. "When you're in that state of mind, you want to rush through it. I don't know if it's normal, but it's a risk. It's a rescue mechanism that we have, that we try to say, 'Let's go, come on.'"

A glaring oversight for Gonzales, who was turned away from the civic center on May 24 because there "were too many people," was the absence of support for the surviving students from Room 112. She searched out the children not as a therapist but as a concerned community member. After listening to them, "she was astonished that so many people, including from the school and community, had not reached out to them. It was mind boggling. I could not believe we might not know who had trauma from Robb," she said.

Panel member Monica Gutierrez, a counseling faculty member at Sul Ross State University in Alpine, Texas, said that the dysfunction—or turmoil—within the community was clearly making it harder to heal. "We have so many different trains of thought from different community entities and you know, we had the ones 'Three months are up you guys, come on now, you should be over this.' 'Okay, now it's six months. Where are y'all now?' 'It's the year; come on. . . . You know, let's move on . . . let's get over this.'" She said, "That's not the way grief and therapy and support work. I think so many people in our own community don't understand."

The enormous disconnect between what the families of victims were experiencing and what much of the community expected to happen was exactly as Gutierrez described. Our reporting had focused on holding institutions accountable and yet there had been virtually no feedback. It was almost as if we were operating in a vacuum. We knew from previous experience that when the lines went silent, it generally meant disapproval.

Arelis Hernandez, a veteran reporter for the *Washington Post* who had covered more than nine mass shootings, directed the next panel, titled "Healing." Straightaway, she asked community advocate Aide Escamilla, "How do you guide members of your community through something called healing when justice and accountability seem not to have descended on this community yet?"

Escamilla suggested that people and healing are complex, so the process was going to be different for everyone, but no one was exempt from mental, emotional or physical pain. "I honestly think that by my estimation that kind of healing is going to take generations to come."

Hernandez questioned whether it was possible to have healing without justice. Panelist Rev. Mike Marsh, rector at St. Philip's Episcopal Church, offered that there were a number of ways to think about justice, not only in terms of the legal system and punishments but also in the sense that whenever there is violence or injustice, needs are created. "And so justice means seeing and responding to those needs. And if we don't do that, then we get stuck in our healing. It can't happen. . . . So I think justice is essential to the healing process. It's not the only thing, but it has to be a part of it."

Escamilla said that before Robb, she had attended only a handful of government meetings—two meetings of commissioners court and a couple of city council meetings. She had not attended any school board meetings. After May 24, attendance became almost mandatory for her, either in person or via livestream, she said. "And I remember looking at the governing bodies and thinking . . . this is why we are in the mess we are in. Look who's running the show and making the decisions," she said. The advocate said she was particularly struck by school trustees and "just the shock and the lack of empathy that was displayed by members of the board . . . and how that hasn't changed in a year's time."

"One of the positive things that I believe has come out of this is now we know, we're on to you now, not only the school board but the city council and commissioners court. We're watching in a way we never have before. And we're going to make sure that whatever steps need to be taken are taken, and I think they are working hard at trying to move in that direction," Escamilla said.

As a counter to the criticisms, all three panelists, including Sister Dolores Aviles, offered praise for the way the community had responded in the immediate aftermath of May 24. The outpouring of food and love reminded Escamilla of the kindnesses demonstrated when her mother died. "I saw that on a community-wide scale and it was beautiful."

Rev. Marsh, who had been immersed in the tragedy since being called to Uvalde Memorial Hospital in the first hours, feared that the community would take care of the immediate needs of mental health care, financial assistance, and the need to build a new school but would fail to address issues like racism, gun violence, bullying, and poverty that existed before the tragedy.

Hernandez recalled reading a letter to the editor in the *Leader-News* urging the families of victims to forgive and move on. She wondered what part that played in the healing process.

Escamilla said she thought it was vital. "It doesn't mean that you condone the behavior. It just means that you kind of let yourself off the hook."

Marsh said that healing and forgiveness go hand in hand. "If I forgive someone, it may do something for them. But I know what it does for me. It releases me from the past and what happened. To withhold forgiveness means that I am somehow stuck in the past of what's happened." He added that turning the other cheek is an act of nonviolent resistance. "It is claiming your humanity and holding it before the oppressor, the persecutor. It's certainly not pacifism and it's not being a doormat," he said.

Uriel Garcia, the man chosen to moderate the panel titled "Recovery," knew Kimberly Mata-Rubio and kindergarten teacher Veronica Mata well. Operating from an office in our newspaper, he had covered the shooting for the *Texas Tribune* from the beginning. He asked the women what feedback they had received from the community on their advocacy.

Kimberly said that for some, "the whole situation is inconvenient for them and they're ready to put it behind them so that Uvalde isn't just remembered for the trauma. But that's not what we want. We just want to honor our children . . . and those two teachers, that they always be remembered. This is their community," she said.

Another question concerned the downtown murals and complaints from some parents that the paintings triggered a negative response in their surviving children.

"But they get to see the children grow up . . . move on and go to college and get married and have children," Veronica replied. "All we get is that mural. We never wanted our children to be gone. We never wanted those children to have to sit there and live with that date."

Asked what sacrifices the women had made to ensure that their surviving children received the attention they needed, Kimberly said it had been difficult to balance frequent trips to Washington and Austin advocating for sensible gun laws and caring for the four children who remained at home.

"Lexi would want her siblings to be happy, she would want them to have the mom she had. I don't know if I could quite deliver that anymore, but I'm really, really trying. I know that their lives have changed and that they need me and [I] try my best to balance being there for them and making sure that Lexi is remembered."

Veronica recounted how she and Jerry had returned to work following the shooting to set an example for Faith, who was insisting on staying home from her senior year at Texas State University. "I mean we make the sacrifices for our children, and I would have made that sacrifice for Tess if I had the opportunity, but I didn't."

Garcia's final question may have been the toughest of all. How did the women feel about criminal charges being brought against officers who failed to press for a quick end to the active shooter on May 24?

Kimberly said she could not say definitively without having read the results of the investigation, but she hoped that 38th Judicial District Attorney Christina Mitchell would pursue charges if they were merited.

"Just say my child's dead immediately. Had they intervened right away, I would [have known] that because there's 77 minutes. What you took from me is closure and answers I'll never know. I don't know how long my daughter was terrified. I don't know those answers, and I've never had them," Kimberly said.

Veronica said, "If there was a slight chance that any of those babies could have survived, then they [law enforcement] weren't doing their jobs. They sat out there for 77 minutes and did nothing."

The day after the *Tribune* event, the *Leader-News* published a column I wrote in response to the question What is Uvalde like a year after the shooting? The question had been posed a few weeks earlier by Katherine Jacobsen of the Committee to Protect Journalists.

I wrote that there was not one Uvalde. There were three or four—perhaps a dozen. The most recent Uvalde consists of the twenty-one families who lost children and parents at Robb and their extended families, friends, and acquaintances and the people who care about all of them.

For them, I dared to answer that Uvalde is a far sadder place, a city where the parents of victims—unsure of their reception—avert their eyes when meeting strangers in the grocery store, where the most comfortable place is in the presence of others who lost loved ones at Robb, and where each day is a fight to live in the present without drifting back to "that day" or a future time when the loss would be no less painful.

As for the other Uvaldes, I could only surmise. My guess was that the majority of residents feel a deep empathy for those who have been traumatized. They may not express it frequently—or even openly, out of fear of losing their jobs or offending others—but it surely was there.

And of course, there was another Uvalde encompassing citizens who have wearied of the yearlong upheaval. They are annoyed by the forceful demands for accountability and pleas for new gun laws. Some accused the families of only wishing to exert a new-found power and to enrich themselves through lawsuits. Many harbored resentment and placed blame on the families for seeking justice from people and agencies that were clearly derelict.

There was also an impoverished Uvalde, where an estimated 25 percent live near or below the poverty level, some of whom had lost children at Robb. For these people, each day presents a struggle to put food on the table and clean clothes on their children. They work as construction and farm laborers and at service jobs where they care for other peoples' children or ensure that our facilities are clean. For them, I was not sure how much Uvalde has changed. It was extremely hard before and certainly no easier now.

In general, the process of reporting the events of May 24, 2022, took a steep toll on our staff. It was not possible to record the individual stories of soul-wrenching loss without absorbing the pain. Nor was it possible to sit through countless governmental meetings where families were denied adequate time to speak or a legitimate response to their concerns. Or to watch families' pleas for laws to prevent fresh gun violence go largely ignored. That had been hard to watch without feeling anger.

The manipulation of state law and people's emotions to shield law enforcement agencies and public officials had been equally galling. The US Constitution begins with three words: "We the people." The government works for *us*, and when essential rights like those embedded in the Freedom of Information Act were denied based on a criminal investigation that is little more than a delaying tactic, my staff and I were deeply troubled.

And finally, I wrote that three governmental entities controlled the evidence gathered from Robb: the Department of Public Safety, the FBI, and the Texas Legislature. Somehow that information had found its way into the hands of national media, not once but repeatedly over the last year. From my perspective, none of it was an accident but was further evidence that people like Texas governor Greg Abbott and Department of Public Safety head Steve McCraw saw the state's accountability in the Robb disaster as an existential threat to their political and material lives.

What is our community like now? A place where people find common cause, respect others' rights while at the same time working to lift each other? Of course, but in the months and years to come we will have to work much harder to prevent the different Uvaldes from growing even farther apart.

Two months after I wrote that column, that conclusion had not changed, especially since the obstacles to healing that were so clearly articulated during the *Texas Tribune* event had not been removed. Most especially, we await the justice that can be attained only when all of the facts surrounding the massacre have been laid bare.

CHAPTER 35

Where to from Here?

One year and nineteen days after the attack, Kimberly rejoined our staff. Months earlier, she had confided to a member of the ABC News film crew that she had decided to "go home," back to the *Uvalde Leader-News*, where she could be herself, where her name was not necessarily Kimberly or even Kim, but Rubio. Where she might once again cover the news instead of being part of the story. Or, as it turned out, where she would move to a different department altogether in advertising.

The thirty-four-year-old imagined that her *Leader-News* family would restore some sense of the normalcy that had been ripped away on May 24, that we would not pamper or pity but would resume our relationship predicated on a passion for community journalism.

Of course, Kimberly was forever changed. In addition to continuing to care for her husband and four children, she had vowed to advocate for laws that would protect others from future gun violence, all in the name of Lexi. That commitment would require occasional absences from home and work, and we were in full support.

Our newspaper staff was also committed—to shining a light on every aspect of what went wrong before, during, and after May 24. For some, the rampage killing was a simple act of evil; no one bore any responsibility except the attacker. That is not how we saw it. The eighteen-year-old killer was indisputably unhinged, but he did not arrive at that place in a vacuum.

The lack of transparency from government entities that had circled the wagons to protect themselves seemed like a betrayal. For those entities, in the face of growing lawsuits, their organization itself—even though those organizations were funded by taxpayers—became paramount over what might have been a shared effort to support and inform the community, to search out the justice that is an indispensable part of healing.

Naturally there had been occasions through the years when we butted heads with governmental bodies. At times, there were longtime acquaintances and sometimes close friends on the other side of an issue, but that is the nature of the watchdog relationship. When those situations arose, we published our best interpretation of what had happened based on facts gathered from different viewpoints. It was seldom pleasant, but it had never before resulted in a complete fracture.

Unfortunately, a year after Robb, a complete fracture is where we found ourselves with the Uvalde school district. It began with Arredondo's disastrous leadership and then the administration's refusal to terminate the man or at the very least suspend him. Tensions continued to mount as administrators and trustees declined to answer questions about security lapses, to interact with grieving family members, or even to reach out to wounded teachers and students, some of whom remained hospitalized for months.

Once Superintendent Hal Harrell and other administrators stepped down, the relationship became more fraught when a new interim superintendent and a new school police chief were hired.

On February 27, we filed open record requests for the separation agreements of seven school district employees who had resigned, retired, or been terminated the previous fall. Our desire was to know what we as taxpayers had spent to sever relations with employees who had been responsible for guiding the district up to and after the Robb tragedy. We received nothing until two and a half months later, on May 11, 2023, when Texas attorney general Ken Paxton issued a ruling that the information was public.

The district's response was to hand over the agreement for Harrell and nothing more. The back-and-forth for the other information continued for months, as district administration cited semantics or claimed the documents did not exist. On June 13, the district released resignation letters only, which included nothing about severance pay.

A separate request for the school records of the attacker was also refused. We wanted to know how he had entered his senior year with only enough credits to qualify as a ninth grader. We wanted to know how a mass murderer had come to be called a "school shooter" on social media without anyone attempting to intervene. How had a young man with a speech impediment and a learning disability not elicited special attention? Although the federal Family Educational Rights and Privacy Act guards the

information of students under the age of eighteen who are still living, that didn't apply
to the killer. And yet we were told the information was off limits due to an ongoing
criminal investigation.

We were also informed that our coverage of the district rendered us persona non
grata. The superintendent told our new education reporter, Sofi Zeman, that she would
have to earn the trust of the district's public information officer. But isn't that all backward? Do they not work for us? It is our job—enshrined in the First Amendment—to
report how Uvalde Consolidated Independent School District spends our tax dollars,
including the various severance agreements with administrators. School officials have
to earn the public trust to keep their jobs, not the other way around.

We continued to wait for a report on the response of the city police force to Robb.
Most of the twenty-eight Uvalde police officers—seventeen on duty and eleven off—
who were among the responders remained on the force and in at least two cases had
received promotions and salary hikes. Maintaining the status quo was entirely inconsistent with a force that utterly failed in its mission to serve and protect.

Reports from the Department of Public Safety, the FBI, and the Department of
Justice were also long overdue. A state district judge ruled at the end of June 2023 in
favor of a consortium of news organizations, including the *Texas Tribune*, ProPublica,
the *New York Times*, the *Washington Post*, ABC News, and six others, that had sued the
Department of Public Safety for records three months after the attack. Now the judge
said that the agency had to turn over its material. Of course, the news organizations
already possessed a trove of leaked information. But much more was being withheld.

The Department of Public Safety insisted—as did the Uvalde district attorney—that
evidence could not be released until the prosecutor determined whether criminal charges
would be filed. That investigation had already taken seven months longer than outlined
the previous summer, and soon after June 2023, the deadline for completion was postponed until 2024. District Attorney Mitchell defended the delay, pointing to the fact that
the federal government's January 6 investigation had taken two and a half years. The comparison between prosecuting the law enforcement response to a rampage shooter at a
rural school and an insurrection to overturn a presidential election was hardly fair.

If and when Mitchell decides to bring charges, the delays are not likely to end.
Defendants' attorneys will certainly appeal, eliciting further arguments that evidence
needs to be kept under wraps. The legal machinations could very well go on for years,
all of which is a defense attorney's dream. Delay and deflect is the golden rule.

We had branded the lies, obfuscation, and misdirection from Gov. Abbott and his
Department of Public Safety director as criminal. As time went on, the validity of that

label grew more certain. With the exception of the firing of one Department of Public Safety trooper, Sgt. Juan Maldonado, who had responded to Robb within minutes, no other state police of the ninety-one who were present that day were terminated. At least seven were placed under investigation in the fall of 2022, including Ranger Christopher Ryan Kindell. The following January, Department of Public Safety director Steve McCraw notified Kindell in a letter that he was being terminated, writing, "You took no steps to influence the law enforcement response toward an active shooter posture."

The firing called for Kindell to receive a hearing before the director, but over a year later, that had not happened. Meanwhile, the discredited officer draws his $90,718 annual pay without lifting a finger. McCraw must feel that keeping the man on ice is a bargain at any price. If the director upholds the firing, Kindell can appeal to the Texas Public Safety Commission. A public hearing there would certainly involve the ranger and others testifying about what went wrong in Uvalde. In other words, it would be more bad press for McCraw and the governor.

In the meantime, Kimberly and the others clawed their way forward. At the end of July 2023, our new advertising executive announced her candidacy for the mayoral seat Don McLaughlin Jr. was vacating. The mayor had jumped at the chance to run for Tracy O. King's seat in the Texas House when the long-serving lawmaker announced his retirement. State law dictated that McLaughlin resign his city post.

Kimberly's news attracted national attention. Social media posts gave encouragement and, in some cases, offers of monetary support. News agencies also reached out for comment. When Pete Luna fielded a call from Telemundo seeking to talk to the candidate, he asked if the network wanted to buy advertising. They declined.

Former mayor Cody Smith revealed his candidacy the same day as Kimberly. A senior vice president at First State Bank of Uvalde, Smith was first elected to the city council in 1994. He served there for thirteen years before being elected to back-to-back two-year terms as mayor. The announcement stories from the two Uvalde natives ran side by side on the front page of the June 27 issue of the *Uvalde Leader-News*.

The race presented an interesting choice for voters. On the one hand, Smith was a known quantity, a man who had served the city for two decades and had been a member of the advisory committee of the Uvalde Forever Fund, which had distributed funds to the families of Robb victims. His experience appealed to residents who felt that the city's future depended on maintaining a certain status quo. The town's economy had never really boomed, but neither had it suffered a debilitating crash. It crept along at a dependable pace, affording a livable income and a pleasant environment for the most fortunate.

Kimberly's announcement called for a recalibration, not radical change. "It would be easy to run away from the issues that plague our town, but I have decided to remain in Uvalde and be part of the change that is long overdue," she said in the *Leader-News* story. "Our town has become stagnant. Our leadership became comfortable, which led to the events that unfolded on May 24, 2022. The aftermath has added to the trauma of a grieving and fractured community. It is my hope to bridge the gap because only when we come together can we evolve to something greater."

The first-time candidate cited her recent advocacy for stronger gun-safety laws, which had brought her into contact with dozens of elected officials at the state and national level. "I have learned much from navigating our country's political system, and I hope to utilize that new-found wisdom as mayor."

Her priorities included lowering the risk to Uvaldeans from high-speed chases involving human smugglers that careened through the city almost weekly and that had resulted in multiple fatalities; improving communications between the city and other entities, including the county and the school district; preserving the city's rich history; and boosting the vitality of locally owned businesses. If elected mayor, she would be the first woman and the third Hispanic mayor.

But she would be far more than that. Kimberly would represent the city's Latino population in a way they had never experienced. People like her now-close friends whose dead children had propelled them into the public arena, a place they never expected or wanted to be.

Before Robb, Kimberly's reporting had provided her with a primer on governmental affairs and confidence in dealing with the public. But she had never delivered a speech or flown in a commercial airliner—much less met face to face with a US senator like Ted Cruz, who listened to Kimberly and Felix for a minute in his DC office and then walked out of the meeting.

As a grieving parent, she had attended city council meetings seeking answers to why city police had failed to breach Robb classrooms. She had fought for the twenty-one memorials to remain on the downtown plaza and had petitioned council members to allow a vertical headstone to identify her daughter's grave in Hillcrest Memorial Cemetery. In her grief and frustration, she had lashed out at her hometown. Now she had determined that staying in Uvalde would be best for her children, and she wanted to make the city a better place.

Win or lose, Kimberly planned to sharpen her skills as an advocate. St. Mary's School of Law had offered her a scholarship to enroll in the university's three-year

Online J.D. Program. Pursuing a law degree at home would give her the flexibility to care for her family and continue occasional travel to speak on behalf of Lives Robbed.

As for our newspaper, I was fully aware that Kimberly's mayoral campaign would put us squarely in the middle of a divided community. Some already felt that the *Leader-News* demanded too much from local institutions and the people who directed them. Our feeling was that much of the poor decision-making during and after the tragedy was the result of well-meaning people unable to function in a crisis.

That failure set us apart from other mass school shootings, especially the nation's deadliest at Sandy Hook. *Newtown Bee* editor John Voket had been in the *Bee* offices on December 14, 2012, when another young man with an assault-style rifle unloaded his existential anger on first graders. We had become friends after he invited me to sit on a panel at the New England Newspaper & Press Association meeting in early May 2023. John's experience was that in the wake of the Newtown tragedy, local institutions had been nothing but cooperative.

Had we been another rural community with a proportional law enforcement presence, the result might have been different. A couple of dozen responders could well have been less confused—and more effective—especially if there had been one leader among them. But because the city was home to a veritable army aimed at protecting the border, the crush of responders—149 Border Patrol officers, 91 members of the Texas Department of Public Safety, 25 officers of the UPD, a 16-member SWAT team from the San Antonio Police Department, 16 employees of the Uvalde County Sherrif's Office, 14 Department of Homeland Security officers, 13 United States Marshalls, 8 Drug Enforcement Agency officers, and 44 police, sheriff's deputies, constables, and firefighters from nearby counties—had been overwhelming.

A statement made only days after Robb by former Uvalde County sheriff Charlie Mendeke still strikes a chord. The sixty-five-year-old, who had held the office for twelve years before retiring at the end of 2021, said that he had outfitted his department's deputies with all the equipment necessary to confront an active shooter, including semiautomatic rifles, shotguns, rifle vests, and helmets. The Uvalde native added with obvious emotion that he had been deeply disturbed by the pleas of parents for officers to save their children.

"[Parents] were yelling 'Get in there, please get in there.' It sickens me to hear that. You are sworn to do the duty. True grit and leadership were missing," Mendeke said.

"True grit and leadership were missing." It sounded like a line John Wayne might have uttered in any of his dozens of movies. But the scripts the Duke read from resonated because they captured the essence of standing up to evil. Simplistic for sure. But sometimes all it takes is one man—or woman—to say "No, that is not how this turns out."

Every man who stood in that hallway and many who should have, including Mendeke's successor, Sheriff Ruben Nolasco, could have made a difference. It did not require a Medal of Honor winner like Audie Murphy or Roy Benavidez. It only required that someone move assertively to employ tactics like firing tear gas or flash-bangs through outside windows and breaching the two classroom doors simultaneously.

There is so much room for blame, and while assessing it will not bring back any of the deceased, a final accounting would give closure. For Lives Robbed mothers like Kimberly and Veronica, it would mean knowing that their children could not have been saved by immediate police intervention. For others, like Gloria Cazares, it is far more difficult. Her daughter Jackie lived for more than an hour after the initial assault. The nine-year-old, who was shot once in the chest, might well have survived.

The release of long-promised investigation reports will empower families across the nation who fear their own children could be confronted by an active school shooter to make educated demands of their schools and governmental bodies, including those who are sworn to protect.

What we learned in Uvalde is that the institutions we trusted for decades were not managed or trained well enough and were not willing enough to safeguard our children and teachers. An equally painful lesson exploded the myth that one good man with a gun can stop one armed bad man. At Robb Elementary School, 376 good men could not pull off that feat.

Afterword

News that the Department of Justice report on Robb would be released January 18, 2024, stirred fresh anxiety among families and in our newsroom. What would it say? Would the Justice Department stamp its approval on the Uvalde response as it had done with Orlando police after the Pulse Nightclub attack? In June 2016, Pulse ranked as the worst mass shooting in US history. A lone gunman professing allegiance to Isis killed forty-nine people and wounded fifty-three others. It took police three hours to eliminate the assailant.

In emails beginning two days prior, we learned that Attorney General Merrick Garland and Associate Attorney General Vanita Gupta would travel to Uvalde on January 17. The officials would brief families of victims that evening, before the press was provided an in-camera review of the report the following morning. An embargo would be imposed until a press conference got under way at 12:30 p.m.

We submitted the names of two reporters who would be permitted to examine the 575-page document and attend the press conference. Melissa Federspill and I met early at the *Uvalde Leader-News* for the short drive to the Herby Ham Adult Activity Center on the eastern edge of the city. I'm certain the people who manage the modern brick building that hosts pickleball, aerobic swim classes, and woodworking courses never expected the US attorney general and hoards of media to crowd its space. The small room into which we were directed was cold and lacked amenities, especially coffee. Visiting journalists seemed not to notice. The veterans arranged themselves at long tables, laptops running and insulated coffee mugs within easy reach.

When bound copies of the report arrived around 8:30 a.m., we learned there was only one copy per media team. The rest of the inventory remained locked in the hold of a jet marooned by weather somewhere back east. If other copies arrived, we would be supplied.

We removed the binder rings, separated the pages and began to read. Melissa turned immediately to the executive summary at the beginning, and I thumbed to the conclusion. We were stunned, not because of startling new information, but because the Department of Justice described the police response exactly as families had experienced it on May 24. Cops wilted in the face of an eighteen-year-old holed up in two classrooms with an "AR."

We learned that officials with the Justice Department's Office of Community Oriented Policing Services spent a total of 54 days in Uvalde to compile the critical incident report. During that time, they looked at 14,000 pieces of evidence and conducted 260 interviews with individuals from more than 30 organizations, including law enforcement, elected officials, hospital staff, and families of victims and survivors.

The "most significant failure" identified in the report was that officers should have immediately recognized the incident as an active shooter situation and used "the resources and equipment that were sufficient to push forward immediately and continuously toward the threat until entry was made into classrooms 111/112 and the threat was eliminated." The words echoed the Texas House committee findings released two months after the attack.

The Justice Department also found police woefully unprepared, as most officers "lacked specialized, advanced training and preparation to handle such situations" and the school district had cultivated "a culture of complacency regarding locked-door policies"—both of which contributed to the challenges in mounting an effective response to the incident.

The failure of anyone to take command, something that never seemed in doubt to any of our reporting staff, leaped from the pages. "Leadership . . . demonstrated no urgency for establishing a command and control structure, which led to challenges related to information sharing, lack of situational statuses, and limited-to-no direction for personnel in the hallway or on the perimeter," the report continued. And counter to well-established active-shooter training methods, Arredondo "directed officers intending to gain entry into the classrooms to stop."

The failed leadership was painfully familiar and at the same time affirming of my editorial published six years earlier that called the creation of a school police force a waste of taxpayer dollars. I reasoned that city police and sheriff's deputies could respond within two minutes to almost any location in the city, which is exactly what happened. And that they would likely bring better training and equipment. The fact that school chief Arredondo had proved more of an impediment than a help made the outcome even worse.

The aftermath, as noted in the report, was made worse by serial misinformation, misguided and misleading narratives, leaks, and lack of communication. Investigators labeled it as "unprecedented" and as having had "an extensive negative impact on the mental health and recovery of the family members and other victims, as well as the entire community of Uvalde."

The last sentence resonated as much as anything in the report. The harm caused by law enforcement was unimaginable, but so was the damage caused by ongoing obfuscation, deceit, and betrayal on the part local and state officials.

At 9:30 a.m., the aide who had delivered the doorstop-sized document caught our attention. CNN had jumped the gun, leaking the Department of Justice investigation nationwide. The embargo was lifted, and the attorney general's press conference moved up to 11 a.m.

We weren't surprised or terribly disappointed. CNN had been the source of repeated leaks over the last twenty months, and we weren't going to beat anyone to the story. We returned to the office, where Melissa finished a piece for our social media and website and I worked on an editorial for Sunday's print edition.

The media briefing began promptly at 11 a.m., with Garland describing "cascading failures" that started with law enforcement and extended to local institutions. "Victims and survivors should never have been trapped with that shooter for more than an hour as they waited for rescue. . . . Lives would have been saved, and people would have survived," if officers had acted faster to confront the gunman.

We sat in the front row, barely eight feet from the smallish, bespectacled man whose red-rimmed eyes reflected the weight of the message. Melissa stifled her own tears, partly from reliving the trauma but perhaps more in relief that the nation's top law enforcement official was confirming what we had long believed and reported.

Garland reviewed the timeline, which by now had become widely known and criticized. Eleven officers arrived within two minutes of the attacker (he began shooting inside the school at 11:33 a.m.), and, hearing gunfire, approached Classrooms 111 and 112. When shots were fired from within the classroom and building debris grazed two of the officers, all responders retreated to cover.

A single officer made an attempt to return at 11:40 a.m., but no one followed. The victims trapped in the classrooms were still waiting at 11:44 a.m. when the subject fired another shot in the classroom. The officers waited at 11:56 a.m. when an officer at the scene told fellow officers that his wife, a teacher, was inside the classrooms and had been shot; they continued to wait at 12:10 p.m. when a student called 911 to report victims in the classroom; they were still waiting at 12:21 p.m. when four more shots were fired in the classrooms. And they waited for another 27 minutes until officers finally entered the classroom and killed the attacker.

Gupta followed her boss to the mic, saying, "It is hard to look at the truth—that the law enforcement response on May 24 was an unimaginable failure and that a lack of action by adults failed to protect children and their teachers."

She added that the failures did not end at 77 minutes but continued at minute 78 when it became clear that because there was no leader, there was no plan to triage victims in classrooms 111/112.

"Victims were moved without precautions and deceased were transported to the hospital in ambulances, while children with bullet wounds were driven to the hospital in school buses without medical attention," Gupta said as she recapped what families had seen and fought against. "In the commotion, one adult victim (teacher Eva Mireles) was placed on a walkway on the ground outside to be attended to. She died there."

The petite woman in an unwavering voice described the reunification process coordinated by the Uvalde school district as "similarly chaotic." Families and survivors received unclear and sometimes conflicting information about where to go to reunite with their loved ones. Many family members waited at the school for hours without status updates, not knowing where their children were—if they were safe or hurt or even alive. These were the same sad stories we had documented in the months after the attack.

She also addressed inaccurate and inconsistent public communications, including social media posts and press conferences that made things infinitely worse. Mentioned specifically was the 12:06 p.m. school district Facebook post, reassuring parents that "students and staff are safe in the buildings." She said that that false reassurance was never corrected. An hour later, law enforcement inaccurately posted on social media that the shooter was in custody (he was dead). That post, too, was never corrected.

I stuck my hand up early in the briefing and was the last to be called on. I said that some people considered Robb to be typical—or even better—among police responses to mass shootings. Why was it a failure if it took 77 minutes and Pulse required three hours?

Garland said that the report described clearly accepted methods for responding to an active shooter, confirmed by experts across the nation. None of that happened at Robb. He then handed the question to the director of the Office of Community Oriented Policing Services, Hugh Clements, who balked at the comparison.

He called the report "comprehensive . . . extensive" and urged us all to read it. "I will say there was an epic or complete lack of leadership, unity of command; there was no incident command set up. That's not the case with the Pulse nightclub."

Another distinction, which was not permissible in the pages of an objective investigation, was that twenty-nine children remained trapped with a killer within a few feet of their rescuers, while a ten-year-old girl risked her life repeatedly to call 911 and beg police to save her and her classmates. Justice Department investigators could not have missed that she was the hero that day.

A second media briefing began in front of the facility shortly after the first concluded. Josh Koskoff, an attorney representing seventeen families, including sixteen who lost children, told the media that his firm was focused on how an eighteen-year-old was able to purchase such destructive weapons along with more than 1,700 rounds of ammunition from an "on-line ammo" dealer. "How could that happen? How are these companies marketing guns to our children? Where is the role of gun companies and marketing in this report?"

Kimberly, Felix, and other Lives Robbed families had not been afforded sufficient time to read the entire report. However, Kimberly zeroed in on one part that had stood out: Pete Arredondo telling other officers intending to enter the classrooms to stop. And still no other leaders emerged to override Arredondo or acting city chief Pargas.

"I hope that the failures end today. And that local officials do what was not done that day: do right by the victims and survivors of Robb Elementary—terminations, criminal prosecutions." She called for state and local governments to do their part by enacting sensible gun laws, "because Robb Elementary began the day an eighteen-year-old was allowed to purchase an AR-15."

Jerry Mata, accompanied by wife, Veronica, and his daughter, Faith, was devastated to hear Garland talk about lives that might have been saved. "I just couldn't believe it. . . . For these officers to sit there and not do anything, and still be out there on the streets like nothing happened, and my daughter's gone—it was hard."

Brett Cross seethed at seeing officers in public that "you know were standing there while our babies were murdered and bleeding out." He hoped the report "lights a fire up under the district attorney's ass because we know that she has not done a damn thing and we refuse to accept that."

Cross added that the weight of the Justice Department report might compel some "to start taking us seriously . . . instead of telling us to move on, telling us to sweep it under the rug."

Vincent Salazar, whose granddaughter Layla died in the shooting, saw deep divisions in Uvalde between those who are seeking answers and accountability and those who want to move on from the tragedy. "Without justice this is going to be a split town," Salazar told the media.

When I reached previous mayor McLaughlin for comment, he expressed appreciation for the investigation but lamented that it had taken 18 months from the time he requested it in the days after the tragedy. He also criticized the Justice Department's failure to include state and federal law enforcement leaders in the botched response.

"There is plenty of blame for all of the agencies. We need to lay our cards on the table . . . and if people need to go, they will," he told me.

Another major story broke the next day, and this time it was all ours. We reported on social media that 38th Judicial District Attorney Christina Mitchell had seated a special twelve-person grand jury to help determine whether criminal charges would be brought against any members of law enforcement.

I didn't envy anybody that duty. Jurors would spend the next six months looking at body cam video, crime scene photographs, and autopsy reports and reviewing interviews with hundreds of first responders and survivors. It would be tedious and emotional—and almost assuredly an act of political expediency. The district attorney had turned what was originally termed a six-month investigation into nineteen months, and the special grand jury felt like more cover.

Few members of the community—and fewer legal experts nationwide—believed Mitchell could successfully prosecute officers for their actions at Robb. To do so would rest on three possible criminal charges: manslaughter, criminally negligent homicide, and abandoning or endangering a child. The first two charges would require the prosecution to prove that the officers "caused the death of" an individual.

Central to that would be the introduction of evidence that any victims might have survived the attack had officers intervened more quickly. Assuming that it was presented to grand jurors, that information would be contained in autopsy reports, which were completed toward the end of 2022 and then sealed by the district attorney.

Similar studies had been performed following other mass shootings, including after the Pulse attack. In that review, researchers reported that sixteen of the forty-nine victims had potentially survivable wounds had they received faster medical care and made it to a hospital within the golden hour. Still, the officers who responded to the shooting weren't criminally charged.

Barely a year after Robb, a Florida jury acquitted former Broward County sheriff's deputy Scot Peterson on seven counts of felony child neglect, three misdemeanor counts of culpable negligence, and one count of perjury, charges that carried a maximum prison sentence of 96.5 years.

Peterson worked as a school resource officer at Marjory Stoneman Douglas High School in Parkland, Florida, when a former student opened fire with an AR-15 on Valentines Day 2018. The officer responded within 2 minutes but failed to enter Building 12. Inside, seventeen people were dead or dying—six of them killed after Peterson took cover behind a nearby building. He would remain there for 48 minutes. Seven other Broward deputies could have entered the building but didn't. Three of them were fired.

Some legal experts speculated that community pressure played a role in the convening of a grand jury in Uvalde. "I think the DA may be trying to create some goodwill in the community and maybe address her political concerns for her future," G. M. Cox, a former chief of police and lecturer at Sam Houston State University told the *Texas Tribune.* "The reality is that it's going to be tough to file a criminal case."

Still, the grand jury was a big story, and once it broke, state and national media scrambled to catch up. Meghann fielded a call from a CNN journalist who asked—bordering on condescension—how we knew the story to be factual. "Because I know," Meg responded. I received a similar call from a San Antonio television station requesting background on the development.

Whether the Justice Department investigation ultimately changed attitudes might soon become apparent. The March 5 Republican Party primary featured three candidates from law enforcement who had been named for failing to assert themselves at Robb: Sheriff Nolasco and incumbent constables Johnny Joe Field and Emanuel Zamora, who oversaw the Southwest Texas Junior College Law Enforcement Academy. Nolasco faced three challengers, while Field and Zamora had drawn two and one, respectively. Pete Arredondo and Mariano Pargas, also cited for failure to lead, no longer held positions in law enforcement.

Kimberly called it "shocking" that the government had singled out the leaders, but hesitated to say she was optimistic about what might actually happen to them—either politically or in the form of criminal conviction. "I think I learned long ago not to be optimistic. You're just going be let down. I'm just hopeful."

And she was grateful to the attorney general, who she described as being "very emotional" during introductions to family members on the evening of January 17. "I appreciate that he allowed himself to be vulnerable in front of us. And that he came all way down here to say what we've all known. Law enforcement failed us that day."

In the days after the report, former sheriff Charlie Mendeke stopped at the office for a cup of coffee. We sat in the conference room for almost an hour, discussing the Justice Department findings and the fate of officers named in the report who were running for county offices in the coming election.

"It's pretty much what I told you," Charlie said, a half-smile creasing his bearded face. "They had everything they needed except the nerve."

Note on Sources

Journalists are trained to verify their sources and to protect them, if need be. In this account, I have followed that training, noting each source in the text, including interviews (the basis for the majority of the text); journals, reports, or newspapers, whether print, broadcast, or online; government sources; archives; or other sources, whether published or not.

That said, I include the following list of sources (other than personal interviews) that I consulted in preparing this narrative.

A Proud Heritage: A History of Uvalde County, Texas (Uvalde: El Progreso
Club, 1975)
ABC News
ACEP Now (American College of Emergency Physicians: https://www.acep.org/)
Austin American-Statesman
CNN
New York Times
ProPublica (https://www.propublica.org/)
San Antonio Express-News
Texas House Committee Report(https://house.texas.gov/_media/pdf
/committees/reports/87interim/Robb-Elementary-Investigative-Committee
-Report.pdf)
Texas Tribune (https://www.texastribune.org/)

US Department of Justice Report (https://www.justice.gov/opa/pr/justice
-department-releases-report-its-critical-incident-review-response-mass
-shooting-robb)
Voces Oral History Center, University of Texas at Austin (https://voces.moody
.utexas.edu/)
Washington Post

Index